D0220132

THE EUROPEAN UNION SERIES
General Editors: Neill Nugent, William E. Paterson

The European Union series provides an authoritative library on the European Union, ranging from general introductory texts to definitive assessments of key institutions and actors, issues, policies and policy processes, and the role of member states.

Books in the series are written by leading scholars in their fields and reflect the most up-to-date research and debate. Particular attention is paid to accessibility and clear presentation for a wide audience of students, practitioners and interested general readers.

The series editors are **Neill Nugent**, Emeritus Professor, Manchester Metropolitan University, and Honorary Professor, University of Salford, UK; and **William E. Paterson,** Honorary Professor in German and European Studies, University of Aston. Their co-editor until his death in July 1999, **Vincent Wright,** was a Fellow of Nuffield College, Oxford University.

Feedback on the series and book proposals are always welcome and should be sent to Stephen Wenham, Palgrave Macmillan, Houndmills, Basingstoke, Hampshire, RG21 6XS, UK, or by e-mail to **s.wenham@palgrave.com.**

General textbooks

Published

Series Standing Order (outside North America only)
ISBN 978–0–333–71695–3 hardback
ISBN 978–0–333–69352–0 paperback
Full details from www.palgrave.com

Visit Palgrave Macmillan's
EU Resource area at
www.palgrave.com/politics/eu/

The major institutions and actors

Published

Renaud Dehousse **The European Court of Justice**
Justin Greenwood **Interest Representation in the European Union (3rd edn)**
Fiona Hayes-Renshaw and Helen Wallace **The Council of Ministers (2nd edn)**
Simon Hix and Christopher Lord **Political Parties in the European Union**
David Judge and David Earnshaw **The European Parliament (2nd edn)**
Neill Nugent **The European Commission**
Anne Stevens with Handley Stevens **Brussels Bureaucrats? The Administration of the European Union**

Forthcoming

Ariadna Ripoll Servent **The European Parliament**
Sabine Saurugger and Fabien Terpan **The European Court of Justice and the Politics of Law**
Wolfgang Wessels **The European Council**

The main areas of policy

Published

Michael Baun and Dan.Marek **Cohesion Policy in the European Union**
Michele Chang **Monetary Integration in the European Union**
Michelle Cini and Lee McGowan **Competition Policy in the European Union (2nd edn)**
Wyn Grant **The Common Agricultural Policy**
Martin Holland and Mathew Doidge **Development Policy of the European Union**
Jolyon Howorth **Security and Defence Policy in the European Union**
Johanna Kantola **Gender and the European Union (2nd edn)**
Stephan Keukeleire and Tom Delreux **The Foreign Policy of the European Union (2nd edn)**
Brigid Laffan **The Finances of the European Union**
Malcolm Levitt and Christopher Lord **The Political Economy of Monetary Union**
Janne Haaland Matláry **Energy Policy in the European Union**
John McCormick **Environmental Policy in the European Union**
John Peterson and Margaret Sharp **Technology Policy in the European Union**
Handley Stevens **Transport Policy in the European Union**

Forthcoming

Karen Anderson **Social Policy in the European Union**
Hans Bruyninckx and Tom Delreux **Environmental Policy and Politics in the European Union**
Sieglinde Gstöhl and Dirk de Bievre **The Trade Policy of the European Union**
Christian Kaunert and Sarah Leonard **Justice and Home Affairs in the European Union**
Maren Kreutler, Johannes Pollak and Samuel Schubert **Energy Policy in the European Union**
Paul Stephenson, Esther Versluis and Mendeltje van Keulen **Implementing and Evaluating Policy in the European Union**

Also planned

Political Union

The member states and the Union

Published

Carlos Closa and Paul Heywood **Spain and the European Union**
Andrew Geddes **Britain and the European Union**
Alain Guyomarch, Howard Machin and Ella Ritchie **France in the European Union**
Brigid Laffan and Jane O'Mahoney **Ireland and the European Union**

Forthcoming

Simon Bulmer and William E. Paterson **Germany and the European Union**
Brigid Laffan **The European Union and its Member States**

Issues

Published

Derek Beach **The Dynamics of European Integration: Why and When EU Institutions Matter**
Christina Boswell and Andrew Geddes **Migration and Mobility in the European Union**
Thomas Christiansen and Christine Reh **Constitutionalizing the European Union**
Robert Ladrech **Europeanization and National Politics**
Cécile Leconte **Understanding Euroscepticism**
Steven McGuire and Michael Smith **The European Union and the United States**
Wyn Rees **The US–EU Security Relationship: The Tensions between a European and a Global Agenda**

Forthcoming

Graham Avery **Enlarging the European Union**
Senem Aydin-Düzgit and Nathalie Tocci **Turkey and the European Union**
Thomas Christiansen, Emil Kircher and Uwe Wissenbach **The European Union and China**
Tuomas Forsberg and Hiski Haukkala **The European Union and Russia**

Cohesion Policy in the European Union

Michael Baun
and
Dan Marek

macmillan education   palgrave

First published 2014 by
PALGRAVE

Palgrave in the UK is an imprint of Macmillan Publishers Limited, registered in England, company number 785998, of 4 Crinan Street, London N1 9XW.

Palgrave Macmillan in the US is a division of St Martin's Press LLC, 175 Fifth Avenue, New York, NY 10010.

Palgrave is a global imprint of the above companies and is represented throughout the world.

Palgrave® and Macmillan® are registered trademarks in the United States, the United Kingdom, Europe and other countries

ISBN 978-0-230-30313-3 hardback
ISBN 978-0-230-30314-0 paperback

This book is printed on paper suitable for recycling and made from fully managed and sustained forest sources. Logging, pulping and manufacturing processes are expected to conform to the environmental regulations of the country of origin.

A catalogue record for this book is available from the British Library.

A catalog record for this book is available from the Library of Congress.

Typeset by Cambrian Typesetters, Camberley, Surrey, England, UK

Printed in China

In memory of Dave Allen, who inspired us and many other colleagues and students with his scholarship and insightful views in this EU policy field

List of Tables and Figures

Tables

Figures

List of Abbreviations

CAP	Common Agricultural Policy
CDU/CSU	Christian Democratic Union/Christian Social Union
CEC	Commission of the European Communities
CEE	Central and Eastern European
CEU	Council of the European Union
CGE	Computable General Equilibrium
CI	Community Initiative
CLLD	Community-led Local Development
COP	Community of Practice on Partnership
COR	Committee of the Regions
CSF	Community Support Framework
CSG	Community Strategic Guidelines
DG	Directorate-General
EAGGF	European Agricultural Guidance and Guarantee Fund
EAFRD	European Agricultural Fund for Rural Development
EC	European Community
ECA	European Court of Auditors
ECB	European Central Bank
ECU	European Currency Units
EES	European Employment Strategy
EESC	European Economic and Social Committee
EFTA	European Free Trade Association
EIB	European Investment Bank
EMFF	European Maritime and Fisheries Fund
EMU	Economic and Monetary Union
EP	European Parliament
ERDF	European Regional Development Fund
ESF	European Social Fund
ESI	European Structural and Investment
ESM	European Stability Mechanism
ETC	European Territorial Cooperation
EU	European Union
EUA	European Units of Account
FCC	Federal Constitutional Court

FIFG	Financial Instrument for Fisheries Guidance
GDP	Gross Domestic Product
GNI	Gross National Income
GNP	Gross National Product
ICT	Information and Communications Technology
IDP	Integrated Development Programme
IGC	Intergovernmental Conference
IMF	International Monetary Fund
IMP	Integrated Mediterranean Programme
IT	Information Technology
LAG	Local Action Group
LDR	Less Developed Region
MA	Managing Authority
MC	Monitoring Committee
MDR	More Developed Region
MEP	Member of European Parliament
MFF	Multi-annual Financial Framework
MLG	Multi-level Governance
NGO	Non-governmental Organization
NRP	National Reform Programme
NSRF	National Strategic Reference Framework
NUTS	*nomenclature d'unités territoriales statistiques* (Nomenclature of Units for Territorial Statistics)
OMC	Open method of coordination
OP	Operational Programme
PPP	Purchasing Power Parity
RCE	Regional Competitiveness and Employment
R&D	Research and development
RTD	Research and Technology Development
SEA	Single European Act
SGP	Stability and Growth Pact
SME	Small and medium-sized enterprise
SPD	Single Programming Document
TEN-T	Trans-European Network-Transport
TEU	Treaty on European Union
TFEU	Treaty on the Functioning of the EU
TR	Transition Region
UK	United Kingdom
UKIP	UK Independence Party
VAT	Value-added tax
YEI	Youth Employment Initiative

Acknowledgements

This book is the outcome of a collaborative partnership that stretches back some fifteen years. Over that period of time we have jointly authored or edited more than a dozen academic journal articles, many of them focusing on EU cohesion policy and its effects, and three books, including *EU Cohesion Policy after Enlargement*, published by Palgrave Macmillan in 2008. This book draws on this previous scholarship while seeking to extend it, with the goal of providing a more comprehensive overview of the evolution, operation and effects of this important EU policy.

As with all major projects, this one could not have been completed without the assistance and support of many others. Michael Baun would like to thank Valdosta State University for providing a work environment conducive to scholarship and for its support of his research activities. In particular, he would like to thank his department chair and immediate supervisor, Dr James Peterson, for his efforts to accommodate the author's research needs. He would also like to acknowledge the memory of Col. Vernon Pizer, through whose generosity the Marguerite Langdale Pizer Chair in International Relations at Valdosta State University was established. He is also grateful to his wife, Julia, and son, Matthew, for their love and encouragement.

Dan Marek would like to thank Palacky University, the Faculty of Arts and the Department of Politics and European Studies for supporting his research activities related to this book project. He would also like to thank Monika Brusenbauch Meislová for her research assistance.

The authors would also like to thank the general editors of Palgrave Macmillan's European Union series, Neill Nugent and Willie Paterson, for their excellent suggestions and encouragement throughout the book-writing process. They would also like to give special thanks to Steven Kennedy at Palgrave Macmillan, who first approached the authors about this project nearly five years ago. Through a judicious mixture of patience and prodding, he deserves a considerable amount of credit for its eventual completion. Thanks also to Stephen Wenham and Madeleine Hamey-Thomas at Palgrave Macmillan for their assistance.

MICHAEL BAUN
DAN MAREK

The authors and publishers would like to thank the European Union for permission to use illustrative material in this book, reproduced under copyright of the European Communities 2007.

Introduction

If one visits the website of the European Commission's Directorate-General for Regional and Urban Policy, the main body responsible for administering EU cohesion policy, in the menu under 'Project examples' you will find the link to a searchable database of activities funded by the structural and cohesion funds in the 2007–13 programming period. The search options allow the user to select one or all of the EU's 28 member states – along with some neighbouring non-member countries or candidate states for EU accession – and one or all of the statistical regions of each member state. It also allows the searcher to select one or all of 12 different project themes, ranging from 'Business support', 'Environment' and 'Health' to 'Tourism and culture', 'Transport' and 'Urban development'. If the viewer selects the 'all countries/all regions', 'all projects' and 'all themes' options and hits the 'Go!' ('Start the search') button, they are presented with a hyperlinked list of hundreds of projects being implemented throughout the wider EU, including 'A Scandinavian model for women-led companies' (Denmark, Sweden and Norway), 'Business support for Turkish entrepreneurs' (Germany, Karlsruhe), 'Urban homes turn green in Baltic Sea Region' (Estonia, Latvia, Lithuania, Poland and Germany) and 'Science and marketing help develop new outlets for traditional Mediterranean wool' (Italy, Sardinia and France, Corsica), to name just a few. The website also proudly informs the visitor that 'Hundreds of thousands of projects throughout the EU have benefited from investment from [cohesion] policy over the years' (DG Regio, 2013).

A visit to the 'Inforegio' website is instructive, for it opens one's eyes to the thematically wide-ranging and geographically extensive nature of EU cohesion policy, while also offering a hint of its operational complexity. Quite simply, cohesion policy seems to be 'everywhere', and to do 'all things'. This is an exaggeration, of course, but it underscores the ubiquity of cohesion policy that is at once viewed as one of its major strengths and also a key weakness. A strength, since the visibility of cohesion policy projects – all marked by the

1

familiar billboards bearing the EU flag emblem and a reference to the EU structural or cohesion fund(s) involved, replaced in most cases by a permanent explanatory plaque once the projects are completed – provides concrete evidence to European citizens of the benefits of EU membership, while also serving as a practical expression of EU solidarity between rich and poor. A weaknesses, since the breadth of activities funded under cohesion policy implies a loss of policy focus (and perhaps effectiveness) and generates substantial confusion over what the main purpose or objectives of cohesion policy really are. Getting a handle on this sprawling, multifaceted and often bewildering EU policy, and gaining an understanding of where cohesion policy came from, how it has evolved and where it might be going, is the basic purpose of this book.

What is cohesion policy?

Cohesion policy can be defined in a number of ways, beginning with its official goals and purposes. Since its creation in the late 1980s, following ratification of the Single European Act (SEA), cohesion policy has been the EU's primary policy tool for strengthening the Union's economic, social and (since ratification of the Lisbon Treaty in 2009) territorial cohesion. While the concept of 'cohesion' can be understood in a number of different ways, for the purposes of cohesion policy it has traditionally been defined as the promotion of 'convergence', or the reduction of economic disparities within the EU between its member states and regions. Through cohesion policy the EU has sought to achieve this goal through planned investments, directed primarily at less wealthy member states and regions, which seek to promote economic development and growth-enhancing structural change. While other EU policies, including agricultural, fisheries, transportation, education, energy and environmental policies, to name just a few, also have implications for economic development and cohesion, it is through cohesion policy specifically that the EU makes its main effort to achieve this important, EU treaty-based objective.

Since 2006, however, cohesion policy has been assigned an additional task, and that is to promote or contribute to the EU's broader economic growth and competitiveness as well as related strategic objectives. As a result, cohesion policy spending is now closely aligned with the goals of the EU's medium-term economic strategy, first the Lisbon strategy for 2000–10, which aimed at making the EU into 'the most competitive and dynamic knowledge-based economy in the world capable of sustainable economic growth with more and better jobs and greater social cohesion', and now the Europe 2020 strategy for promoting 'smart, sustainable and inclusive growth'. Consequently, while the promotion of regional economic development and convergence remains a major goal of cohesion policy, it is now pursued in alignment with the Union's growth and competiveness agenda, through targeted investments that address the EU's strategic economic priorities. Cohesion policy today thus has a dual mission or purpose – the promotion of cohesion/convergence *and* growth and competitiveness, or in other words both equity and efficiency (Dhéret, 2011).

A brief look at how cohesion policy funds are spent shows just how it seeks to accomplish these dual objectives. In the 2007–13 programming period, in which cohesion policy was aligned with the goals of the Lisbon strategy, the main areas of cohesion policy investment and their relative shares of appropriations were as follows:

1. Knowledge and innovation: 24 per cent of all cohesion policy spending, including investments in such areas as research centres and infrastructure, technology transfer and innovation in firms, and the development and diffusion of informatics and communication technologies.
2. Transport: 22 per cent, aimed at improving the accessibility of regions, supporting the construction of Trans-European transport Networks (TEN-T), and investing in environmentally sustainable transport facilities, particularly in urban areas.
3. Human resources: 22 per cent, for spending on education, training, employment and social inclusion schemes.
4. Environmental protection and risk prevention: 19 per cent, including support for water and waste-treatment infrastructures, the decontamination of land in order to prepare it for new economic use and protection against environmental risks. (CEC, 2008: 3)

Although the deadline for the use of EU funds allocated for 2007–13 was still several years away, in July 2013 the Commission announced a number of concrete achievements generated by cohesion policy programmes in the funding period, including:

1. the creation of 400,000 new jobs by the end of 2011, including more than 15,600 research jobs and 167,000 jobs in small and medium-sized enterprises (SMEs);
2. support provided for 53,240 Research and Technology Development (RTD) projects and 16,000 cooperation projects between private enterprises and research institutions;
3. support provided for 53,160 business 'start-ups';
4. the provision of broadband Internet access to nearly 1.9 million people;
5. the creation of 1,222 megawatts of additional electricity generation capacity from renewable sources;
6. the completion of water supply projects serving 2.6 million people and waste-water projects serving 5.7 million people;
7. support provided for over 5,000 transport projects, with 460 km of TEN-T roads and 334 km of TEN-T rail completed;
8. access provided to improved urban transport for nearly 3.4 million people;
9. support provided for over 19,000 educational infrastructure projects, mostly in the area of Information Technology (IT), benefitting 3.4 million students. (CEC, 2013b: 9)

In the 2014–20 programming period, cohesion policy spending will target a number of thematic priorities linked to the objectives of the Europe 2020 strategy, including: the strengthening of research, technological development and innovation; enhancing the competitiveness of SMEs; supporting the shift to a low-carbon economy; promoting climate change adaptation; promoting sustainable transport and removing bottlenecks in key transport network infrastructures; and investing in education, training and vocational training for skills and lifelong learning (OJEU, 2013a: 343). Cohesion policy in 2014–20 will also contribute to the fight against youth unemployment, especially in member states like Spain, Greece and Portugal that have been badly impacted by the euro-zone debt crisis. It will also make investments aimed at improving institutional capacity and the quality of public administration in recipient countries, especially poorer southern and Central and Eastern European (CEE) member states, which is another thematic priority for cohesion policy in the new programming period.

Aside from its official goals and purposes, cohesion policy also has an important unofficial purpose or function that is well understood but not formally acknowledged, and that is its role as a compensatory mechanism that facilitates intergovernmental bargaining and agreement within the EU. In the past, cohesion policy spending has been used in this fashion to broaden support among the member states for further integration, both deeper economic and political integration ('deepening') and the accession of new member states ('widening'). Indeed, the very creation of cohesion policy and the expansion of EU structural spending in the late 1980s is generally viewed as a 'side payment' made by wealthier countries to poorer member states to secure their agreement to further economic liberalization and integration (the single market and Economic and Monetary Union (EMU)). More recently, special cohesion policy allocations have become an important means of adjusting net budgetary balances and facilitating intergovernmental agreement in negotiations on EU Multi-annual Financial Frameworks (MFFs). This compensatory function gives cohesion policy a political utility that helps explain why structural spending has grown over the years, but also why cohesion policy has been so difficult to reform.

Cohesion policy can also be defined in terms of the share of the EU budget it absorbs and its role in EU budgetary politics. Since the mid-1990s cohesion policy has accounted for roughly a third of the EU budget, making it the second largest area of EU expenditure after the Common Agricultural Policy (CAP). This places cohesion policy squarely in the middle of EU budgetary politics, which is increasingly characterized by the fierce struggle for resources between relatively wealthy, primarily northern European, member states that are net contributors to the EU budget, and less wealthy, mainly southern and CEE, member states that are net recipients and the primary beneficiaries of cohesion policy. As such, cohesion policy plays a major role in the EU's growing 'north–south' economic and political divide. While the amount spent on cohesion policy is ultimately relatively modest – the entire EU budget only amounts to about 1 per cent of the EU Gross Domestic Product (GDP), after all – these funds take on greater significance in times of economic hardship and fiscal constraint, such as those experienced by Europe as a consequence of the global financial and euro-zone crises. Cohesion policy's budgetary share also makes it even more publicly visible and the object of often critical attention in discussions about the focus and effectiveness of EU spending.

Cohesion policy is also defined by the way in which it operates and the unique multi-level character of its implementation system. Cohesion policy operates through the programmed use of the so-called structural funds, the most important of which are the European Regional Development Fund (ERDF), the European Social Fund (ESF) and the Cohesion Fund. The amounts dedicated to the various structural funds, and thus the financial envelope for cohesion policy, are decided on a multi-annual basis, in negotiations between the member states on multi-annual budgetary or financial frameworks, now covering seven years, and since 2009 formally referred to as the MFF. These negotiations proceed on the basis of budgetary proposals from the Commission, and since the 2009 ratification of the Lisbon Treaty their outcome must be approved by the European Parliament.

The rules for how the structural funds will be used for the same multi-annual period – for which priority objectives, the geographic eligibility criteria, and the rules for how the funds will operate – are determined in a parallel set of intergovernmental negotiations, once again on the basis of Commission proposals, that are closely tied to the budgetary negotiations. The outcome of these negotiations – the agreement on a set of formal 'regulations' for the structural funds –must also be approved by the European Parliament as part of the EU's usual legislative process. The main actors in this process are the Commission, especially its Directorate-General (DG) for Regional and Urban Policy (DG REGIO) and for Employment, Social Affairs and Inclusion (DG EMPL), the member states, acting within the EU Council (or Council of Ministers) and the European Council (of heads of government or state), and the European Parliament, with consultative roles for the Committee of the Regions (COR) – a body representing subnational regional and local authorities – and the European Economic and Social Committee (EESC), which represents the interests of employers and organized labour. However, in drafting its legislative proposals the Commission also consults broadly with various interested partners and stakeholders in EU cohesion policy, including regional and local authorities, non-governmental organizations and academic experts, as well as national government representatives.

While decision-making on the basic design or architecture of cohesion policy and its funding occurs mainly at the European level, in a process involving EU institutions and the member states, the implementation of cohesion policy is a truly multi-level process that takes place mainly at the national and subnational (regional and local) levels. Implementation also involves a variety of public actors at different levels, including the Commission, national governments and subnational authorities, as well as relevant private interests and non-governmental groups in accordance with the key operational principle of 'partnership'. The partnership principle and the unique multi-level character of cohesion policy implementation has attracted considerable scholarly interest and spurred debate about the implications of cohesion policy for multi-level governance in the EU more broadly. Indeed, the promotion of multi-level governance and the diffusion of the partnership approach and other innovative governance norms can be considered an important 'side effect' or secondary objective of cohesion policy (Tarschys, 2003: 76–8).

Why study cohesion policy?

Cohesion policy is an important topic to study because of all that it is – the EU's main policy tool for promoting economic development, growth and competitiveness; a compensatory mechanism that facilitates intergovernmental bargaining and consensus; a major area of EU expenditure with a central role in EU budgetary politics and the Union's growing north–south divide; and a unique multi-level policy with implications for EU governance norms and practices more broadly. Indeed, each of these aspects of cohesion policy alone would be an interesting and important subject to examine. Studying cohesion policy as a whole, however, allows us to investigate the linkages between the different faces or dimensions of this complex and controversial policy.

Cohesion policy is also an important topic to study because of what it can tell us about the EU itself. In many ways, cohesion policy is a reflection of the EU – a complex, multi-level system that integrates a great diversity of interests and moves forward on the basis of painfully negotiated trade-offs and package deals. An examination of cohesion policy, therefore, can reveal a great deal about what the EU is and how it operates, and also where it is going. It can also shed light on questions of consensus and legitimacy and on the relationship between values and interests in the EU polity. The creation of cohesion policy in the late 1980s was in many ways an expression of solidarity between rich and poor and a statement of the EU's basic commitment to this value, as well as being an outgrowth of the EU's consensus-based system of decision-making. An examination of cohesion policy's development since that point can thus tell us a great deal about the continued relevance of this principle in the EU today, in difficult economic and political circumstances, as well as the balance between national self-interest and solidarity in the EU going forward.

Book organization and plan

This book is a study of EU cohesion policy. It examines the historical origins and evolution of cohesion policy and the various political and economic factors that have influenced its development, the key role of cohesion policy in EU budgetary politics, especially its traditional use as a compensatory mechanism and its role in the EU's growing 'north–south' divide, and the ongoing debates about the impact of cohesion policy on multi-level governance and on economic growth and convergence. It also discusses the future prospects of cohesion policy in an unfavourable economic and political climate. In the process, it attempts to explain the importance of cohesion policy and its historical significance and role in the process of European integration and the 'building of Europe' (Leonardi, 2005).

To cover these topics and questions, the book is divided into seven chapters, organized as follows. The first two chapters examine the historical development of cohesion policy from its origins to the present. Chapter 1 examines the creation of cohesion policy, tracing its development from the Rome Treaty and establishment of the ERDF in 1975 to the major reform of the structural funds in 1988 that marked the birth of cohesion policy. It also discusses the creation of the Cohesion Fund and the relatively minor policy reform of 1993, and the 1999 reform of cohesion policy which occurred in the shadow of the EU's pending enlargement to Central and Eastern Europe. The chapter explains the main political and economic factors influencing these developments and the reasons why cohesion policy became such an important policy and a major area of EU expenditure.

Chapter 2 examines the evolution of cohesion policy after 2000, in response to the challenge of Eastern enlargement and the EU's growing focus on economic growth and competitiveness. In particular, it examines the major reorientation of cohesion policy that has occurred since 2006, through its alignment with the Lisbon and Europe 2020 strategies for creating a more economically dynamic and competitive Europe. It also looks at the impact of the 2008 global financial crisis and the subsequent euro-zone crisis on cohesion policy, including its increased use as an instrument of EU economic governance and structural reform. The chapter examines the main political and economic factors affecting decision-making on cohesion policy in this period which explain its reorientation and the changes to its basic goals and objectives.

Chapter 3 examines the role of cohesion policy in EU budgetary politics, including its use as a compensatory mechanism or 'side payment' to facilitate intergovernmental agreement on both EU widening and deepening. It also looks at how cohesion policy has been used in EU budgetary negotiations to deal with the tricky issue of member state net balances, thereby helping to achieve final agreement on the complex multi-annual budgetary frameworks that have been a feature of the EU since the late 1980s, as well as the implications of such deal-making for the coherence and effectiveness of cohesion policy. The chapter also examines the growing 'north–south' cleavage in EU budgetary politics between wealthy and poor member states and its implications for cohesion policy.

The next three chapters focus on the implementation of cohesion policy, once the basic decisions on policy design and budgetary allocations have been made, and on its consequences for multi-level governance and economic growth and convergence. Chapter 4 examines the different stages of the cohesion policy implementation process, including the determination of which geographical areas will be eligible for EU assistance, strategic planning and programming, the monitoring and management of operational programmes, and programme evaluation and reporting. It also discusses changes to implementation rules and procedures that have occurred over the years and the reasons for them, including the changing role of the Commission in the implementation process, and some key problems in cohesion policy implementation.

Chapter 5 looks at the impact of cohesion policy on multi-level governance. After discussing the evolution of the partnership principle and its relationship to the academic concept of multi-level governance, it examines the application of the partnership principle in different programming periods. It then examines the debate over whether cohesion policy has promoted both vertical and horizontal multi-level governance in the EU, with a look at the experiences of different member states. The chapter concludes with a brief look at the new Community-led Local Development (CLLD) instrument of cohesion policy that was introduced for 2014–20 as another means of promoting a participatory approach in the use of EU funds.

This is followed in Chapter 6 by an examination of the debate over whether cohesion policy has been effective in promoting economic growth and convergence. After discussing why the economic effects of cohesion policy are so difficult to evaluate, it surveys different views on this question, both pro and con, put forward by critics and supporters of cohesion policy alike. It also discusses why there is so much divergence in these assessments of the impact of cohesion policy.

Chapter 7 concludes the book with a discussion of the future of cohesion policy. It begins by discussing important aspects of the economic and political context that are likely to influence future decision-making on cohesion policy, including the euro-zone crisis and its impact on the European economy, the growing dominance in the EU of Germany and its economic vision, the EU's deepening north–south divide, and the growth of euroscepticism and populist nationalism and its impact on domestic and EU politics. In view of this context, the chapter then addresses some key questions about the future of cohesion policy, concluding that cohesion policy is likely to survive in basically its present form but also as an increasingly contested policy.

Chapter 1

The Origins and Early Evolution of Cohesion Policy

Cohesion policy was not an original policy of the EU, like the CAP or the common commercial policy. While the preamble of the 1957 Rome Treaty, the founding treaty of the European Community (EC, later the EU), referenced the desire of the signatory states to reduce regional disparities in the Community, it was not until nearly 20 years later that an EC regional policy was finally established. What we now know as cohesion policy was only created in the late 1980s, following the signing and ratification of the SEA, which among other things established the strengthening of economic and social cohesion as a core objective of the EC. The creation of cohesion policy was accompanied by a dramatic expansion of structural funds spending, and by the late 1990s cohesion policy had grown to account for more than a third of the EU budget, making it the second largest area of EU expenditure after the CAP.

How cohesion policy came to be and how it evolved in its initial years is the subject of this chapter. The chapter begins with the creation of the ERDF in 1975 and the subsequent development of EC regional policy. It then examines the major reform of the structural funds in 1988, exploring both the reasons for this reform and the design of the new cohesion policy to which it gave birth. The chapter then discusses the relatively minor reform of cohesion policy in 1993 and the creation of the Cohesion Fund in connection with the Maastricht Treaty. It ends with the 1999 reform of cohesion policy, which occurred in the shadow of the EU's pending enlargement to Central and Eastern Europe and marked the end of the first era of cohesion policy. Chapter 2 continues the historical narrative, focusing on the impact of enlargement and the major reorientation of cohesion policy after 2006 to align it with the EU's growth and competitiveness strategies.

From Rome to the ERDF: the creation of EC regional policy

The problem of uneven regional development and its implications for the functioning of the common market was something that European leaders were well aware of as they gathered in the mid-1950s to negotiate the EC's founding treaties (Molle, 2007). The outcome of these negotiations, the 1957 Treaty of Rome, contained no specific provisions for a Community regional policy, however, with such a policy being viewed as either unnecessary or too ambitious by most of the signatory states. Not only were most national governments reluctant to grant competencies in this sensitive policy area to a new European authority, but it was widely believed that increased integration itself would eventually reduce economic and social imbalances in Europe through the promotion of interregional trade. As a result, while the goal of reducing regional disparities and the 'backwardness of the less favoured regions' was mentioned in the Rome Treaty's preamble, the treaty itself addressed the regional issue only indirectly, through its provisions for common policies in the areas of agriculture, transport and state aid, all of which had regional development implications (Manzella and Mendez, 2009: 5). The only financial instrument created by the treaty for promoting regional development was the European Investment Bank (EIB), which could provide low-interest loans and guarantees to national governments for projects aimed at assisting less developed regions (CEC, 1957: 45). The Rome Treaty also provided for the establishment of two financial instruments with regional development implications, the ESF, created to assist workers affected by industrial restructuring, and the European Agricultural Guidance and Guarantee Fund (EAGGF), which contained a small ceiling under its Guidance section to support the adaptation of underdeveloped rural areas (CEC, 1957: 17, 43–4). These were the first of the so-called structural funds, which along with the ERDF and the Cohesion Fund would later provide the main financial instruments for cohesion policy.

The idea of a common regional policy nevertheless had its supporters. Among these was the newly created European Commission, which over the next decade worked tirelessly to promote the creation of an EC regional policy. These efforts included the organization of a major conference on regional economies in Brussels in 1961 that was attended by national regional policy officials, and which had the aim of outlining the future shape of a Community regional policy (Bache, 1998: 35). The conference was followed by a process of study and reflection, which included the establishment of a network of working groups in order to compare national regional policy practices and experiences. These consultations and deliberations provided the basis for the publication of two memos ('communications') in 1965 and 1969 in which the Commission laid out its argument and initial proposals for a common regional policy (CEC, 1965, 1969). The Commission also created a new Directorate-General for Regional Policy (DG XVI) in 1968, even though a Community regional policy did not yet exist and regional development measures still only accounted for 3 per cent of the EC budget (Santos, 2008: 2). In addition to the Commission's efforts, support for a Community regional policy also came from the European Parliament, in the form of a series of resolutions between February 1959 and February 1964 (Wozniak Boyle, 2006: 33–44; Manzella and Mendez, 2009: 7, fn 15).

It wasn't until the early 1970s, however, that a convergence of economic and political developments enabled the regional policy issue to rise to the top of the EC's agenda. One was the emergence of severe economic structural problems in different parts of Europe, which created an increased focus on unemployment and drew attention to the close linkage between declining industries and the problems of specific regions (Manzella and Mendez, 2009: 7). Another was the decision of EC leaders, taken at the December 1969 Hague summit, to pursue the goal of EMU, which led to concerns about the economic impact of EMU on Europe's less developed regions as well as the problems for monetary union that regional disparities might pose (Allen, 2005: 217; Manzella and Mendez, 2009: 7; Ujupan, 2009: 5; Werner Report, 1970). Also playing a role were the Commission's plans, approved by the Council in 1971, to restrict member state aids to wealthier regions in favour of poorer ones, thereby placing constraints on national regional policy and generating increased interest in a Community-level approach (Bache, 1998: 36-7).

The main factor in the establishment of EC regional policy, however, was the Community's pending first enlargement. In 1970, Denmark, the United Kingdom (UK) and Ireland began negotiations to enter the EC (along with Norway, which eventually did not join the Community in 1973 together with the other three), and the prospect of their accession raised issues that could only be solved through the creation of a common regional policy. For starters, enlargement would add two countries to the EC – the UK and Ireland – with severe regional problems, thus both increasing regional disparities in the Community and expanding the coalition of member states supporting a common regional policy (Balchin *et al.*, 1999: 16; Reiner, 1999: 7). The prospect of enlargement also raised the issue of net budgetary balances, because of the dominant role in the Community budget of the CAP, which by this point accounted for close to 75 per cent of EC spending (Ujupan, 2009: 5; Manzella and Mendez, 2009: 8). While Ireland, as an agricultural country, would qualify for CAP allocations, it seemed likely that the UK, with its relatively small, highly efficient and modern agricultural sector, would become a net contributor to the EC budget, even though it had to deal with significant industrial reconversion and a high rate of unemployment (Keating, 1995: 19; Paraskevopoulos, 2001: 33; Ujupan, 2009: 5). Especially because the UK was afraid that some of its declining industrial regions would not be able to compete with their continental counterparts, it eagerly supported the establishment of a Community regional policy (and a corresponding reduction in the proportion of the EC budget absorbed by the CAP) as a way to compensate the UK for its anticipated large net contributions to the budget while at the same time granting assistance to its declining regions (Allen, 2005: 217; Kengyel, 2000: 6). The creation of EC regional policy, therefore, became part of the general package deal that allowed the 1973 enlargement to go forward.

At the October 1972 Paris summit, EC leaders announced that the member states had 'agreed to give top priority to correcting the structural and regional imbalances in the Community which could hinder the achievement of Economic and Monetary Union'. They also declared that the member states would coordinate their regional policies and establish a Regional Development Fund, and they invited the Commission to draft a report that would analyse regional problems in the Community and propose appropriate solutions (Bulletin of the EC, 1972: 18–19). Responding to this request, in May 1973 the Commission published its 'Report on the Regional Problems in the Enlarged Community' – better known as the Thomson Report, after the British Commissioner for Regional

Policy, George Thomson – in which it outlined the political and economic rationales for a common regional policy and an interregional transfer of resources within the Community (Behrens and Smyrl, 1997: 12). According to the report:

> No Community could maintain itself nor have a meaning for the people which belong to it so long as some have very different standards of living and have cause to doubt the common will of all to help each Member State to better the condition of its people ... Unless the Community's economic resources are moved where human resources are, thus sustaining living local communities, there is bound to be disenchantment over the idea of European unity. The long history and diversity of the European people, the historical and cultural values which are the moral wealth of each region, make the maintenance or establishment in each region of the groundwork of an up-to-date economy a matter of capital importance. (CEC, 1973a: 4)

The Commission submitted its formal legislative proposal in July 1973, in which it called for the creation of a European Regional Development Fund with a budget of 2.25 billion European Units of Account (EUA) for a three-year period. According to the Commission's proposal, the ERDF would disburse its funds according to 'objective Community indicators' rather than national quotas; however, ERDF support would only be given to regions designated by national governments for domestic assistance, thus enabling the member states to determine eligibility (CEC, 1973b). Nevertheless, the Commission later published its own proposal for which areas should be eligible to receive the funds (CEC, 1973c).

The subsequent negotiations were lengthy and difficult, characterized by strong divisions among the member states and between national governments and the Commission. Among the member states, the UK, Ireland and Italy, the presumed major beneficiaries of the ERDF, were the strongest supporters of the Commission's plans and called for a larger regional fund, while Germany, the likely main paymaster for the scheme, had the deepest reservations and favoured a much smaller fund. There was also disagreement over how funds would be distributed. Germany, along with the Netherlands and Denmark – other potential net contributors – favoured a greater concentration of ERDF funding, hoping this would limit the size of the fund, while Ireland and Italy also favoured concentration but with a larger fund. The UK and France, meanwhile, wanted greater flexibility in geographical targeting and less Commission interference in the domestic allocation of economic development resources. Also hindering negotiations was the Israeli–Arab Yom Kippur War in October 1973 and the subsequent oil crisis and economic recession, which made Germany and other likely net contributors even more reluctant to accept a larger regional fund, a reluctance that only grew with the UK's refusal to supply oil from newly discovered deposits in the North Sea to its EC partners at a preferential price. Through it all, the Commission, with the backing of the European Parliament and in alliance with the poorer member states, continued to push for the ERDF while submitting new proposals (Bache, 1998: 39–40; Wozniak Boyle, 2006: 52–7).

The combination of Commission efforts and the election of new German (Helmut Schmidt) and French (Giscard d'Estaing) leadership led to renewed movement on the regional policy issue by the fall of 1974. Also instrumental to achieving an agreement was the threat of the Irish and Italian governments to 'sabotage' the scheduled Paris summit in December unless the other member states agreed to establish a regional development fund and give a firm commitment on its size (Bache, 1999: 30). As a result, EC leaders agreed in Paris to establish the European Regional Development Fund, and the regulation formally creating the ERDF was approved by the Council in March 1975 (Bache, 1998: 41; Wozniak Boyle, 2006: 55–7; OJEC, 1975).

Because of the intergovernmental compromises required to create the ERDF, its initial size and scope were fairly modest. The fund's budget of EUA 1.3 billion for the period 1975–8 was significantly below the Commission's original suggestion of EUA 3 billion, made at the 1972 Paris summit, or even the EUA 2.25 billion mentioned in its July 1973 legislative proposal. At the agreed level the ERDF accounted for only 4.8 per cent of the total Community budget, which itself represented only 0.5 per cent of the EC GDP (Bouvet and Dall'erba, 2010: 504). As such, the ERDF was too small in its early years to have a significant impact on welfare differences across the regions and its operations remained very modest. The Commission was also not successful in having ERDF funds allocated according to 'objective Community indicators'; instead, at member state insistence, the funds were allocated according to a system of national quotas set in annual negotiations between the member states. National governments also retained the right to determine which regions would be eligible for Community support, by limiting ERDF funds to areas targeted by the member states' own regional policies. Applications for project financing were channelled through national governments as well, giving them the primary role in project selection (Manzella and Mendez, 2009: 10). As a result of these provisions, the Commission's role in regional policy decision-making was very limited; nor did subnational authorities have much involvement, as the Commission had originally hoped (Leonardi, 2005: 2). It would not be until the 1988 reform of the structural funds that this basic policy model would be revised. In the meantime, however, two smaller reforms introduced some significant adjustments that would provide the basis for more substantial later changes.

The 1979 and 1984 reforms

The creation of the ERDF was followed by two minor policy reforms in 1979 and 1984. In the former, the member states, responding to the prospective accession of Greece and growing regional disparities in the context of European economic stagnation, as well as the European Parliament's insistence on a higher allocation for regional policy, approved a 50 per cent increase in the ERDF's budget (OJEC, 1979). As a consequence, regional policy spending grew to a little over 6 per cent of the EC budget.

The 1979 reform also made some changes to the design of regional policy. These included the creation of a new 'non-quota' section for Community actions managed by the Commission, although this accounted for only 5 per cent of total ERDF resources. The Commission could use these funds to support economic development projects and programmes in areas not designated by national governments for regional policy assistance; however, the distribution of non-quota funding was subject to unanimous decision by the Council rather than qualified majority voting, thus limiting the Commission's discretion in using these funds (Bache, 1998: 55–7). The reform also allowed a greater role for regional development programmes – packages of interrelated measures rather than single projects, drawn up in agreement with member states in the form of a contract – and it broadened the types of activities eligible for Community assistance. It also allowed for the combined use of different Community funds with regional implications – the ERDF, ESF, EAGGF (Guidance section) and EIB loans – something long sought-after by the Commission, creating the possibility for 'integrated' development programmes. Using its new prerogatives, the Commission launched a series of small-scale Integrated Development Programmes (IDPs) in several member states in the early 1980s. The new legislation also assigned the Commission more of a strategic role, by giving it the responsibility for preparing periodic reports on the social and economic situation of the Community's regions; within these reports, the Commission could propose new regional policy priorities and guidelines (Manzella and Mendez, 2009: 11–12; Paraskevopoulos, 2001: 35; Leonardi, 2005: 34–5, 44–5).

A second regional policy reform in 1984 resulted in further changes (OJEC, 1984). The ERDF's budget was once again increased, although its share of total EC spending remained relatively stable (at about 7.5 per cent of the EC budget until 1986, when it rose to 9.1 per cent due to additional allocations for Spain and Portugal, which joined the Community that year). A new system of financial allocations to the member states was created, replacing the old system of fixed national quotas with a system of indicative ranges (minimum and maximum), although in reality the lower limit represented a guaranteed minimum amount of ERDF funding for member states if they submitted a sufficient number of acceptable applications within a specified time. The 1984 reform also increased the share of ERDF spending to be delivered through integrated programmes, thus significantly reinforcing the programme approach to regional policy favoured by the Commission. This funding could take the form of Community Programmes, drawn up by the Commission in consultation with member states to serve Community objectives (and generally concerning the territory of more than one state), or National Programmes of Community Interest, drawn up by the member states in consultation with the Commission and subnational authorities and focused on national regional development priorities. For the approval of Community Programmes, only a qualified majority vote in the Council was now needed, rather than unanimity as before, while the use of National Programmes gave the Commission further scope to align national regional policies to Community priorities (Manzella and Mendez, 2009: 12; Bache, 1998: 61–3; Paraskevopoulos, 2001: 34).

The 1984 reform represented the end of the first phase of EC regional policy with a new era set to begin with the more radical reforms in 1988. While the 1979 and 1984 reforms had increased the Community orientation of regional policy and given the Commission enhanced discretion and more of a strategic role, EC regional policy before 1988 remained essentially a transfer payment system between the Community and the member states, with the Commission acting basically as paymaster and playing very little or no role in planning how regional funds were used, or in overseeing their use and evaluating the impact of EC-funded projects in the regions and countries where they occurred. Thus, according to Leonardi (2005: 65), before the 1988 reform of EC regional policy 'no explicit policy to stimulate socio-economic development [was] ... in place at the European level'.

The SEA and 1988 reform of the structural funds: the creation of cohesion policy

By the mid-1980s several factors necessitated a more fundamental reform of EC regional policy. These included widening regional disparities in the Community, as Europe underwent economic structural changes that resulted from deindustrialization, rising energy prices and increased competitive pressures from lower-cost producers worldwide. The main impetus for reform, however, was provided by the dual process of EC enlargement ('widening') and intensified economic integration ('deepening') which occurred at this time. The accession of Spain and Portugal in January 1986 brought two poor countries with serious development problems into the Community and further enlarged the coalition of member states favouring increased EC efforts to strengthen economic and social cohesion (Manzella and Mendez, 2009: 13). At the same time, the EC's plan to deepen integration through adoption of the single market programme, with its goal of creating a barrier-free internal market by the end of 1992, raised concerns about the ability of weaker countries and regions to compete in a more integrated Europe.

The need for regional policy reform was stressed by Commission President Jacques Delors in a speech to the European Parliament in early 1985:

> Over the past 15 years regional disparities within the Community have widened. The underdeveloped regions of the periphery of the industrial heart of Europe have been joined by a number of old industrial regions whose traditional economic base is in structural decline. But the two are fundamentally different. The Community's Structural Funds should – provided, of course, that they have sufficient resources – make it possible for the Community to support structural conversion and adjustment projects in regions in difficulty. The Commission aims to reverse the trend towards treating these funds as a mere redistribution mechanism (CEC, 1985).

The intergovernmental negotiations on the single market programme and other changes to the Rome Treaty – which were launched in September 1985 and eventually concluded in February 1986 with the signing of the SEA – provided an opportunity for poorer member states and the proponents of a stronger regional policy to press for reform and increased regional spending. In the Intergovernmental Conference (IGC), the poorer member states – Greece, Ireland and Italy, joined later by Spain and Portugal – with the strong support of Commission President Delors, argued for a major increase in regional policy spending to compensate them for the anticipated negative effects of the single market and economic liberalization. In fact, these member states indicated, in the words of a report drafted by an intergovernmental committee preparing the negotiations (the Dondelinger Group), that they considered such 'appropriate provisions ... a condition for [their] acceptance of the proposals on the Internal Market' (cited in Moravcsik, 1998: 367). The wealthier member states, which would be the main source of these increased funds, were reluctant to make such a commitment but they needed the support of the poor member states in order to reach an SEA agreement, unanimity being required for treaty approval.

In the end, the IGC agreed to introduce a new treaty section (Title V) on 'economic and social cohesion' and to make economic and social cohesion a core objective of the EC. According to Article 130a of the SEA:

In order to promote its overall harmonious development, the Community shall develop and pursue its actions leading to the strengthening of its economic and social cohesion. In particular the Community shall aim at reducing disparities between the various regions and the backwardness of the least-favoured regions.

Article 130b specified the means by which the objectives of 'cohesion policy' would be achieved, including the three structural funds – the ERDF, ESF and EAGGF (Guidance Section) – loans from the EIB and other existing financial instruments and the coordination of member state economic policies. The role of the ERDF specifically was defined in Article 130c: 'The [ERDF] is intended to help redress the principal regional imbalances in the Community through participating in the development and structural adjustment of regions whose development is lagging behind and in the conversion of declining industrial regions' (SEA, 1986: 13–14).

The SEA contained no specific provisions concerning the financial resources for cohesion policy, however. In the draft text agreed to at the December 1985 summit, the European Council only declared that the reformed structural funds would be 'adequately financed so far as budgetary resources permit' (European Council, 1985: 15). In the final treaty text, even this vague commitment disappeared. Instead, Article 130d obligated the Commission to submit a 'comprehensive proposal' to the Council for reforming the 'structure and operational rules' of the structural funds, so that they could more effectively achieve the objectives of social and economic cohesion and the reduction of regional disparities (SEA, 1986: 14). Although the subject of financial resources was not specifically mentioned in this directive, the clear implication was that the Commission's proposal would deal with the issue of funding in a manner that would satisfy the demands of the less wealthy countries. Despite the lack of hard evidence for such a deal (Allen, 2000: 249), therefore, the eventual intergovernmental agreement two years later to double structural funds resources has prompted the widespread view that increased regional policy spending was a 'side payment' made by wealthier member states to the Community's poorer members to secure their agreement to the single market programme and deeper integration (see, for example, Moravcsik, 1991: 62; 1998: 367, 374; Pollack, 1995: 365–6; Ross, 1995: 40).

While the SEA provided the legal basis for policy reform, a programmatic basis was provided by the Integrated Mediterranean Programmes (IMPs), a special development programme for southern member states (Greece, Italy and France) that was approved in 1985 as compensation for the presumed costs of admitting Spain and Portugal to the EC (CEC, 1989a: 2–5; Allen, 2005: 218). Created for a seven-year period and drawing on the experiences of the first integrated operations in the early 1980s, the IMPs further applied the multi-annual programming, integrated planning and participative approach to Community regional policy favoured by the Commission, while also providing for the 'continuing involvement of the Commission in all aspects of programming' (Manzella and Mendez, 2009: 12; Hooghe, 1996: 11). Altogether, the IMPs covered 29 programmes in the three countries and accounted for ECU 6.6 billion, making them the largest and most financially significant experimental programmes attempted by the Commission before 1989 (Leonardi, 2005: 45–6; Paraskevopoulos, 2001: 35). According to Leonardi (2005: 46), however, the most important aspect of the IMPs was that 'a new regulation had to be formulated ... to allow them to operate, and that regulation became the model for the 1988 reform that was to revolutionize regional policy in the Community and member states from 1989 onwards'.

The Commission presented its general ideas for reform of the structural funds in February 1987, as part of an ambitious five-year plan (the so-called Delors I package) for remaking the EC budget and policies to align them with the goals of the SEA. In its Communication to the Council, the Commission justified reform of the structural funds and its request for a doubling of structural funds resources primarily in economic efficiency terms, arguing that regional economic disparities in the Community, which had grown with the accession of Greece, Portugal and Spain, could impede the completion and effective functioning of the single market, and hence undermine European economic growth and competitiveness. To avoid this outcome, the Commission argued that the structural funds must be made into 'instruments of economic development' and a more effective means for strengthening economic and social cohesion, the new EC core objective established by the SEA, and which the Commission defined primarily in terms of achieving 'greater convergence' (CEC, 1987: 6–7). The 'main objective' of the reformed structural funds – 'the real crux when it comes to cohe-

sion' – according to the Commission, was assistance to economically less developed regions, to enable them to 'catch up' or
converge with wealthier parts of the Community (CEC, 1987: 14).

The Commission's detailed proposals for structural funds reform
were presented in April 1987. Despite the radical nature of the
proposed reforms, most of the intergovernmental debate over the
next months centred on the amount of structural funds spending as
well as other major elements of the Delors I package (CAP reform,
the budgetary ceiling, the move to GNP-based contributions to the
EC budget, the UK rebate). As a result, there was little real debate on
the structural funds proposals themselves, with most member states
appearing to broadly accept them (Wozniak Boyle, 2006: 148–66).

In the budgetary negotiations, the main impediment to agreement
was the British government of Prime Minister Margaret Thatcher,
which opposed the general idea of cohesion but also a budget deal that
might worsen the UK's net budgetary position. Later in the negotiations, it was joined by France, which opposed CAP reform and also
expressed concern about the impact of increased structural funds
spending on its net budgetary position. The poor member states,
meanwhile, led by Spain, continued to insist on increased regional
spending in exchange for their support for further economic liberalization. In the end, after months of difficult negotiations that drifted
past the December 1987 (Copenhagen summit) deadline, agreement
on the Delors I package was finally achieved in February 1988. British
opposition was overcome when the UK was assured that it could
retain its special budget rebate, and German Chancellor Helmut Kohl
helped pressure other national leaders while agreeing to essentially
subsidize the new budgetary arrangement (Ross, 1995: 42; Dinan,
2012). As requested by the Commission, the agreement provided for
a doubling in real terms of the annual financial resources available to
the structural funds, from approximately ECU 7 billion in 1987 to
over ECU 14 billion in 1993 (European Council, 1988: 15). As a
result, structural spending would rise from 16.2 per cent of the EC
budget in 1987 to 30.7 per cent in 1993, making it the second largest
area of expenditure after the CAP (CEC, 2009: 80).

The design of cohesion policy

The Delors I deal also included agreement in principle on the regulatory guidelines for the structural funds, which were subsequently

implemented through five new Council regulations that became effective in January 1989: a framework regulation and four implementation regulations, one defining the horizontal coordination of the actions of the structural funds and other financial instruments, and the other three specifying new governance norms for each of the structural funds.

The new regulations introduced four complementary principles according to which the structural funds were supposed to operate:

1. 'Concentration' – requiring that Community assistance be concentrated in areas of greatest need, as defined by established objectives.
2. 'Programming' – requiring that the structural funds be used to support multi-annual programmes drawn up by the member states, in line with Community objectives and priorities and approved by the Commission, rather than for individual projects.
3. 'Partnership' – requiring involvement of the Commission, national governments and subnational bodies in the planning and implementation of cohesion policy.
4. 'Additionality' – requiring that member states spend regional policy allocations in addition to their own domestic expenditure, so that EC funds do not substitute for national expenditures but rather complement them; the receipt of structural funds assistance, in other words, should not lead to a reduction of national expenditure on regional development policy. (CEC, 1989b: 13–55, 21)

In accordance with the principle of concentration, the new regulations established six 'priority objectives' to guide the use of the funds, three of which had an explicitly regional focus:

1. Objective 1 – assisting development and structural adjustment in economically backward regions, defined as having a per capita GDP below 75 per cent of the Community average;
2. Objective 2 – promoting the conversion and restructuring of areas seriously affected by industrial decline;
3. Objective 5b – assisting rural areas facing problems of structural adjustment linked to the decline of agriculture. (OJEC, 1988: 13–16)

Another three objectives concentrated on specific problems rather than on regions and covered the entire Community:

1. Objective 3 – combatting long-term unemployment;
2. Objective 4 – facilitating the occupational integration of young people;
3. Objective 5a – assisting the development of rural areas. (OJEC, 1988: 15–16)

EC assistance under each of the six objectives would be provided – up to 75 per cent of total costs for Objective 1, 50 per cent for other objectives – by one or more of the structural funds, with member states expected to provide the rest from a mix of public and private funding sources (OJEC, 1988: 17). Of the six priority objectives, Objective 1 was allocated the lion's share of resources, accounting for about 70 per cent of the structural funds budget for the 1989–93 programming period (see Table 1.1). Regions in seven member states qualified for Objective 1 assistance in 1989–93, including the entire territory of Greece, Ireland and Portugal, the majority of Spain, and parts of Italy, France (the overseas departments) and the UK (Northern Ireland). Altogether, more than 43 per cent of the EC12 population was covered by the three regional objectives, with about half (21.7 per cent) living in areas eligible under Objective 1 (CEC, 1996: 151).

To facilitate the geographical targeting of structural funds assistance, the Commission devised a new territorial classification scheme, known as the 'NUTS' system after the French *nomenclature d'unités territoriales statistiques* (or Nomenclature of Units for Territorial Statistics). The largest units in this classification scheme were NUTS 1 regions, defined as 'major socio-economic regions,' which consisted of entire countries or groupings of smaller regions within countries. The next level consisted of NUTS 2 regions, defined as the 'basic regions for the application of regional policies', while NUTS 3 regions were even smaller in size (Eurostat, 2013a). Thus, while eligibility for Objective 1 assistance was assessed on the basis of NUTS 2 regions, assistance under Objectives 2 and 5b was generally directed at NUTS 3 units.

The guidelines for cohesion policy incorporated many of the principles long advocated by the Commission going back to the 1960s. These included the use of integrated, multi-annual programming for

TABLE 1.1   *Structural funds resources by Objective, 1989–93*

	Funds	Financial resources, ECU million (1988 prices)	Share of total structural funds resources (%)
Regional Objectives			
Objective 1	ERDF, ESF, EAGGF Guidance	43,818	69.6
Objective 2	ERDF, ESF	6,130	9.7
Objective 5b	ERDF, ESF, EAGGF Guidance	2,232	3.5
Total		**52,180**	**82.8**
Community-wide Objectives			
Objective 3 and 4	ESF	6,669	10.6
Objective 5a	EAGGF Guidance	4,102	6.5
Total		**10,771**	**17.1**
Total		**62,951**	**100.0**

Source: CEC (1989b: 14, 1996: 145) © European Union.

all structural funds assistance. Instead of Community financing for individual projects, support would now be provided for multi-year, multifaceted development programmes with financial commitments running over larger periods of time (CEC, 1989b: 21, 30–1). This change ensured greater coherence in formulating regional develop-ment strategies, while it also brought stricter budgetary discipline and provided for a certainty and predictability in funding that had formerly been missing (Bache, 1998: 73; CEC, 2010a: 3). The new guidelines also adopted the participative approach to decision-making that the Commission had long favoured through introduc-tion of the partnership principle, which required the involvement of subnational governmental actors in the planning and implementa-tion of structural funds assistance.

The 1988 reform also greatly expanded the Commission's discre-tionary authority and role in the administration of the structural funds (Bouvet and Dall'erba, 2010: 504; Paraskevopoulos, 2001: 37). The Commission was given the authority to determine the eligibility criteria for EC-funded development programmes and to formulate the rules for managing them (Leonardi, 2005: 35). It also gained the right to draw up and manage separate spending programmes co-financed by the structural funds, the so-called Community Initiatives (CIs), which eventually accounted for about 8 per cent of the structural funds budget for 1989–93 (CEC, 1996: 145). Altogether, the Commission adopted about a dozen CIs in this period, focused on such issues as cross-border cooperation, environmental protection, energy and telecommunications networks, research and development (R&D) and innovation and equal opportunity for women (CEC, 1993: 28).

While the Commission's increased management role might have been expected to generate opposition among the member states, the doubling of structural funds resources and the shift of spending towards poorer, mostly new member states also increased the interest of wealthier net contributors in having greater Commission oversight and supervision of the use of EU assistance. According to Pollack (1995: 372), from the perspective of wealthier countries 'the idea of greater Commission oversight [now] seemed less like an intrusion into the internal affairs of one's own state, where EC spending was minimal, and more like a necessary oversight of the poor member states where the bulk of EC money was being spent'.

In summation, the 1988 reform was a watershed, as it transformed EC regional policy 'from an essentially intergovernmental budgetary transfer to ... a genuine regional development tool with the potential to provide effective solutions to the problems faced by the Community's regions' (Manzella and Mendez, 2009: 13). Whereas previously Community assistance was provided via a redistributive mechanism to member states to support their own domestically determined priorities, it would now be provided on the basis of EC-approved multi-annual programmes, in pursuit of Community-determined objectives and in accordance with eligibility criteria that were also determined at the Community level. For the first time as well the various structural funds would be used in a coordinated fashion to achieve these objectives. Because it created the means for pursuing the EC's new core objective of economic and social cohesion, the 1988 reform also marked the birth of EC cohesion policy (Leonardi, 2005: 1–2).

The Maastricht Treaty and 1993 reform

The first reform of cohesion policy took place in the context of another major treaty revision and the further deepening of economic and political integration. The Treaty on European Union (TEU) was signed in Maastricht in February 1992 and came into force in November 1993, after a more difficult-than-expected ratification process. After the formal completion of the single market, the Maastricht Treaty marked a new era in European integration by providing for the stage-by-stage establishment of economic and monetary union. The Maastricht Treaty also had consequences for cohesion policy, however, as it reaffirmed the importance of economic and social cohesion and made it one of the EU's main priorities alongside the single market and EMU. It also restated the basic objectives of cohesion policy introduced by the SEA, but added 'rural areas' as a focus of EU efforts to reduce regional dispar-ities (TEU, 1992: 4, 26).

The Maastricht Treaty also expanded the Commission's role in cohesion policy somewhat, requiring it to 'submit a report ... every three years on the progress made towards achieving economic and social cohesion' and the contribution of cohesion policy to this progress. Moreover, the report was to be accompanied, if necessary, by the Commission's 'appropriate proposals' for policy reform. The treaty also provided for the establishment of a new EU institution with a consultative role in cohesion policy, the Committee of the Regions, which was to be made up of the representatives of regional and local authorities in order to give them a voice in EU debates and policy-making, especially on matters affecting their interests (TEU, 1992: 26, 39–40).

The Maastricht Treaty also established a new structural instru-ment, the Cohesion Fund, which was designed to help poorer member states (not regions) with a per capita GDP below 90 per cent of the EU average (at the time Greece, Ireland, Spain and Portugal) (TEU, 1992: 27). The creation of the Cohesion Fund was essentially a concession to Spain and the other poor member states, who in the intergovernmental negotiations were demanding a further large increase of EU assistance as a condition of their support for the treaty (Ross, 1995: 152, 182, 190; Moravcsik, 1998: 446, 449). The Cohesion Fund would support projects in the fields of transport, energy, and telecommunications infrastructure and the environment, thereby allowing recipient countries to spend public funds on economic development while working towards meeting the strict EMU 'convergence criteria', which placed limits on levels of government deficits and debt in order to qualify for EMU (Rumford, 2000: 32). The Cohesion Fund provided up to 85 per cent of project costs, a higher rate than any of the structural funds, and its operations, which were not initially programmed together with the structural funds, did not have to adhere to the same strict governance rules – additionality, partnership, etc. – that applied to the structural funds (Bache, 1998: 89–90).

The priority given to economic and social cohesion in the Maastricht Treaty was later reflected in a substantial increase of the financial resources for cohesion policy, thus meeting the demands of Spain and the other poor member states. While in the treaty negotiations the wealthier member states refused to commit to increased spending, through Commission President Delors they delivered the message that if the poor member states signed the treaty, they could expect a sizeable increase in structural funding when the new multi-annual budgetary perspective was agreed in 1992 (Moravcsik, 1998: 446). In the end, the Delors II package for 1994–9 that was approved at the Edinburgh summit in December 1992 contained a further doubling of the annual resources allocated to cohesion policy over the next six years. As a result, structural funds spending in 1994–9 amounted to ECU 141.5 billion (at 1992 prices), equalling a third of the EU budget, while an additional ECU 15.2 billion was allocated for the Cohesion Fund (European Council, 1992: 68–9).

A new set of regulations for the structural funds was adopted by the Council in July 1993. The new regulations slightly revised the priority objectives of cohesion policy: Objective 3, originally aimed at combatting long-term unemployment, was extended to include the integration of young people and people excluded from the labour market into working life; a reformulated Objective 4 now aimed at helping workers adapt to industrial changes and changes in production systems; and while Objective 5a maintained its initial goal of assisting the development of rural areas, it now also included aid for modernizing and restructuring fisheries (CEC, 1993: 11). To support this objective a fourth structural fund, the Financial Instrument for Fisheries Guidance (FIFG), was created.

The three regional Objectives (1, 2 and 5b) remained more or less unchanged, although the member states were given more input into

TABLE 1.2   *Structural funds resources by Objective, 1994–9*

	Funds	Financial resources ECU million (1994 prices)	Share of structural funds resources (%)
Regional Objectives			
Objective 1	ERDF, ESF, FIFG, EAGGF Guidance	93,991	68.0
Objective 2	ERDF, ESF	15,352	11.1
Objective 5b	ERDF, ESF, EAGGF Guidance	6,860	5.0
Objective 6	ERDF, ESF, FIFG, EAGGF Guidance	697	0.5
Total		**116,900**	**84.6**
Community-wide Objectives			
Objective 3	ESF	12,938	9.4
Objective 4	ESF	2,246	1.6
Objective 5a	EAGGF Guidance, FIFG	6,155	4.4
Total		**21,339**	**15.4**
Total		**138,239**	**100.0**

Source: CEC (1993: 24, 1996: 145) © European Union.

the selection of eligible areas under Objectives 2 and 5b, rather than this being decided unilaterally by the Commission as was previously the case. With the accession of Austria, Finland and Sweden in 1995, a new Objective 6 was introduced to assist the sparsely populated northern regions of the two Nordic member states, thus ensuring that these countries would also be eligible for regional support as they did not fit the existing objectives of cohesion policy (Allen, 2010: 235; CEU, 1995). Altogether, in 1994–9 the spatial coverage of cohesion policy's regional objectives increased from 43 per cent of the EU population to 52 per cent, with much of this increase attributable to the relaxation of regional eligibility criteria for assistance under Objective 1, which now covered 26.6 per cent of the EC population (CEC, 1996: 151). Objective 1 also continued to absorb the greatest share, about 68 per cent, of structural funds resources in the new programming period (see Table 1.2).

The 1993 reform also made changes to the Community Initiatives, including the creation of a management committee with member state representatives to oversee the CIs, thereby limiting somewhat the discretionary power of the Commission in operating these programmes (CEC, 1993: 27). It also identified seven new priorities for the CIs:

1. cross-border, trans-national and interregional cooperation and networking;
2. rural development;
3. development of the most remote regions;
4. employment and development of human resources;
5. management of industrial change;
6. development of urban areas hit by a crisis;
7. restructuring of the fishing industry.

Based on these priorities, by mid-1994 a set of 13 CIs was launched:

ADAPT (training and job creation in areas of industrial and techno-
    logical change);
EMPLOYMENT (labour market measures for disadvantaged groups);
INTERREG (interregional cooperation);
KONVER (defence-industry dependent regions);
LEADER II (rural development);
REGIS (integration of the most remote regions);
RECHAR (areas affected by coalfield closures);
PEACE (peace and reconciliation process in Northern Ireland and
    the border regions of the Republic of Ireland);
PESCA (areas dependent on the fishing industry);
RESIDER II (areas affected by closures in the steel industry);
RETEX (textile dependent regions);
SME (small and medium-sized enterprises in less favoured regions);
URBAN (urban areas with serious socio-economic problems).

About 10 per cent of the structural funds budget for 1994–9 was set aside for these various programmes (CEC, 1996: 109–12).

The new regulations retained the basic governing principles of cohesion policy, but these were modified somewhat to create more flexibility for national governments. For example, the additionality requirement was watered down to allow economic circumstances to be taken into account; and while the partnership principle was extended to specify a role for the economic and social partners in the implementation of cohesion policy, the new regulations allowed national governments to designate the appropriate partners in accordance with established national rules and practices (CEC, 1993: 19–20, 25–6). Changes were also made to the programming process, including the replacement of the previous five-year programming period with a six-year term that matched the time-frame of the new financial perspective (CEC, 1993: 21–2).

Thus, while the 1993 reform made only modest changes to the design of cohesion policy, through these changes the member states were able to reclaim some of the policy prerogatives they had ceded to the Commission in 1988, especially when it came to implementation (Pollack, 1995: 384). In addition to the dilution of the additionality principle, the establishment of a Cohesion Fund that did not operate according to structural funds rules, the greater input of national governments into the selection of eligible areas for structural funds assistance, and the creation of a management committee for the CIs were all steps that lessened the restrictiveness of EU rules for the member states and limited the Commission's discretion in the operation of cohesion policy. Thus, according to Bache (1998: 90), 'While the context of the 1988 reform gave the Commission considerable scope for advancing its policy preferences, the 1993 reform represented a reassertion of national government control in key areas.'

The 1999 reform: preparing for Eastern enlargement

The next reform of cohesion policy came in 1999 and covered the 2000–06 programming period. Once again, the prospect of enlargement, in this case the accession of a number of post-communist Central and Eastern European states, formed an important part of the context of cohesion policy reform, even though it was not yet clear how many new member states would enter the EU and when this would occur. Eventually, 10 new member states joined the EU in May 2004 – Cyprus, the Czech Republic, Estonia, Hungary,

Lithuania, Latvia, Malta, Poland, Slovakia and Slovenia – with Bulgaria and Romania joining in January 2007.

As the most extensive enlargement ever undertaken, the 'Eastern enlargement' of the EU resulted not only in an unprecedented expansion of the Union (both territorially and in terms of the number of new member states), but also a massive increase in its economic diversity (Begg, 1999: 9). Because the CEE countries had much lower GDPs than the EU15 average, almost their entire territory would be eligible for Objective 1 assistance once they joined the EU (Ujupan, 2009: 8). In 2000, Slovenia was the richest of the CEE group, with a per capita income around 70 per cent of the EU average, higher than Portugal and at approximately the same level as Greece. The Czech Republic, Hungary and Slovakia had per capita incomes around 50 per cent of the EU15 average, Poland and Estonia about 40 per cent, and Latvia and Lithuania around or below 30 per cent (Boldrin and Canova, 2003: 39).

The Eastern enlargement thus posed a more serious challenge for the EU than previous enlargements. As Begg (1999: 9) argues, the 1973 and 1995 enlargements were 'much easier to accommodate because they brought in countries with similar living standards and levels of economic development'; and while the accession of Greece and the Iberian countries in the 1980s 'added substantially to the number of less-favoured regions ... the degree and scale of diversity remained manageable'. Enlargement to Central and Eastern Europe, however, would greatly increase economic disparities within the EU and the number of claimants for EU assistance, thus posing a tremendous test for cohesion policy and the EU budget (Funck *et al.*, 2003: 1).

Also affecting cohesion policy reform was the difficult economic climate of the late 1990s, with most member states experiencing only very slow economic growth following the recession of the early 1990s, while Germany, Europe's economic engine, struggled to pay the costs of unification and the incorporation of its poorer eastern *Länder*. In this context there was growing concern about unemployment, which peaked at 11 per cent across the EU in 1996. In the 1997 Treaty of Amsterdam, which amended the TEU, the achievement of a 'high level of employment' was made a basic objective of the EU. The Treaty of Amsterdam also included a new title on employment and provided for the creation of a European Employment Strategy (EES), through which the member states would coordinate their employment policies to promote job creation and boost the employability of workers. EU leaders also indicated that they wanted the structural funds to be used to support the EES. Thus, at the November 1997 Luxembourg summit at which the EES was formally launched, the European Council expressed its 'hopes that the forthcoming reform of the Structural Funds ... [would] make optimum use of the Funds to serve employment needs wherever possible in the framework of the objectives assigned to them while respecting their primary purpose, which is to enable regions lagging behind to catch up' (European Council, 1997). There were also strong fiscal consolidation pressures across the EU, partly associated with the pending introduction of the euro and the requirement that member states reduce their budget deficits and debt levels in order to qualify for euro-zone membership (Manzella and Mendez, 2009: 16). In this difficult economic climate, the negotiations on the 2000–06 financial perspective were certain to be difficult.

The Commission first revealed its plans for cohesion policy reform in its July 1997 'Agenda 2000' report, a detailed medium-term strategy for strengthening the EU in the perspective of Eastern enlargement. In the report, the Commission declared that economic and social cohesion 'must remain a political priority' for an enlarged EU, and that the structural funds should remain a vital instrument for achieving this goal and strengthening the economies of underdeveloped regions. To achieve its objectives within budgetary limits, however, cohesion policy needed to become more effective, efficient and transparent, with the principles of concentration, efficiency and simplification being the keystones of future reform. To this end, the Commission proposed reducing the number of priority objectives for cohesion policy from seven to three – two regional objectives and one horizontal objective for human resources – and the number of CIs to three. It also proposed allocating ECU 275 billion (at 1997 prices) for structural and cohesion spending in 2000–06, with ECU 45 billion set aside for the new member states (CEC, 1997: 21–6).

The Commission's proposals were cautiously received by the member states. While most agreed that reform was necessary, and there was general acceptance of the Commission's proposed reorganization of the priority objectives, among nearly all member states there was concern about the loss of structural funds for specific regions due to the redefinition of objectives and the tightening of eligibility requirements. These concerns were not much allayed by the Commission's formal legislative proposals, presented in March 1998, which provided more details on transition arrangements for areas losing assistance and included provisions for a 'safety net' that would limit the loss of structural funds for individual member states (CEC, 1998).

The biggest split between the member states was on the budgetary front, where there was a strong difference of views between wealthier net contributors to the EU budget, especially Germany and the Netherlands, and poorer member states such as Spain who were the main beneficiaries of cohesion policy. While the former opposed further increases in EU spending to pay for enlargement – in keeping with their demand for a reduction in net contributions and out of concern that they would pay the lion's share of the costs of enlargement – the latter argued that it would be unfair to pay for enlargement by reducing the amount of assistance given to the poorest EU15 countries. Spain led the latter group in questioning whether enlargement could be accomplished without an increase in EU spending, declaring that the poorer member states were not prepared to 'foot the bill' for enlargement. The Spanish government also strongly rejected Germany's suggestion that member states joining the euro-zone should forfeit their rights to receive Cohesion Fund assistance (Baun, 2000: 150).

After months of difficult bargaining, final agreement on the Agenda 2000 package was reached at the Berlin European Council in March 1999. In Berlin, EU leaders agreed to a total of €213 billion for cohesion policy in the next six-year period, representing about one-third of the overall EU budget, a figure that was considerably below the Commission's initial proposal. Of this amount, €195 billion was allocated to the four structural funds and €18 billion to the Cohesion Fund, for which the four poorest EU15 member states would continue to be eligible, provided their per capita GNP remained less than 90 per cent of the EU average. The Berlin agreement also included €3.12 billion per year for pre-accession aid to the candidate countries, and an additional €40 billion in structural assistance for the new member states after their accession to the EU (European Council, 1999).

A new set of regulations for cohesion policy was subsequently approved by the Council between May and July 1999. As proposed by the Commission, the number of priority objectives for cohesion policy was reduced from seven to three:

Objective 1 – to assist regions whose development was lagging behind and which faced the most serious difficulties in terms of income, employment and infrastructure;

Objective 2 (formerly Objectives 2 and 5b) – to assist economic and social restructuring in areas experiencing structural difficulties;

Objective 3 – to help member states modernize their systems of education, training and employment in areas not targeted by Objectives 1 and 2 (OJEC, 1999: 8–10).

Among these objectives, Objective 1, which provided assistance to the EU's poorest regions, continued to receive the lion's share of resources, accounting for nearly 70 per cent of structural funds spending in 2000–06 (see Table 1.3). Stricter application of the eligibility criteria for Objective 1, however, meant that assistance under this objective targeted just 22.2 per cent of the EU15 population in 2000–06, compared with 26.6 per cent in 1999. In addition, a maximum coverage rate for Objective 2 assistance was set at 18 per cent of the EU 15 population, which was less than the 25 per cent rate for Objectives 2 and 5b combined in 1999 (CEC, 1999:10, 12). Assistance under Objective 3, and the ESF in general, was closely tied to the fight against unemployment and the goals of the EES. Thus, according to the new regulations, proposals for Objective 3 assistance would be assessed by the Commission in terms of their compatibility with national employment plans adopted under the EES (OJEC, 1999: 16).

As a result of the reform, the Commission succeeded in its goal of reducing the share of the EU population eligible for support under cohesion policy's regional objectives, from over 50 per cent in 1994–9 to 41 per cent in the new programming period (CEC, 2001a: 123). However, transitional assistance was given to all regions which no longer met the relevant eligibility criteria and for which assistance was being phased out. Also in the spirit of concentration, the number of Community Initiatives was reduced from 13 to four – INTERREG, LEADER, URBAN and EQUAL (transnational cooperation to combat all forms of discrimination and inequalities in the labour market) – with 5.4 per cent of the structural funds budget allocated for these programmes (CEC, 1999: 17–19). To keep the cost of enlargement manageable but also to address the limited capacity of the new member states to absorb EU funds once they became eligible, a cap of 4 per cent of GDP for

TABLE 1.3 *Structural funds resources by Objective, 2000–06*

	Funds	Financial resources € million (1999 prices)	Share of total structural funds resources (%)
Regional Objectives			
Objective 1	ERDF, ESF, FIFG, EAGGF Guidance	135,900	69.7
Objective 2	ERDF, ESF	22,500	11.5
Total		**158,400**	**81.2**
Objective 3	ESF	24,050	12.3
Fisheries (outside Objective 1)	FIFG	1,110	0.6
Community Initiatives	ERDF, ESF, EAGGF Guidance	10,440	5.4
Transitional and innovative measures		1,000	0.5
Total		**195,000**	**100.0**

Source: CEC (1999: 19–20) © European Union.

structural assistance was imposed for all member states. To ensure that EU funds were used in a timely and efficient manner, the new regulations also introduced the rule that funds would be automatically 'de-committed' by the end of the second year following the year of commitment – the so-called n + 2 rule (OJEC, 1999: 8–11, 20, 26).

Significant changes were also made to the programming and implementation procedures for cohesion policy, with an emphasis on greater simplification and decentralization and a corresponding reduction of the Commission's role in the management of EU-funded programmes. This reduced management role was offset, however, by the enhanced 'strategic' role given to the Commission, which was now responsible for establishing general priorities ('indicative guidelines') for the use of the structural funds, and by strengthened financial controls and evaluation requirements (CEC, 1999: 22–3, 28–30).

Upon acceding to the EU in May 2004, the 10 new member states were allocated a total of €13.5 billion (1999 prices) in structural funds resources between them. Almost all (98 per cent) of these funds were allocated under Objective 1, with much of this assistance dedicated to spending on basic infrastructure and regional development. The new member states also were granted €7.6 billion from the Cohesion Fund for investments in transportation and the environment (CEC, 2004a: 186). In the next programming cycle beginning in 2007, however, the new member states would be even greater beneficiaries of cohesion policy, since they would be entitled to funding for the entire multi-year period. They would also be full participants in the next round of budgetary negotiations and decision-making on cohesion policy reform. Enlargement, therefore, along with the EU's growing focus on economic growth and competitiveness, would be the main factors shaping the evolution of EU cohesion policy going forward.

Conclusion

The 1999 reform marked the end of the second era of EU regional or cohesion policy. The first era began with the creation of the ERDF and EC regional policy in 1975, while the second commenced with the 1988 reform of the structural funds and the creation of cohesion policy per se, as a means for pursuing the new economic and social cohesion objective established by the SEA. Since the 1988 reform, cohesion policy has developed into a major EU activity and area of expenditure. By the late 1990s, it accounted for more than a third of the EU budget, while funding operations in every member state and nearly all of the EU's regions.

The evolution of cohesion policy is closely linked to the dual process of EU widening and deepening. Successive enlargements since 1973 have increased economic disparities in the EU, thereby increasing the need for cohesion policy, while also expanding the coalition of member states favouring greater regional and cohesion spending. Efforts to deepen economic integration, on the other hand – first the single market programme and SEA, followed by the Maastricht Treaty and EMU – have generated concern about the ability of poorer countries and regions to compete in a more integrated Europe, while also creating opportunities for poorer member states to demand compensation in the form of increased cohesion policy spending in return for their agreement to new EU treaties. Cohesion policy was created and has grown, in other words, because of both objective economic needs and the politics of inter-governmental bargaining over further EU economic integration and liberalization.

This chapter has also identified the major actors in the development of cohesion policy. These include, first and foremost, the member states acting through the Council. Through intergovernmental bargaining and agreement on treaty reforms, MFFs and new policy regulations, the member states determine the scope and direction of cohesion policy and the financial resources allocated to it. Also playing an important role, however, is the Commission. After the Rome Treaty, the Commission was instrumental in getting regional policy onto the Community agenda, and since the creation of the ERDF it has been a major factor in the expansion and evolution of cohesion policy, serving as an advocate of increased spending and policy reform, an initiator and framer of policy proposals, and an intermediary in intergovernmental budgetary and legislative negotiations, where it has been a key ally of member states and regions favouring a stronger and more well-funded cohesion policy. The Commission also plays an important role in the multi-level process of implementing cohesion policy once the basic decisions about budgets and policy design are made, a topic that is explored further in Chapter 4. The European Parliament has also played a significant role as a supporter of regional policy and increased cohesion policy spending.

By the late 1990s cohesion policy had reached something of a 'high water mark', at least in terms of the share of the EU budget and GDP that it accounted for. In the negotiations on the 2000–06 financial framework and cohesion policy reform, the focus was on budgetary consolidation and the greater concentration of available financial resources. There were also calls to link cohesion policy spending more closely to the pursuit of other EU priorities, especially the struggle against unemployment. Among the main reasons for this shift of focus was the pending enlargement to Central and Eastern Europe, which would dramatically increase the number of poor member states and intra-EU economic disparities, and a much less favourable economic climate. Major contributors to the EU budget, especially Germany, were also becoming more reluctant to support EU spending. In the development of cohesion policy after 2000, these factors would continue to dominate, especially with the onset of the global financial crisis in 2008 and the subsequent euro-zone crisis. As a consequence, cohesion policy would undergo a fundamental thematic reorientation, from a focus on convergence and regional economic development to alignment with the EU's broader growth and competitiveness strategies, as the policy's supporters sought to demonstrate its continued relevance and EU 'value added'. This reorientation process and the factors influencing it are the subject of the next chapter, which examines the evolution of cohesion policy from the 2006 reform to the present.

Chapter 2

The Transformation of Cohesion Policy: Alignment with the EU's Growth and Competitiveness Strategy

After 2000 EU cohesion policy underwent a major thematic reorientation, adopting a new focus on economic growth and competitiveness in alignment with the EU's Lisbon and Europe 2020 strategies. While the promotion of economic convergence and the reduction of regional disparities remained official goals of cohesion policy, they would now be pursued in the context of efforts to make the EU as a whole more economically dynamic and competitive. This reorientation was necessitated by changing economic and political conditions, and by the need to demonstrate the continued relevance and added value of cohesion policy in a period of slow economic growth, high unemployment and tight budgetary constraints. The 2008 global financial crisis and the subsequent euro-zone crisis only added to the pressures on cohesion policy spending, but also provided cohesion policy with a potential new role as a source of growth-inducing public investment in a period of national fiscal austerity. As a consequence of these developments and the 2006 and 2013 policy reforms, cohesion policy has entered a new era with new goals and changes to its basic purpose or rationale. These changes, and the various economic and political factors influencing them, are the focus of this chapter.

The economic and political context of cohesion policy reform

The debate on cohesion policy reform began soon after the approval of the new regulations for 2000–06. Greatly influencing this debate was Eastern enlargement, which as expected posed a major challenge for the EU and cohesion policy. The accession of eight Central and Eastern European countries, plus Malta and Cyprus in 2004, significantly increased economic disparities in the EU, a situation that would be further amplified by the accession of Romania and Bulgaria in 2007. In its *Third Report on Economic and Social Cohesion*, the Commission stated that enlargement presented 'an unprecedented challenge for the competitiveness and internal cohesion of the EU'. According to the Commission, enlargement would 'lead to a widening of the economic development gap, a geographical shift in the problem of disparities towards the east and a more difficult employment situation: socio-economic disparities will double, and the average [per capita] GDP of the Union will decrease by 12.5 per cent' (CEC, 2004a: xxv).

In 2004, all 10 of the CEE countries had per capita GDPs under 90 per cent of the EU average, with most of them far below this level. As a consequence, the gap between rich and poor member states in an enlarged EU was quite dramatic. GDP per capita in Romania and Bulgaria, the poorest (at that time prospective) member states, was only 34 and 35 per cent of the EU average respectively, compared with 77 per cent of the EU average in Portugal (the poorest EU15 country), and 253 per cent in Luxembourg (the wealthiest). In regional terms the disparities were even greater. According to a Eurostat report, the poorest EU27 NUTS 2 region in 2004, Nord-Est in Romania, had a per capita GDP only 27 per cent of the EU average, compared with 303 per cent for Inner London, which was the richest. Moreover, the 15 poorest EU27 regions were all in Bulgaria, Romania, and Poland, and of the 70 regions with a per capita GDP under 75 per cent of the EU average, the threshold for Objective 1 assistance, 48, or nearly 70 per cent, were in nine CEE countries (all except Slovenia) (Eurostat, 2007: 1). In all, around 92 per cent of the population of the ten countries joining the EU in 2004 lived in regions with a GDP per capita below 75 per cent of the EU average while, taking Bulgaria and Romania into account, the EU population living in regions with a GDP per capita below the Objective 1 threshold would double from what it was in the EU15, as would the gap between their average income per capita and the EU average (CEC, 2004a: ix–x).

An 'inevitable and politically sensitive consequence' of enlargement, therefore, to be reflected in the next funding cycle, would be the 'budgetary shift in Cohesion policy resources from the EU15 to the new Member States' (Manzella and Mendez, 2009: 18). Enlargement would also significantly enlarge the coalition of member states favouring greater spending on cohesion policy. Another consequence was the so-called statistical effect of enlargement, resulting from the lowering of the EU's average GDP per capita as a consequence of the accession of a number of much poorer member states. According to the Commission, because of this statistical effect, 18 regions with a per capita income below 75 per cent of the EU15 average before enlargement would no longer be below this threshold for Objective 1 assistance after May 2004, although their structural economic development situation would not have improved. How to ensure that these regions continued to qualify for structural funds assistance after enlargement was yet another challenge for cohesion policy after 2006.

Also influencing the debate on cohesion policy reform was the unfavourable economic climate and the increased importance of the EU's growth, jobs and competitiveness agenda. Concerned about continued high levels of unemployment and the ability of the European economy to meet the challenges posed by globalization and the 'knowledge-driven economy', in March 2000 the European Council approved the so-called Lisbon strategy, which set the strategic goal of making the EU by 2010, 'the most competitive and dynamic knowledge-based economy in the world, capable of sustainable economic growth with more and better jobs and greater social cohesion'. To this end, the Lisbon strategy set goals for the improvement of high-tech infrastructure; investments in research and development; the promotion of innovation, entrepreneurship and small and medium-sized enterprises (SMEs); and completion of the internal market, especially in the areas of energy, communications, transportation networks and services. It also called for the modernization of education and training policies to prepare citizens for 'working and living in the knowledge economy', active employment policies to create 'more and better jobs', and policies to promote social inclusion for certain target groups, including the young, minorities, and the elderly and disabled. To achieve these objectives, the Lisbon strategy would be implemented using the 'new open method of coordination' (OMC), featuring EU guidelines with timetables for member states to achieve specific targets, the use of quantitative and qualitative indicators and benchmarks to measure progress and compare best practice, and 'periodic

monitoring, evaluation and peer review organised as mutual learning processes' (European Council, 2000).

The Lisbon strategy also set specific targets for 2010, including:
annual economic growth of 3 per cent of GDP; the creation of 20
million new jobs; an overall employment rate of 70 per cent; an
employment rate for women of over 60 per cent, and 50 per cent for
older workers; and (in March 2002) overall spending on R&D
approaching 3 per cent of GDP with two-thirds of this coming from
the private sector (European Council, 2000; 2002: 20). In June 2001
the European Council, meeting in Gothenburg, expanded the
Lisbon agenda to include the goal of 'sustainable development', thus
adding an 'environmental dimension' to the Lisbon strategy
(European Council, 2001: 4–8).

The Lisbon strategy proved difficult to implement in practice,
however, and after several years European economic performance
remained lacklustre. In November 2004, a high level committee
headed by former Dutch Prime Minister Wim Kok issued a critical
review of the Lisbon strategy which blasted the EU and its member
states for 'failing to act on much of the Lisbon strategy with sufficient urgency'. While national governments bore much of the blame
for their 'lack of determined political action', the report also criticized the design of the Lisbon strategy for being too broad and unfo-
cused, with its 'overloaded agenda, poor coordination and
conflicting priorities' (Kok Report, 2004: 6).

In a scheduled mid-term review, the new president of the
European Commission, José Manuel Barroso, drew on the findings
of the Kok report to call for a radical overhaul of the Lisbon strategy that would greatly simplify and streamline it while placing
renewed focus on the key priorities of growth and jobs. To achieve
the Lisbon goals, the Commission called for a new partnership
between the EU and national governments, including the creation of
Integrated Policy Guidelines at the EU level (proposed by the
Commission and approved by the Council) and National Reform
Programmes (NRPs) to be implemented by the member states (CEC,
2005a). The Commission's proposals were subsequently approved
by the European Council in March 2005, thereby formally re-
launching the Lisbon strategy. At the same time the European
Council decided to reduce the number of key targets for 2010 to two
– an overall employment rate of 70 per cent, and overall spending on
R&D approaching 3 per cent of GDP – while it identified four prior-

ity areas for EU and national action: knowledge and innovation, improving the business environment (making the EU a more 'attractive area in which to invest and work'), employment and labour markets, and energy and climate change (European Council, 2005: 2–14).

The Commission's 2004 proposals

For the Commission the Lisbon strategy presented an opportunity and the way out of a dilemma. The dilemma was caused by the bleak economic picture and the budgetary constraints imposed by EMU, which, combined, were making wealthier member states increasingly reluctant to subsidize EU spending. In December 2003, a group of six net contributors – Germany, the UK, Sweden, the Netherlands, Austria and Finland – had publicly called for a reduction of EU spending. In addition, Germany and France had already agreed that there would be no significant cuts to CAP spending in the next financial framework, meaning that the focus would be on cohesion policy as the place to cut for those wanting to reduce EU spending. The wealthier member states were also suggesting that, as a way to reduce spending, cohesion policy assistance in the future should only be given to the poorest member states and regions, while wealthier countries would resume full responsibility for regional development policies within their own borders (Euractiv. com, 2003).

For the Commission, therefore, the challenge was twofold: how to maintain the level of cohesion policy spending in the face of demands for budgetary retrenchment; and how to preserve cohesion policy as an EU-wide policy that applied to all member states and regions not just the poorest, thus maintaining the Commission's 'influence on Cohesion policy throughout the EU' (Bachtler and Mendez, 2007: 545). Linking cohesion policy spending to the Lisbon strategy provided a means to resolve this dilemma, while providing a new, forward-looking rationale or purpose for cohesion policy.

The Commission put forward its proposals for cohesion policy reform in February 2004, in the context of its *Third Report on Economic and Social Cohesion*. The Commission began by recalling that cohesion policy was not just a policy for transferring 'resources between Member States via the [EU] budget', it was also 'a dynamic policy that seeks to create resources by targeting the factors of economic competitiveness and employment, especially where unused potential is high'. It went on to declare that the EU continued to require an 'ambitious' and well-funded cohesion policy to meet the challenges of enlargement, globalization, and technological and demographic change. The Commission also stated that cohesion policy needed to be viewed as 'an integral part of the Lisbon strategy' and that it needed 'to incorporate the Lisbon and Gothenburg objectives and to become a key vehicle for their realisation via the national and regional development programmes' (CEC, 2004a: xxv–xxvi). The Commission thus proposed a 'new architecture' for cohesion policy, with investment targeted on 'a limited number of Community priorities, reflecting the Lisbon and Gothenburg agendas, where Community intervention can be expected to bring about a leverage effect and significant added value'. For regional programmes specifically, these priorities were 'innovation and the knowledge economy, environmental and risk prevention, accessibility and services of general interest' (CEC, 2004a: xxvii).

The new design of cohesion policy would jettison the old system of priority objectives in favour of three new objectives: 'Convergence', focusing on the least developed NUTS 2 regions with a per capita GDP less than 75 per cent of the EU average, thus essentially replacing Objective 1; 'Regional and Competitiveness and Employment' (RCE), targeting regions (mainly in the EU15) not eligible for Convergence assistance with the aim of encouraging innovation, entrepreneurship and environmental protection and accommodating structural change, thus essentially replacing Objectives 2 and 3; and 'European Territorial Cooperation' (ETC), comprising cross-border and transnational programmes with a thematic emphasis on research and development and information society, and incorporating the Community Initiatives INTERREG, URBAN, EQUAL and LEADER. The instruments linked to rural development and fisheries, meanwhile, EAGGF-Guidance and FIFG, would be integrated into the CAP. Funding for Convergence programmes would come from the ERDF and ESF as well as the Cohesion Fund, which would remain targeted at member states with a GDP per capita under 90 per cent of the EU average. Both the ERDF and ESF would provide funding for Regional Competitiveness and Employment programmes, while ETC programmes would be funded by the ERDF. To deal with one key consequence of enlargement, the Commission also proposed transitional ('phasing out') assistance for regions no longer qualifying for assistance under the Convergence heading because of the 'statistical effect' of enlargement. Similarly, regions eligible for Objective 1 assistance in 2000–06 but which would lose that eligibility in the next programming period, even without the statistical effect, would be eligible for transitional ('phasing in') support under the RCE heading (CEC, 2004a: xxvii–xxviii and xxx).

The Commission's proposals also included changes to the implementation process for cohesion policy. These included ideas for a more 'strategic' approach that would aim at achieving better synergy with the Lisbon and Gothenburg agendas and other EU priorities. This would involve an 'overall strategic document' proposed by the Commission and approved by the Council before the beginning of the new programming period, and national strategic documents prepared by the member states in negotiation with the Commission. The national documents would be in compliance with the Commission's strategic guidelines and serve as the framework for thematic and regional operational programmes, which would then be approved by the Commission. The Commission would also submit to the Council and the European Parliament annual reports summarizing national progress towards meeting the overall strategic goals. The Commission also proposed further simplification of the programming process, including a reduction of the number of funding instruments from six to three, and a one fund per programme ('mono-fund') rather than multi-fund approach to programme funding. It also proposed further decentralization of programme management, the enhancement of partnership, and a 'stronger accent on performance and quality' of national and regional programmes (CEC, 2004a: xxxv–xxxviii).

As for financial resources, the Commission proposed a total of €336.3 billion for cohesion policy in 2007–13, amounting to 0.41 per cent of EU27 GNI (0.46 per cent with transfers to the proposed single rural and fisheries instruments), and representing a 30 per cent increase in cohesion policy spending over the previous funding period. Of this amount, 'around' 78 per cent would be allocated for the Convergence objective, 18 per cent for RCE, and 4 per cent for ETC. The Commission also proposed the creation of two reserve funds designed to promote the efficient and effective use of EU funds: a 'Community performance reserve', a modified version of the existing performance reserve, to be used by the Commission to reward member states and programmes making the most progress towards the agreed objectives; and a 'national reserve', through which member states would set aside a small portion of their allocations, giving them the capacity to respond to unexpected economic shocks. Funds from the national reserve would be utilized by member states in agreement with the Commission. The Commission also proposed retaining the 4 per cent of GDP absorption cap and the 'n+2' automatic de-commitment rule that had been introduced in 1999 (CEC, 2004a: xxxviii–xxxix).

The 2006 reform and the 'Lisbonization' of cohesion policy

The Commission submitted its formal legislative proposals for cohesion policy to the Council in July 2004, and these were debated as part of the broader negotiations on the 2007–13 financial perspective. As in 1999, the budgetary negotiations pitted net recipients and the main beneficiaries of cohesion policy, now including the new member states that had joined the EU in 2004, who favoured an increase in cohesion policy spending, against wealthier net contributors who opposed budget increases – in fact, they requested a reduction in EU expenditure to at most 1 per cent of EU GNI – and wanted to restrict cohesion policy assistance to only the poorest member states and regions (Mrak and Rant, 2007: 21–2; Ujupan, 2009: 9).

The budgetary negotiations began in the fall of 2004, and after many difficult months they finally concluded with a European Council agreement in December 2005 (CEU, 2005; Bachtler *et al.*, 2007). On the basis of this deal, an inter-institutional agreement was reached in April 2006 which set the allocation for cohesion policy in 2007–13 at €308 billion (in 2004 prices), or about 35.7 per cent of the total EU budget (OJEU, 2006a). While this amount represented an increase in absolute terms from the previous period, it continued the trend of reduced expenditure for cohesion policy as a percentage of EU GDP since its peak in 1999 (see Figure 2.1). The budget deal for 2007–13 also saw a large shift in cohesion policy spending to the new member states, which would receive 51 per cent of cohesion policy resources in this period, even though they

FIGURE 2.1   *Cohesion policy spending 1989–2013*

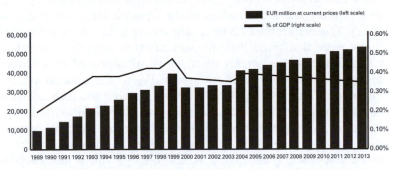

Source: CEC (2007b: 174) © European Union.

accounted for less than one-third of the EU population. Many of the older member states, on the other hand, would experience sharp declines in cohesion policy funding (Baun and Marek, 2008a, 4).

The regulatory package that was approved in July 2006 represented the most radical reform of cohesion policy since 1988 (Manzella and Mendez, 2009: 19). Among other changes, the new regulations confirmed the thematic re-orientation of cohesion policy, from an instrument for pursuing the EU treaty objective of strengthened economic and social cohesion to one that would also support the Union's new strategic economic priorities. According to the framework regulation, actions 'taken under the [structural and cohesion] Funds shall incorporate ... the Community's priorities in favour of sustainable development by strengthening growth, competitiveness, employment and social inclusion and by protecting and improving the quality of the environment' (OJEU, 2006b: 36).

As proposed by the Commission, the new regulations replaced the previous three priority objectives with three new priorities for cohesion policy spending – Convergence, Regional Competitiveness and Employment and European Territorial Cooperation. They also introduced a more strategic approach to targeting EU economic priorities through cohesion policy spending, by linking EU assistance to the Lisbon strategy goals. This linkage was ensured through the practice of 'earmarking', an idea introduced in the late stages of the budgetary negotiations by Commission President Barroso (Mendez, 2012: 164). Under this procedure, member states would be required to allocate a certain percentage of the assistance received under the Convergence and RCE objectives to programmes related to the Lisbon goals, although this requirement was voluntary for the new member states. According to the Commissioner for Regional Policy, Danuta Hübner (2006), earmarking would ensure that EU funds were dedicated 'for investments that directly strengthen competitiveness and job creation'. A list of approved expenditure categories was provided in an annex (IV) to the regulation, and included the following 'priority themes': research and technological development, innovation and entrepreneurship; information society; transport; energy; environmental protection and risk prevention; increasing the adaptability of workers and firms, enterprises and entrepreneurs; improving access to employment and sustainability; improving the social inclusion of less favoured persons; and improving human capital (OJEU, 2006b: 76-8).

The new Convergence objective essentially replaced Objective 1, and retained the traditional cohesion policy focus on 'speeding up the convergence of the least developed Member States and regions'. In the new Lisbonized cohesion policy, however, this goal was to be accomplished

> by improving conditions for growth and employment through the increasing and improvement of the quality of investment in physical and human capital, the development of innovation and of the knowledge society, adaptability to economic and social changes, the protection and improvement of the environment, and administrative efficiency.

Under the earmarking procedure, member states were required to allocate 60 per cent of the financial assistance received under the Convergence objective to pursuit of the Lisbon goals, although this requirement was voluntary for the new member states (OJEU, 2006b: 37–8).

Financed by the ERDF, the ESF and the Cohesion Fund, the Convergence objective was allocated over 81 per cent of the total budget for cohesion policy in 2007–13 (see Table 2.1). About 70 per cent of this sum was allocated for Convergence regions, defined by the previous Objective 1 standard of regions with a per capita GDP less than 75 per cent of the EU average, while 5 per cent was reserved for transitional support to 'phasing out' regions which had previously qualified for Objective 1 assistance but were no longer

TABLE 2.1   *Structural and cohesion funds resources for 2007–13*

	Funds	Financial resources € million (2008 prices)	Share of total cohesion policy resources (%)
Objectives			
Convergence	ERDF, ESF, Cohesion Fund		
– Convergence		199,322	57.4
– Phasing out		13,955	4.0
– Cohesion Fund		69,578	20.0
Total		**282,855**	**81.4**
Regional Competitiveness and Employment	ERDF, ESF		
– RCE		43,556	12.5
– Phasing in		11,409	3.3
Total		**54,965**	**15.8**
European Territorial Cooperation	ERDF		
– Cross-border		6,440	1.9
– Transnational		1,830	0.5
– Interregional		445	0.1
Total		**8,723**	**2.5**
Technical assistance		868	0.3
Total		**347,410**	**100.0**

Source: CEC (2007a: 24–5; 2008: 9) © European Union.

eligible because of the statistical effect of enlargement. The remaining 25 per cent of the total allocated for the Convergence objective was for the Cohesion Fund (CEC, 2008: 2, 8).

Altogether, 84 regions in 18 member states, with a total population of 154 million – about 31 per cent of the EU27 population – qualified as Convergence regions in 2007–13 (CEC, 2008: 8). These regions encompassed the entire territory of the 10 CEE new member states – with the exception of the wealthier Prague (Czech Republic), Budapest (Hungary) and Bratislava (Slovakia) regions – and the entire island of Malta, as well as parts of Greece (Anatoliki Makedonia, Thraki, Thessalia, Ipeiros, Ionia Nisia, Dytiki Ellada, Peloponnisos, Voreio Aigaio, Kriti), Portugal (Norte, Centro, Alentejo, Região Autónoma dos Açores), Spain (Andalucía, Castilla-La Mancha, Extremadura, Galicia), Italy (Calabria, Campania, Puglia, Sicilia), Germany (Brandenburg-Nordost, Mecklenburg-Vorpommern, Chemnitz, Dresden, Dessau, Magdeburg, Thüringen), France (Guadeloupe, Guyane, Martinique, Réunion) and the UK (Cornwall and Isles of Scilly, West Wales and the Valleys) (CEC, 2007a: 14).

Transitional support under the Convergence objective was given to 16 'phasing out' regions in eight member states, with a combined 16.4 million inhabitants, or about 3.3 per cent of the EU27 population: Belgium (Province du Hainaut), Germany (Brandenburg-Südwest, Lüneburg, Leipzig, Halle), Greece (Kentriki Makedonia, Dytiki Makedonia, Attiki), Spain (Ciudad Autónoma de Ceuta, Ciudad Autónoma de Melilla, Principado de Asturias, Región de Murcia), Austria (Burgenland), Portugal (Algarve), Italy (Basilicata) and the United Kingdom (Highlands and Islands) (CEC, 2007a: 14; 2008: 8).

Assistance from the Cohesion Fund, now programmed together with the ERDF and ESF under the Convergence objective, continued to be provided to member states whose per capita GNI was below 90 per cent of the EU average, although EU15 member states who no longer qualified because of the statistical effect of enlargement also continued to benefit from transitional assistance, similar to the phasing out regions. Altogether, 15 member states were eligible for Cohesion Fund assistance in 2007–13: Portugal, Greece and all of the new member states that joined in 2004 and 2007, while Spain was subject to phasing out assistance. In 2007–13, the Cohesion Fund provided support for actions concerning trans-European transport networks, the environment and sustainable development as well as improving administrative capacity and the effectiveness of public administration (CEC, 2007a: 16, 120).

The Regional Competitiveness and Employment objective targeted regions not covered by the Convergence objective. It aimed at strengthening regions' competitiveness and attractiveness as well as employment by anticipating economic and social changes, including those linked to the opening of trade, through the increasing and improvement of the quality of investment in human capital, innovation and the promotion of the knowledge society, entrepreneurship, the protection and improvement of the environment, and the improvement of accessibility, adaptability of workers and businesses as well as the development of inclusive job markets.

Member states were required to earmark 75 per cent of the assistance received under this objective for programmes related to the Lisbon and Gothenburg goals, although once again this procedure was voluntary for the new member states (OJEU, 2006b: 37–8).

Financed by the ERDF and ESF, approximately 16 per cent of the total resources for cohesion policy were allocated to the RCE objective in 2007–13. While ERDF assistance was used to help regions anticipate and promote change in industrial, urban and rural areas by strengthening competiveness, ESF funds were intended to support policies aimed at full employment (Allen, 2005: 227). Specifically, four priorities within the European Employment Strategy were financed by the ESF: improving the adaptability of workers and businesses, increasing social inclusion, improving access to employment and implementing reforms in the fields of employment and inclusion (Molle, 2007: 156).

In contrast to the former Objective 2, in which assistance was restricted to areas facing structural change, the new RCE objective was more thematic in approach, with full responsibility granted to the member states to determine the geographic areas eligible for RCE assistance (Schröder, 2008: 12). On this basis, 168 regions in 19 member states, representing 314 million inhabitants, received assistance under the RCE objective in 2007–13 (CEC, 2008: 8). Moreover, these regions were heavily concentrated in EU15 member states, most notably Germany, France and the UK.

Among the regions covered by the RCE objective were 13 'phasing in' regions, former Objective 1 regions which had outgrown this status and were no longer eligible even after taking into account the statistical effect of enlargement. About 21 per cent of RCE resources (€11.4 billion) was allocated in 2007–13 for special transitional assistance to such regions, including regions in Ireland (Border,

Midland and Western), Greece (Sterea Ellada, Notio Aigaio), Spain (Canarias, Castilla y León, Comunidad Valenciana), Italy (Sardegna), Cyprus (the whole territory), Hungary (Közép-Magyarország), Portugal (Região Autónoma da Madeira), Finland (Itä-Suomi) and the UK (Merseyside, South Yorkshire) (CEC, 2007a: 18; 2008: 8–9).

The European Territorial Cooperation objective aimed at

> strengthening cross-border cooperation through joint local and regional initiatives, strengthening transnational cooperation by means of actions conducive to integrated territorial development linked to the Community priorities, and strengthening interregional cooperation and exchange of experience at the appropriate territorial level. (OJEU, 2006b: 37)

While the ETC objective incorporated the previous Community Initiative programmes, in contrast to the emphasis of the CIs on traditional infrastructure projects, ETC programmes focused on such Lisbon-related goals as promoting research and development, creating a knowledge-based society and the establishment of SMEs. The ETC objective served as a complement to the Convergence and RCE objectives, since eligible regions also qualified for assistance under the other two objectives (CEC, 2007a: 20).

Specifically, the ETC objective provided assistance for three types of cooperation programmes:

Cross-border programmes
Eligible regions were situated along all EU internal and some external land borders as well as maritime borders separated by a maximum of 150 km (CEC, 2007a: 20). Altogether, 53 cross-border programmes along internal EU borders were funded, including programmes in the following areas: entrepreneurship and SMEs; cross-border trade; tourism and culture; environmental management; transport, informatics and communication networks; water, waste and energy management; the joint use of health, culture and education infrastructure; and judicial and administrative cooperation (CEC, 2008: 24).

Transnational programmes
These covered larger geographical areas such as the Baltic Sea,

Alpine and Mediterranean regions, and channelled aid to interregional projects focused on innovation, environment and risk prevention, accessibility and sustainable urban development (CEC, 2008a: 24). While all regions were eligible for assistance, the Commission – in consultation with the member states – identified 13 specific transnational cooperation zones in which it would fund programmes (CEC, 2007a: 20).

Interregional programmes
Interregional programmes provided a framework for the exchange of experiences between regional and local institutions in different countries within two priorities, innovation and the knowledge economy, and environment and risk prevention (CEC, 2008: 24). Operating at a pan-European level with all EU regions being eligible, interregional cooperation encompassed the following programmes: INTERREG IVC, structured around two priorities addressing innovation and the knowledge economy and environment and risk prevention; URBACT II, bringing together actors at local and regional level in order to exchange experiences and facilitate learning on urban policy themes; the European Spatial Planning Observation Network (ESPON), providing scientific information for the development of regions and larger territories through applied research, analysis and tools; and INTERACT II, offering services and tools on the management of cooperation programmes (CEC, 2008: 24–5).

Financed by the ERDF, the ETC objective was allocated 2.5 per cent of the cohesion policy total in 2007–13, split as follows: 74 per cent for cross-border programmes; 21 per cent for transnational programmes; and 5 per cent for interregional cooperation programmes (CEC, 2008: 9). The population living in cross-border areas amounted to about 182 million, almost 38 per cent of the EU27 population, but all EU regions and citizens were covered by at least one of the 13 transnational cooperation areas and were therefore eligible for both transnational and interregional cooperation assistance (CEC, 2008: 9; OJEU, 2006b: 7).

Beyond revamping the priority objectives of cohesion policy and linking EU assistance to the pursuit of the Lisbon strategy goals, the 2006 reform also introduced a new process of strategic planning for cohesion policy. In the new system, general goals for cohesion policy were identified in the Community Strategic Guidelines (CSG) on economic and social cohesion, which were proposed by the Commission and adopted by the Council, taking into account the views of the European Parliament. The CSG then guided the preparation of National Strategic Reference Frameworks (NSRFs) by the member states which, in turn, provided the basis for the development of operational programmes. As a result of these changes, which are discussed further in Chapter 4, the Commission's role in cohesion policy implementation shifted even more from national-level programming towards EU-level strategic goal-setting (OJEU, 2006b: 42–4; Schröder, 2008: 20–1, 32). Otherwise, the new regulations retained the main governing principles of cohesion policy, while adding a new emphasis on 'decentralization' and 'simplification'. They also introduced the principle of 'proportionality', requiring that spending on the administration, financial control and monitoring of specific projects should not be disproportionate to total expenditure on the project (OJEU, 2006b: 39; Schröder, 2008: 10, 23).

In some areas the new regulations departed from the Commission's original proposals, as a result of member state pushback and intergovernmental bargaining. At the insistence of the member states, greater flexibility in planning and less onerous reporting requirements were introduced, such as the shift from annual to triennial reports by the member states (Bachtler *et al.*, 2007: 53–4; OJEU, 2006b: 43–4). Also in response to member state demands, the Community reserve for quality and performance was changed to a 'national performance reserve' and its creation by individual member states was now optional. Moreover, funds from the reserve would be awarded to programmes of the member state concerned, rather than among all member states as the Commission had initially proposed. The funds would also be allocated (by the end of 2011) by the Commission on the basis of proposals from the member states and in consultation with them, thus substantially reducing Commission discretion. In addition, the creation of a national contingency reserve was also now optional and member states were given more control over how to allocate it (OJEU, 2006b: 51).

Changes were also made to the absorption cap, with agreement on a new graduated scale that set a maximum level of assistance of 3.79 per cent of GNI for member states with a per capita GNI less than 40 per cent of the EU25 average, declining in steps to 3.24 per cent for member states with a per capita GNI between 70 and under 75 per cent of the EU25 average. Thereafter, the cap was reduced by 0.09 per cent of GDP for each increment of five percentage points of per capita GNI compared with the EU25 average (OJEU, 2006b: 72). The new member states were also granted a more generous co-financing rate of 85 per cent, a relaxation of the automatic de-commitment rule to allow an additional year to use allocated funds, a waiver of the Lisbon earmarking requirement and other changes to the rules governing cohesion policy to compensate for reduced levels of funding (OJEU, 2006b: 38, 65 and 75). These changes to the rules were not welcomed by the Commission, which complained about a 'two-speed' and more divided Europe as a result. According to Regional Policy Commissioner Hübner, the agreement 'risk[ed] creating something we have never had: two distinct cohesion poli-cies for Europe, one for the "old" Member States, and one for the "new"' (cited in Wozniak Boyle, 2006: 266).

In the end, both enlargement and the EU's new growth and competitiveness agenda left their mark on the 2006 reform of cohe-sion policy, which was framed and negotiated in the context of a fierce budgetary conflict between the member states. The redesigned cohesion policy was thematically re-oriented to align it with the goals and priorities of the Lisbon strategy, and it featured a major shift of resources towards the EU's newer and poorer member states. As a result, the cohesion policy of 2007–13 looked very different from the cohesion policy of previous programming peri-ods. The transformation of cohesion policy would continue with the next policy reform, which took place in an even more difficult economic and political environment.

The Lisbon Treaty, economic crisis and Europe 2020

The most recent reform of cohesion policy occurred in the wake of further changes to the EU's treaty structure and in the midst of economic crisis. As a replacement to the failed Constitutional Treaty, the more modest Treaty of Lisbon was signed in December 2007 and came into force two years later. The Lisbon Treaty introduced the concept of 'territorial cohesion' and recognized it as a fundamental EU objective along with the strengthening of economic and social cohesion. It also designated economic, social and territorial cohesion as an area of 'shared competence' between the EU and the member states. Significantly, the Lisbon Treaty changed the legislative process for cohesion policy, replacing the 'assent procedure' with the 'ordinary legislative procedure', thereby giving the European Parliament more of a voice in cohesion policy decision-making. It also gave the EP a role in decision-making on the multi-annual financial perspectives, now formally referred to as the Multi-annual Financial Framework (MFF), requiring its consent to MFF agreements adopted by the European Council (OJEU, 2007: 11, 47, 85, 122).

Also influencing cohesion policy reform was the global financial crisis that began in September 2008 in the United States and quickly spread to Europe, helping to trigger the euro-zone debt crisis which began in the following year. The euro-zone crisis, which began in Greece in late 2009 but soon engulfed Ireland, Portugal, Spain, Italy and other southern member states, resulted in severe fiscal consolidation pressures throughout Europe and harsh austerity policies in many countries, especially those receiving EU/IMF bailout assistance (Greece, Ireland, Portugal and later Cyprus). As a result, most of Europe entered a severe economic recession that it only began to pull out of in late 2013, with soaring levels of unemployment especially in the hard-hit southern member states.

In response, cohesion policy resources were mobilized by the EU as a counter-cyclical tool to address the crisis. In March 2009, the European Council endorsed the Commission's decision to advance payments from the structural and cohesion funds as part of the EU's €400 billion fiscal stimulus package (European Council, 2009: 4). The Commission also introduced greater flexibility to cohesion policy rules to make it easier to use EU funds, for example, by extending the deadline for using unspent funds from the 2000–06 programming period, and by waiving or reducing requirements for national co-financing. It also raised the project approval threshold to €50 million, allowing member states to launch EU-funded projects below this level without prior Commission approval, and hence more quickly (Jacoby, 2014: 65–6).

In December 2011, the Commission proposed a 'Youth Opportunities Initiative', which involved the re-prioritization of €30 billion of unspent ESF funds for 2007–13 to support actions aimed at reducing youth unemployment in member states affected by the euro-zone crisis, including apprenticeship schemes and support for young entrepreneurs (CEC, 2013a). And at its June 2012 meeting, the European Council approved the French government's proposal for a 'Compact for Growth and Jobs', which included an option for member states to use unspent structural funds to guarantee European Investment Bank loans to support growth-enhancing investments in knowledge and skills, resource efficiency, strategic infrastructure and access to finance for small and medium-sized enterprises (European Council, 2012: 12). In May 2013, the Commission proposed additional measures to help crisis-afflicted countries, including granting Romania and Slovakia additional time to spend cohesion policy funds allocated for 2007–13, and a higher co-financing rate (up to 95 per cent) for Greece, Portugal and Cyprus that would provide them collectively with an additional €520 million in assistance (Giannoulis, 2013). In these various ways, therefore, as one of the few, if relatively modest in size, fiscal instruments available to the EU, cohesion policy spending was used to buffer the economic shock generated by the euro-zone crisis, and to support measures aimed at renewing economic growth and reducing unemployment (Jacoby, 2014: 65–6).

In this difficult economic environment, the European Council approved a new medium-term economic strategy for the EU in March 2010 – the 'Europe 2020' strategy for 'smart, sustainable and inclusive growth'. A successor to the now-expired Lisbon strategy, the Europe 2020 programme emphasized the need for innovation, employment and social inclusion while also including a strong focus on environmental challenges and the problem of climate change (European Council, 2010).

The Commission's 2010 proposals

As it prepared its new proposals for cohesion policy reform, the Commission faced the same general challenge as before: how to justify an adequately funded and EU-wide cohesion policy in a difficult economic climate, in this case exacerbated by the effects of the global financial and euro-zone debt crises. Once again, the Commission addressed this challenge by linking cohesion policy to broader EU strategic priorities that concerned all member states and regions, not just the poorest.

Following an extended consultation process with various governmental and non-governmental stakeholders, the Commission revealed its ideas for cohesion policy reform in November 2010, in the context of its *Fifth Report on Economic, Social and Territorial Cohesion*. In the report, the Commission touted the contributions of cohesion policy to reducing economic, social and territorial disparities in Europe, but it also stressed cohesion policy's role in helping the EU deal with other pressing economic, social and environmental problems, including the challenges posed by globalization and the need for increased competitiveness, the reduction of unemployment and poverty and the transition to a low-carbon economy. Once again, the Commission emphasized the value of cohesion policy for the entire EU, not just its poorer regions and member states. 'The explicit linkage of Cohesion Policy and Europe 2020 provides a real opportunity', it asserted, 'to continue helping the poorer regions of the EU catch up, to facilitate coordination between EU policies, and to develop Cohesion Policy into a leading enabler of growth, also in qualitative terms, for the whole of the EU, while addressing societal challenges such as ageing and climate change' (CEC, 2010b: xxiii).

The Commission thus proposed a further 'ambitious reform' of cohesion policy that would enhance its 'European value added' by linking it closely to the goals of the Europe 2020 strategy for 'smart, sustainable and inclusive growth'. Responding to the demands of some wealthier member states that cohesion policy assistance be limited to only the poorest countries, the Commission proposed revising the territorial architecture of cohesion policy to enable it to address the needs of all EU regions. It also proposed strengthening the governance mechanisms of cohesion policy and creating a more streamlined and simpler delivery system (CEC, 2010b: xxiii–xxxiii).

In its formal legislative proposals, presented in October 2011, the Commission identified two main goals for cohesion policy going forward – 'investment for growth and jobs' and 'European territorial cooperation' – with spending on the first of these goals accounting for the great majority (over 96 per cent) of the cohesion policy budget in 2014–20. According to the Commission, both of these goals would be pursued through a reinforced strategic approach, in which the operation of the structural and cohesion funds would be closely aligned with the goals of the Europe 2020 strategy and coordinated within a Common Strategic Framework drawn up by the Commission. Another new feature was the use of Partnership Contracts, agreed between the Commission and each member state, which would set out the terms for the use of cohesion policy assistance. The Partnership Contracts would specify the actions each member state would take to achieve the Europe 2020 goals with the help of EU assistance, along with measurable targets and indicators (CEC, 2011a).

The Commission also proposed a new three-tier territorial scheme for allocating cohesion policy resources, distinguishing between:

1. less developed regions (LDRs), with a per capita GDP less than 75 per cent of the EU-27 average;
2. transition regions (TRs), having a per capita GDP between 75 and 90 per cent of the EU average;
3. more developed regions (MDRs), with a per capita GDP above 90 per cent of the EU average.

While LDRs would continue receiving the lion's share of cohesion policy resources, with a continued emphasis on economic catching up, in MDRs the focus would be on the challenges of global competition in the knowledge-based economy, the shift to a low-carbon economy and social inclusion. In budgetary terms, the Commission proposed allocating a total of €336 billion for cohesion policy in next programming period, with almost half of this amount going to LDRs. Moreover, with the application of minimum shares for the ESF for each category of regions, the ESF would account for €84 billion (or 25 per cent) of the cohesion policy budget for 2014–20 (CEC, 2011a).

Member state responses to the Commission's proposals varied, with wealthier member states generally welcoming them while calling for reduced levels of cohesion policy spending. Poorer member states, on the other hand, were critical of the Commission's proposal to lower the cap for cohesion policy allocations to 2.5 per cent of GDP, provisions for making the disbursement of EU funds conditional on adherence to EU economic governance rules on public deficits and debt ('macro-conditionality') and the creation of a new, intermediate category of regions which they viewed as unnecessary and a scheme to divert resources to the wealthier member states (Kovacheva, 2012a). Also highly critical of the Commission's proposals for macro-conditionality were regional and local authorities, who argued that they should not be punished for the failings of national governments (Euractiv.com, 2011a).

The Multi-annual Financial Framework (MFF) negotiations began in June 2011 with publication of the Commission's formal budgetary proposal, which called for allocating €336 billion to cohesion policy in 2014–20 (updated in July 2012 to €339), amounting to about one-third of total EU expenditure for this period (CEC, 2011b; 2012b). Once again the negotiations pitted poorer net recipients against wealthier net contributors, only this time in the context of fiscal consolidation and austerity associated with the euro-zone crisis. As expected, the negotiations were extremely difficult and extended beyond the initial deadline for achieving an agreement. After a special budgetary summit in November 2012 produced no deal, EU leaders pledged to reach an MFF agreement early in the next year (Euractiv.com, 2012a). Meeting on 7–8 February 2013, the European Council finally agreed to a budget of €960 billion for 2014–20, representing 1 per cent of EU GNI and amounting to a 3.5 per cent decrease in spending from the previous period, marking the first net reduction of the EU budget in history. The amount allocated for cohesion policy was €325, about 34 per cent of total spending, but almost a 9 per cent reduction from 2007–13 and an €14 billion reduction from the Commission's proposal (Euractiv.com, 2013a, 2013b).

Under the new decision-making procedures for the MFF established by the Lisbon Treaty, however, the European Council agreement required the consent of the European Parliament before the MFF could become law, and in that body there was considerable dissatisfaction with the budgetary deal. As a result, in March 2013 the European Parliament voted overwhelmingly to reject the MFF, necessitating tough negotiations between the EP and Council to reach an inter-institutional compromise (Euractiv.com, 2013c). Finally, in late June the EP and Council reached an agreement on the MFF that left the budgetary amounts unchanged from the European Council agreement but introduced greater flexibility in the use of allocated funds, shifted some funding to more future-oriented areas such as youth employment programmes and research, and provided for a mid-term review of the budget in 2016 (Vogel, 2013a). With the MFF agreement finalized, negotiations between the Council and EP on the new regulations for cohesion policy were finally concluded in November 2013, and the new regulations were formally adopted by the Council in December.

The new design of cohesion policy for 2014–20

The new regulations for cohesion policy that were approved in December 2013 established a new common strategic framework and set of rules for what were now referred to as the European Structural and Investment (ESI) funds – the ERDF, ESF, Cohesion Fund, the European Agricultural Fund for Rural Development (EAFRD) and the European Maritime and Fisheries Fund (EMFF). According to the general regulation, the ESI funds would be used in a targeted manner to support a limited number of thematic objectives linked to the priorities of the Europe 2020 strategy, as well as the treaty-based objectives and missions of specific funds. These thematic objectives are:

strengthening research, technological development and innovation;
enhancing access to, and use and quality of, Information and Communications Technology (ICT);
enhancing the competitiveness of SMEs, of the agricultural sector (for the EAFRD), and of the fishery and aquaculture sector (for the EMFF);
supporting the shift towards a low-carbon economy in all sectors;
promoting climate change adaptation, risk prevention and management;
preserving and protecting the environment and promoting resource efficiency;
promoting sustainable transport and removing bottlenecks in key network infrastructures;
promoting sustainable and quality employment and supporting labour mobility;
promoting social inclusion, combatting poverty and any discrimination;
investing in education, training and vocational training for skills and lifelong learning;
enhancing institutional capacity of public authorities and stakeholders and efficient public administration. (OJEU, 2013a: 343)

Regarding the ERDF, ESF and Cohesion Fund specifically, the new regulations confirmed the thematic re-orientation that had begun with the 2006 reform and declared a new dual mission for cohesion policy: henceforth the three funds were to support actions contributing both to the strengthening of economic, social and territorial cohesion in the EU – the EU treaty objective that provided the original rationale for cohesion policy – and 'to delivery of the Union strategy of smart, sustainable and inclusive growth' (OJEU, 2013a: 381–2).

As proposed by the Commission, the new regulations replaced the previous three objectives for cohesion policy spending with two new goals: 'investment for growth and jobs' and 'European territorial cooperation'. They also established a new territorial architecture for cohesion policy assistance, providing that financial resources supporting the 'investment for growth and jobs' goal – drawn from the ERDF, ESF and Cohesion Fund – would be allocated according to a new three-tier classification of EU regions:

1. less developed regions (LDRs), similar to the previous Convergence regions, with eligibility defined as a per capita GDP less than 75 per cent of the EU27 average;
2. transition regions (TRs), with a per capita GDP between 75 per cent and 90 per cent of the EU27 average;
3. more developed regions (MDRs), consisting of all regions with a per capita GDP above 90 per cent of the EU27 average. (OJEU, 2013a: 382–3)

Of these three categories, the new intermediate category of TRs represented the biggest change from the previous period. While in 2007–13 transitional region status, whether Convergence 'phasing out' or RCE 'phasing in', was determined on the basis of eligibility for Objective 1 assistance in the previous programming period, in 2014–20 TR status is based on current per capita GDP, regardless of whether a region held Convergence status previously (Mendez *et al.*, 2013: 22–3). The new regulations also include a 'safety net' provision for regions previously eligible under the Convergence objective, providing them with additional support – amounting to 60 per cent of their 2007–13 allocation – beyond what they would receive as transition or more developed regions. An additional safety net provision applies to the member states, specifying that a member state's minimum allocation for the structural and cohesion funds in 2014–20 should equal 55 per cent of its total allocation for 2007–13 (OJEU, 2013a: 432).

On the basis of 2007–09 per capita GDP data, the geographical coverage of the LDR category is 24.8 per cent of the EU27 population, somewhat less than the 31.7 per cent under the previous Convergence designation. Moreover, Germany no longer has any regions in the Convergence/LDR category and Spain only one region (Extremadura). Malta also lost its Convergence/LDR status, as did the capital city regions of Poland, Slovenia and Romania. Transition regions, meanwhile, cover 14 per cent of the EU27 population, with such regions heavily concentrated in Germany, Spain, France and the UK, with the residual MDR category covering the rest (Mendez *et al.*, 2013: 22–3).

In keeping with the traditional focus of cohesion policy on assisting the poorest regions, the majority of financial resources in the new programming period are allocated to LDRs. Thus, in 2014–20, less developed regions will receive almost 52 per cent of the total cohesion policy budget compared with 10 per cent for transition regions and just over 15 per cent for more developed regions (see Table 2.2). Different co-financing rates apply to each category of region, up to 85 per cent for less developed regions and for the Cohesion Fund, 60 per cent for transition regions (although up to 80 per cent in exceptional cases) and 50 per cent for more developed regions (OJEU, 2013a: 396-7).

Different rules also apply across regional categories when it comes to the thematic concentration of EU assistance. While MDRs are required to dedicate 80 per cent of their ERDF funds to at least two of four priority investment areas related to the Europe 2020 goals – research and innovation, ICT, support for SMEs and the shift to a low-carbon economy – and at least 20 per cent to the latter area, transition regions are only required to devote 60 per cent of their ERDF resources to these four priority areas, of which 15 per cent to the shift to a low-carbon economy, while for less developed regions the corresponding figures are 50 per cent and 12 per cent. For all types of regions, however, a minimum of 5 per cent of ERDF resources must be used for sustainable urban development (OJEU, 2013b: 293, 296). More developed regions are also required to devote a greater percentage of their ESF funds (80 per cent) to Europe 2020-related investment priorities than are transition (70 per cent) and less developed regions (60 per cent); however, at least 20 per cent of the ESF in all member states must be allocated for promoting social inclusion and combatting poverty (OJEU, 2013c: 476). Also, in order to ensure sufficient resources for investments in these areas and efforts to combat youth unemployment and

TABLE 2.2   *Structural and cohesion funds resources for 2014–20*

Goals	Funds	Financial resources € million (2014 prices)	Share of total cohesion policy resources (%)
Investment for Growth and Jobs	ERDF, ESF, Cohesion Fund		
– less developed regions		182,171.8	51.8
– transition regions		35,381.1	10.1
– more developed regions		54,350.5	15.5
Cohesion Fund		63,399.7	18.0
Outermost and northern sparsely populated regions		1,555.4	0.4
Total		336,858.5	95.8
European Territorial Cooperation	ERDF	9,623.4	2.7
Youth Employment Initiative (additional allocation)		3,211.2	0.9
Other		2,161.1	0.6
Total		351,854.2	100.0

Source: CEC (2014b) © European Union.

improve labour mobility, the new regulations require that at least 23.1 per cent of a member state's financial allocation under the 'investment for growth and jobs' goal must be from the ESF (OJEU, 2013a: 383).

Also financing the 'investment for growth and jobs' objective is the Cohesion Fund, which continues to provide assistance to member states with a per capita GDP less than 90 per cent of the EU average. Accounting for 18 per cent of total cohesion policy resources in 2014–20, the Cohesion Fund maintains its traditional focus on supporting investments in transportation (especially TEN-T networks) and the environment, including climate change adaptation and the promotion of energy efficiency and renewable energy (OJEU, 2013a: 382–3; 2013d). Based on EU27 data, only Cyprus would lose its eligibility for the Cohesion Fund among the 2007–13 beneficiaries (although this was before the 2013 banking crisis and bailout), while Croatia now qualified after joining the EU in July 2013 (Mendez *et al.*, 2013: 21).

The European territorial cooperation goal, financed by the ERDF and accounting for less than 3 per cent of total resources for cohesion policy, continues basically unchanged from the previous ETC objective, with allocations for the same three strands: cross-border cooperation (74 per cent); transnational cooperation (20 per cent) and interregional cooperation (6 per cent). In keeping with the general strategic orientation of cohesion policy, investments funded under the ETC objective also had to target specific thematic priorities related to the Europe 2020 goals (OJEU, 2013e: 265–8).

Cohesion policy in 2014–20 also incorporates the Youth Employment Initiative (YEI), a programme to support unemployed young people not in education or training programmes in regions with a youth unemployment rate above 25 per cent. After being proposed by the Commission in December 2012, the YEI was approved by the European Council in February 2013 and allocated a total of €6 billion for the new programming period. Half of this amount will come from targeted investments from the ESF, while an additional €3 billion 'top-up' was added from a dedicated budget line under the cohesion policy budget subheading. At the member state level, all YEI measures are programmed within the ESF under the 'investment for growth and jobs' goal (CEC, 2013a). Through its role in the YEI, cohesion policy further demonstrates its capacity to serve as a flexible fiscal instrument for dealing with new economic challenges and priorities.

The new regulations also further reduced the absorption cap for cohesion policy, setting a maximum level of 2.35 per cent of GDP for the transfer of ESI funds to individual member states. A slightly higher limit of 2.59 per cent was allowed for EU27 member states whose average real GDP growth in 2008–10 was less than –1 per cent, however. This reduction of the capping limit was justified by the need to achieve both an 'adequate concentration of cohesion funding on the least developed regions and Member States' and a 'reduction in average per capita aid intensities', but the need to spread fewer resources across even more member states was certainly also a factor (OJEU, 2013a: 432).

The 2013 reform also made a number of changes to the programming and implementation rules and procedures for cohesion policy. As proposed by the Commission, a reinforced strategic approach to programming was introduced. This featured a Common Strategic Framework, drawn up by the Commission to provide 'strategic guiding principals' for all of the ESI funds, and the use of Partnership Agreements, which are prepared by each member state in cooperation with the Commission. The latter documents set out the terms for the use of cohesion policy assistance, to ensure that EU funds are used effectively and that they contribute to efforts to achieve the Europe 2020 goals (OJEU, 2013a: 343–6).

The new regulations also include a number of conditionality provisions that link cohesion policy to the fulfilment of EU institutional, regulatory and economic governance requirements, and whose main purpose is to ensure that EU funds are used more effectively: '*ex ante* conditionalities', which concern institutional, regulatory and policy conditions that must be met before EU funds are disbursed, and, more controversially, 'macroeconomic conditionalities', which establish a closer link between cohesion policy and EU economic governance rules and allow for the possible suspension of EU assistance in cases of persistent non-compliance (OJEU, 2013a: 349–53, 438–56). The 2013 regulations also reintroduced the mandatory performance reserve, which had been abandoned in the previous programming period. Consisting of 6 per cent of the resources allocated to the ERDF, ESF and Cohesion Fund for programmes under the 'investment for growth and jobs' goal, funds from this reserve would be allocated to better performing programmes in each member state following a mid-term performance review in 2019 (OJEU, 2013a: 347–9). These and other changes to programming and implementation procedures are discussed further in Chapter 4.

Conclusion

As a result of the 2006 and 2013 reforms cohesion policy has been substantially transformed. From a policy focused primarily on strengthening economic and social cohesion through the reduction of regional disparities, cohesion policy has been transformed into a common investment tool for addressing the EU's strategic economic priorities – increased economic growth, improved competitiveness, more and better jobs, and a sustainable energy future. As a result, cohesion policy spending now targets such areas as innovation, support for SMEs, information and communications technologies, energy efficiency and the shift to a low-carbon economy. While the promotion of convergence and the reduction of economic disparities remain key objectives of cohesion policy, these goals are now pursued in the context of the EU's growth and competitiveness agenda, as the latter set of objectives has joined with convergence and cohesion to form a new dual mission for cohesion policy.

The transformation is explained by several factors, including a worsening economic climate and the declining willingness of wealthier member states to continue making large net contributions to the EU budget. In this context, the Commission viewed the linkage of cohesion policy to the EU's new growth and competitiveness agenda, embodied in the Lisbon and Europe 2020 strategies, as a way to preserve a well-funded cohesion policy that would continue to operate throughout the EU. The trade-off was a thematic re-orientation from convergence and cohesion to growth and competitiveness, or at least a reinterpretation of the former goals in terms of the latter.

The 'broadening' of cohesion policy and the expansion of its official goals raises the question, however, of whether the objectives of convergence and cohesion, on the one hand, and growth and competitiveness, on the other, are fundamentally compatible, or whether the pursuit of one set of objectives perhaps undermines efforts to achieve the other (Begg, 2010: 93). It also raises the issue of 'goal congestion', whereby public policies that attempt to do too many things end up doing none of them well (Tarschys, 2003: 85; Sapir Report, 2003: 124). The adaptation of cohesion policy to new economic and political realities, in other words, may result in policy incoherence and the effectiveness of cohesion policy could be undermined.

With its new dual mission, cohesion policy remains the EU's second largest area of expenditure, after the CAP, and continues to account for about a third of the total EU budget, although the absolute level of cohesion policy spending –and EU spending over-all – will decline slightly in 2014–20 for the first time. This means that cohesion policy continues to be a highly contested aspect of EU budgetary politics, as member states battle to maximize their receipts and improve their net budgetary positions. This budgetary struggle and the role of cohesion policy in EU budgetary politics is the topic of the next chapter.

Chapter 3

Cohesion Policy and the EU Budget

As the second largest area of EU expenditure after the CAP, it is not surprising that cohesion policy should play a major role in EU budgetary politics. Historically, cohesion policy spending has been utilized as a compensatory mechanism to secure the agreement of poorer member states to further economic integration and liberalization, a fact that accounts for the very creation of cohesion policy and the expansion of EU structural spending after 1988. In a similar manner, but on a much smaller scale, special allocations under cohesion policy have become an increasingly utilized means for adjusting the net balances of individual member states and securing intergovernmental agreement on complex multi-annual budgetary packages. Spending on cohesion policy has also become a major issue in the growing split within the EU between net budgetary contributors and recipients, who are also generally the main beneficiaries of cohesion policy. While this north–south divide has always been a factor in EU budgetary politics, it has become a more significant cleavage since the late 1990s because of a worsening economic climate and the budgetary and fiscal constraints imposed by EMU. Enlargement to Central and Eastern Europe has also exacerbated the north–south divide, by increasing economic disparities in the EU and enlarging the group of member states pushing for more cohesion policy spending.

This chapter takes a closer look at cohesion policy and EU budgetary politics. It begins with a brief discussion of the decision-making processes for the Multi-annual Financial Framework and the annual budget. It then examines the basic dynamics of intergovernmental bargaining on the EU budget, including the issue of net balances and the conflict between net contributors and recipients. The next section examines the special role of cohesion policy as a compensatory mechanism, focusing on both its historical role as a

71

'side payment' used to pave the way for further integration, and its more typical use today as a means for adjusting net balances and facilitating agreement in multi-annual budgetary negotiations. The chapter then discusses the EU's growing north–south split and its implications for cohesion policy, before closing with a look at the 2014–20 MFF negotiations.

The EU budget decision-making processes

Prior to 1988, the EU budget was determined annually in negotiations between the member states. Since then, however, it has been determined on the basis of agreement on a multi-annual financial perspective or framework, a system that not only eliminates the need for continuous bargaining over successive annual budgets, but also offers the advantage of guaranteed funding for EU policies over a given number of years. The financial perspective fixes the overall ceiling for EU expenditure (the size of the overall budget), and within that ceiling the amounts dedicated to specific policy headings – agriculture, cohesion, etc. – for each year of a specific multi-annual period. It also determines the amounts received by each member state from spending on EU policies. Concerning cohesion policy specifically, the multi-annual agreements include not only a decision on the total financial amount dedicated to cohesion policy, but also an indicative annual sum for each member state for each year of the financial framework. On the revenue side, the financial perspectives determine the sources of revenue for the EU budget and the total contributions of individual member states for the multi-annual period (Laffan and Lindner, 2005: 191; Neheider and Santos, 2011: 633–4; Molle, 2007: 139) Since 1988, the largest EU revenue source ('own resource') has been national contributions based on a percentage of member state GNI, followed by one based on a percentage of national value-added tax (VAT) receipts. In 2012, for instance, the GNI-based resource accounted for 71 per cent of EU budget revenues, and the VAT-based resource 11 per cent (CEC, 2014a).

Between 1988 and 2007 four separate financial perspectives were approved, each covering a period of five to seven years: the Delors I package for 1989–93; the Delors II package for 1994–9; the Agenda 2000 financial perspective for 2000–06; and the financial perspective for 2007–13. Decision-making on these framework deals was an inter-institutional process, involving: a budgetary proposal from the Commission; negotiations between the member states and final, unanimous, agreement by the European Council; approval ('assent') by the European Parliament; and a formal inter-institutional agreement between the EP, Council and the Commission, such as the inter-institutional agreement for the 2007–13 financial perspective that was agreed to in May 2006 (OJEU, 2006a).

Prior to the Lisbon Treaty, which came into force in December 2009, the multi-annual budgetary agreements did not have a legal basis in the EU treaties or other Community legislation. The Lisbon Treaty, however, confirmed the established practice of working with a multi-annual financial framework, now formally referred to as the MFF, with Article 312 conferring a legally binding status on it. According to the Lisbon Treaty, the MFF, which is to be established for a period of at least five years, determines 'the amounts of the annual ceilings on commitment appropriations by category of expenditure and of the annual ceiling on payment appropriations. The categories of expenditure, limited in number, shall correspond to the Union's major sectors of activity' (OJEU, 2007).

The title of the expenditure category ('heading' or 'subheading') for cohesion policy has varied over the years. In the 2000–06 MFF cohesion policy was listed as heading 2, 'Structural Operations'. In 2007–13, reflecting the new focus on growth and competitiveness, it was listed as subheading 1b, 'Cohesion for Growth and Employment', under the budget heading for 'Sustainable Growth'. In the 2014–20 MFF cohesion policy is subheading 1b, 'Economic, Social and Territorial Cohesion', under the heading 'Smart and Inclusive Growth'.

The Lisbon Treaty also established the inter-institutional process for decision-making on the MFF. According to the treaty, 'The Council, acting in accordance with a special legislative procedure, shall adopt a regulation laying down the multiannual financial framework'. Moreover, 'The Council shall act unanimously after obtaining the consent of the European Parliament, which shall be given by a majority of its component members' (OJEU, 2007). The Lisbon Treaty thus significantly strengthened the European Parliament's role in the budgetary decision-making process, as it abolished the former distinction between compulsory spending (obligatory, required by EU treaty agreements), mainly the CAP, and non-compulsory (non-obligatory) expenditure, which covered just about everything else. It thereby gave the EP the power of decision in all expenditure categories and thus influence over the entire budget, in essence, making it equal in budgetary matters to the Council. While this change does not make much of a difference in the case of cohesion policy specifically, since it qualified as non-compulsory expenditure previously, it enables the EP to veto and amend the entire budgetary package of which cohesion policy is a part. In this manner, the EP can influence the amount of cohesion policy spending and its share of the EU budget relative to other policy headings, as well as the way in which budgeted funds are spent.

The annual budget

The use of MFFs has greatly limited the room for manoeuvre in decision-making on the annual budget, which also follows a specified procedure established by the EU treaties (the current procedure, established by the Lisbon Treaty, is detailed in Article 314 of the Treaty on the Functioning of the EU, (TFEU)). Similar to the MFF procedure, the annual budgetary process begins with a proposal from the Commission, from which the final budget agreement usually does not diverge significantly. In preparing its draft budget the Commission – led by the Budget Commissioner and Directorate-General – must work within the parameters of the MFF, but there remains some flexibility below the established expenditure ceilings and within expenditure headings which, however, has not been greatly exploited (Nugent, 2010: 413). Since enactment of the Lisbon Treaty, the Commission is required to present its draft budget by 1 September of the year prior to the budget concerned.

Before 2010, the Council and EP each had two readings of the Commission's budget proposal, but the Lisbon Treaty reduced this to one. In the current procedure, after receiving the Commission's draft budget the Council must adopt a position and forward it to the Parliament by 1 October, along with an explanation of its position. Thereafter, the EP has 45 days to either adopt the budget or propose amendments. Before 2009, these amendments could only concern non-compulsory spending, but with the elimination of this distinction by the Lisbon Treaty the EP can now propose amendments for all expenditure categories.

If the EP proposes amendments the Council can either adopt them within 10 days or a conciliation committee is established, consisting of an equal number of representatives of both the Council and EP. The committee has 21 days to produce a compromise joint text, or else the Commission must submit a new proposal. If it succeeds, the budget can be adopted in one of three ways:

1. both the Council (by a qualified majority) and the EP (by a majority) approve the joint text;
2. either the Council or EP approves the joint text and the other fails to act;
3. the EP approves the joint text and the Council rejects it, but the Parliament overrides the Council with a supermajority vote (an absolute majority of MEPs and at least two-thirds of the votes cast).

However, the joint text cannot be adopted if both institutions reject it or fail to act, one rejects it and the other fails to act, or the Council approves it but the EP rejects it by an absolute majority. Following approval, the budget is formally signed into law by the presidents of both the Council and EP in a December signing ceremony. In the event that a budget is not agreed before the beginning of the year, the EU continues to function on a month-to-month basis, with the monthly budget being one-twelfth of the previous year's budget ('provisional twelfths'), until a new budget is finally agreed and implemented.

After approval, the Commission is responsible for managing the EU budget and spending, but its handling of the budget must be formally approved by the EP after the fact. The so-called discharge procedure (detailed in Article 319 of the TFEU) begins late in the following year (e.g. 2013 for the 2012 budget), and involves a report by the European Court of Auditors (ECA) on the Commission's expenditures. On the basis of a recommendation by the Council to grant discharge, the EP formally votes on whether to grant discharge, usually by April of the second year after the budgetary year concerned (e.g. 2014 for the 2012 budget). The granting of discharge is not a foregone conclusion, however, and the EP has delayed discharge in the past as a means of censuring or expressing unhappiness with the Commission (Dinan, 2010: 318–21).

Intergovernmental bargaining and the EU budget

Decision-making on the EU budget has always been a highly politically sensitive issue, but it has become even more so since the late 1990s, in the context of difficult economic times, the budgetary and fiscal constraints imposed by EMU and the EU's growing north–south divide. The economic climate for budgetary negotiations deteriorated even further with the 2008 global financial crisis and the subsequent euro-zone debt crisis. In this harsh economic environment, the differences of interest between national governments have become even sharper and the achievement of EU budgetary agreements even more difficult.

A major cleavage in EU budgetary politics is the division between wealthier member states that are net contributors to the budget and poorer member states that are net recipients, with the latter also tending to be the primary beneficiaries of cohesion policy. According to a generally accepted principle, poor member states receive more from the EU budget than they contribute while the richer member states are net contributors. In this respect, the EU budget is redistributive in effect, with cohesion policy being the largest item in the budget and the main EU policy with explicit redistributive objectives (Molle, 2007: 139, 144). As a consequence, wealthier member states generally favour a smaller EU budget, while poorer member states prefer more EU spending, with this division accentuated in economically difficult times. Because of its explicit redistributive objectives and effect, cohesion policy has been specifically targeted in recent budgetary negotiations by net contributors wanting to reduce EU spending, while it has been strongly defended by poorer member states seeking to preserve their benefits.

To a significant extent, this intra-EU cleavage is along geographical lines, with net contributors found mainly among the more prosperous older member states of north-west Europe (for instance Germany, Sweden, the Netherlands and the UK), while the main net recipients or beneficiaries are found among the poorer countries of southern Europe (Greece, Portugal and Spain) and among the new member states of Central and Eastern Europe (see Table 3.1). This north–south division has been accentuated by the euro-zone debt crisis, which has mainly affected the poorer southern member states and Ireland, while wealthier northern member states, especially Germany, have been the main source of bailout assistance for the troubled countries.

TABLE 3.1 *Member state operating budgetary balances, 2012*

	Net contributors			Net recipients	
Member state	Net balance € million	% GNI	Member state	Net balance € million	% GNI
Germany	−11,953.8	−0.44%	Poland	+11,997.2	+3.30%
France	−8,297.5	−0.40%	Portugal	+5,027.2	+3.12%
UK	−7,366.1	−0.39%	Greece	+4,544.9	+2.33%
Italy	−5,058.1	−0.33%	Spain	+3,999.0	+0.39%
Netherlands	−2,364.5	−0.39%	Hungary	+3,280.4	+3.59%
Sweden	−1,925.1	−0.46%	Czech Republic	+3,045.2	+2.14%
Belgium	−1,493.7	−0.39%	Romania	+2,031.6	+1.56%
Denmark	−1,126.0	−0.45%	Slovakia	+1,597.0	+2.28%
Austria	−1,073.3	−0.35%	Lithuania	+1,514.0	+4.82%
Finland	−658.8	−0.34%	Bulgaria	+1,329.7	+3.43%
Luxemburg	−79.5	−0.25%	Latvia	+955.9	+4.29%
Cyprus	−25.2	−0.15%	Estonia	+785.3	+4.84%
			Ireland	+670.6	+0.50%
			Slovenia	+572.2	+1.63%
			Malta	+71.4	+1.14%

Source: CEC (2014a) © European Union.

Beyond this basic division between net contributors and recipients, all member states pay careful attention to the costs and benefits that the EU budget represents for them, with a focus on improving their net position with respect to contributions and receipts. For the most part, in budgetary negotiations all member states try to reduce the amount they contribute to the EU budget while maximizing their benefits, thus achieving the most advantageous net position possible (Lefebvre, 2005: 20). This effort to get back from the EU as much as (or perhaps more than) a member state has paid to it is known as *juste retour*, which is a more dignified term for what is often referred to as 'pork-barrel' politics (Begg, 1999: 4). To describe the position of the member states in bargaining over the EU budget the analogy of a restaurant bill has sometimes been used: 'if I have to pay a certain sum of the total bill I want to be entitled to an extra glass of wine or so' (Molle, 2007: 147). Another commonly used term to describe this bargaining logic and the outcome it generally produces is 'something for everyone'.

Domestic politics is a key driving force behind the concern for net balances. According to Dhéret (2011), since national governments and finance ministries 'need to justify to their citizens how public money is spent, each member state tends to support EU expenditure in policy areas where it traditionally gets what it regards as juste retour'. Budgetary flows to the member states are also highly visible, and in this respect it is easy to identify 'winners' and 'losers' in the budgetary negotiations (Laffan and Lindner, 2005: 192). Indeed, change in a member state's net position, whether positive or negative, is among the most commonly used indicators of whether a government was successful or not at defending its national interests in EU negotiations. Net positions thus tend to be 'a driving force in budget negotiations and are persistently used as a reference point for [the] negotiations' (Neheider and Santos, 2011: 632). In this manner, the amount of support a country receives in one set of negotiations becomes the base line and minimal outcome for the next negotiation round, creating a 'ratchet effect' that is difficult to stop or reverse (Ederveen *et al.*, 2003: 51).

While the preoccupation with net balances is perhaps 'inevitable' (Neheider and Santos, 2011: 632), it produces a number of unfortunate consequences from the perspective of cohesion policy. For one, it complicates the effort to target EU funds on areas 'of real deprivation' (De Rynck and McAleavey, 2001: 541), thus reducing 'the effectiveness of cohesion policy in achieving its goal of convergence' while limiting also its redistributive effects (Ederveen *et al.*, 2003: 51–2). According to Neheider and Santos (2011: 632), the focus on net balances also makes it more difficult to accurately assess the contributions of cohesion policy, since net balances 'do not capture many of the economic benefits from European integration and tell us little about the effects of EU policies, as they depict merely a cash flow of input'. In other words, according to Lefebvre (2005: 19), 'a mere calculation of the return of each country over its contribution does not take all the other external effects of common policy into account', a point which is also emphasized by Begg (2009: 8), who notes that the focus on net balances is often based on 'dubious calculations that leave out feedback flows'.

Cohesion policy as a compensatory mechanism

In the context of EU widening and deepening, the growing divide between rich and poor member states and the preoccupation with net balances, cohesion policy has traditionally played an important role in EU budgetary politics as a compensatory instrument or mechanism. It has played this role in two key ways: as a 'side payment' to gain the agreement of poorer member states to further deepening or widening, and as a means for addressing member state concerns about net balances in multi-annual budgetary negotiations. In either respect, the use of cohesion policy as a compensatory mechanism to facilitate intergovernmental bargaining and agreement is an important, if unstated, aspect and role of cohesion policy, existing, if uneasily, alongside its official purpose of strengthening cohesion and promoting economic growth and competitiveness. This compensatory function has also played an important role in the historical development of cohesion policy itself, being a major reason for the creation of cohesion policy and the expansion of EU structural spending over the years. In the remainder of this section, both uses of cohesion policy as a compensatory mechanism are examined briefly.

Cohesion policy as a 'side payment'

Since the establishment of the ERDF, regional or cohesion policy spending has been used to compensate poorer member states for the prospective disadvantages or costs to them of further EU widening or deepening, thereby gaining their support for new intergovernmental treaties and agreements. In this regard, cohesion policy has played an important role in the European integration process, by facilitating intergovernmental agreements that led to further economic integration or allowed for the accession of new member states. Frequently conceptualized as a bribe or 'side payment' to purchase the consent of reluctant member states, this function of cohesion policy is an outgrowth of the EU decision-making process, which requires unanimity for some key decisions – treaty reform and enlargement, for instance – and thus puts resistant or negatively affected member states in a strong position to demand compensation as a condition of their vote in favour (Bouvet and Dall'erba, 2010: 502).

An initial instance of regional spending being used in this manner was the creation of the Integrated Mediterranean Programmes in 1985. Claiming that the planned accession of Spain and Portugal would harm it economically because of the similarity of their agriculturally based economies, Greece threatened to block the so-called Iberian enlargement unless it received additional EC assistance as compensation. With this threat as leverage, and with the support of France and Italy, which also claimed they would be harmed economically by enlargement, Greece successfully pushed for the creation of a special development programme for southern Europe, with the resulting IMPs accounting for an additional ECU 6.6 billion in EC regional development funds for a seven-year period beginning in 1986 (CEC, 1989a: 2–5; Bache, 1998: 67–8; Schneider, 2009: 165; Allen, 2005: 18).

As discussed in Chapter 1, the creation of cohesion policy and the significant expansion of structural spending in 1988 have also commonly been viewed as a side payment, in this case to gain the consent of poorer southern member states to the SEA and plans for further economic integration (Moravcsik, 1991: 62; Pollack, 1995: 365–6; Allen, 2000: 249). In the intergovernmental negotiations on the SEA the poor member states, led by Spain and Portugal, expressed concerns about the negative consequences for weaker countries and regions of the planned single market, arguing that deeper integration would mainly favour the wealthier and more developed regions of Europe's economic 'core' (the so-called Golden Triangle – an area of north-west Europe embracing southern

England, north-eastern France, Belgium, the Netherlands and north-western Germany, as well as northern Italy), resulting in a further concentration of wealth and increased disadvantages for the weaker countries and regions of Europe's 'periphery' (Bache, 1998: 69). In return for their agreement to the SEA, therefore, the poor member states demanded further EC assistance to help them deal with the challenges of increased integration and greater economic liberalization (Molle, 2007: 141–2; Ujupan, 2009: 6). These demands were backed by France and Greece, which also had a number of peripheral and declining regions, as well as by Commission President Delors, who presented the need for cohesion policy as 'an interventionist counterbalance to the Single Market' (De Rynck and McAleavey 2001: 544). As a result, the SEA made the strengthening of economic and social cohesion a core objective of the EC, and it called on the Commission to propose a wholesale revamping of the structural funds to enable them to help achieve this goal, while the Delors I budgetary package for 1989–93 included a doubling of the financial resources available for the structural funds.

The 1991 decision to create the Cohesion Fund was also a compensatory gesture, in this case aimed at securing approval of the Maastricht Treaty and its provisions for EMU (Begg 1999: 1). Once again the poorer member states – Spain, Portugal, Greece and Ireland – were concerned about the negative consequences of deeper integration, fearing that they could be left behind in a two-speed EMU that would relegate them to a permanent second-class status. They also worried that attempting to meet the strict 'convergence criteria' required for joining the common currency area, especially those placing limits on government budget deficits and levels of public debt, would stifle their efforts to develop and catch up economically with the more advanced countries of northern Europe. They thus threatened to veto the treaty unless certain compensatory measures were adopted (Molle, 2007: 142; Moravscik, 1998: 446). The result was the creation by the Maastricht Treaty of the Cohesion Fund, a new structural instrument designed to assist the EU's poorest member states, followed by agreement in December 1992 on the Delors II budgetary package for 1994–9, which provided for a further doubling of cohesion policy spending. Prompting the latter decision was the threat by Spain and other poor member states to block a budget deal if it did not include a substantial increase of structural spending, an action that would have delayed the beginning of accession negotiations with four European Free Trade Association (EFTA) applicants – Austria, Sweden, Finland and Norway – which were scheduled to begin in January 1993 (Baun, 1996: 117; Ujupan, 2009: 7).

The compensatory role of cohesion policy was once again evident in the March 1999 Agenda 2000 agreement, which opened the door for Eastern enlargement. In the budgetary negotiations, Spain and other poor member states opposed any reductions of their cohesion policy benefits because of the need to pay for enlargement. Spain also rejected the German government's suggestion that it and other poor countries joining the euro-zone should give up their rights to Cohesion Fund assistance, and it threatened to block enlargement unless assured that it would continue to be eligible for Cohesion Fund support. In the end, the German government agreed that Spain and other poor member states could continue receiving Cohesion Fund assistance even if they belonged to the euro-zone, provided their GDPs remained less than 90 per cent of the EU average. It was also decided to limit the amount of financial assistance that would flow to the new member states by imposing a 4 per cent of GDP cap on total cohesion policy receipts. This provision, along with the agreement on generous transitional assistance for regions losing their eligibility for Objective 1 assistance and various 'special provisions' (see below), helped Spain and the other poor member states maintain their levels of EU funding in the 2000–06 period, thus removing a potential barrier to Eastern enlargement (Baun, 2000: 150–4, 161–2).

Cohesion policy has also played a compensatory role by providing a means for addressing the thorny issue of net budgetary balances, beginning with the creation of the ERDF in 1975 as a way to compensate the UK for its anticipated large net contributions to the Community budget. More recently, in successive rounds of budgetary negotiations since the early 1990s, cohesion policy spending has been used to address member state concerns about net balances, whether through changes to the eligibility or allocation rules for EU assistance that benefitted certain member states, or through country-specific 'special provisions' (payments) under the cohesion policy heading that helped achieve intergovernmental agreement on multi-annual financial perspectives.

Equilibrating net balances

In addition to its use as a side payment to secure intergovernmental agreement on EU widening and deepening, cohesion policy has been an important means for dealing with the thorny issue of net balances in successive rounds of budgetary negotiations. Concern about net balances has influenced decision-making on how cohesion policy resources are allocated among the member states, including changes to allocation methods and eligibility rules for EU assistance. Cohesion policy has also been used in the latter stages of budgetary negotiations to award country-specific 'special provisions', which have become increasingly important for achieving final agreements on multi-annual financial frameworks.

The creation of the ERDF itself, and hence EC regional policy, was viewed as a means of addressing net budgetary imbalances. Specifically, it was viewed as a way to compensate the UK for its anticipated large net contributions to the EC budget after it joined the Community in 1973. At the time, the EC budget was over-whelmingly dominated by the CAP. Because of its relatively small and efficient agricultural sector, however, the UK stood to receive little in the way of CAP benefits to offset its large contributions due to the size of its economy. Receipts from EC regional policy, there-fore, provided a way to rectify this imbalance, while also providing the UK with much-needed assistance for its declining industrial regions (Allen, 2005: 217; Kengyel, 2000: 6).

Moreover, in the early days of EC regional policy ERDF spending was allocated according to national quotas that were set in annual negotiations between the member states, with national percentages determined more by net balances than objective regional development needs (Leonardi, 2005: 42–3; Manzella and Mendez, 2009: 10). The concern with net budgetary positions continued with the onset of multi-annual financial planning in 1988, although with the Delors I package the focus was more on the absolute level of spending and the controls the Commission would exercise over the use of EC funds by the poorer member states. However, the new regulations for the struc-tural funds also specified that regions whose per capita GDP exceeded the 75 per cent of EC average threshold could receive Objective 1 assistance for 'special reasons', and on this basis the French overseas departments and Northern Ireland in the UK were able to qualify for Objective 1 support (OJEC, 1988: 13; CEC, 1993: 12).

In the 1993 reform of cohesion policy, agreed to as part of the Delors II package, the eligibility criteria for some objectives were relaxed considerably, allowing wealthier net contributors to claim a larger share of available resources. These changes included a relaxation of the criteria for receiving Objective 1 assistance, with the member states insisting that EU support be extended to more regions for 'special reasons'. As a result, Objective 1 assistance became newly available for Merseyside and the Scottish Highlands and Islands in the UK, the Hainaut region in Belgium, Flevoland in the Netherlands and parts of Nord-Pas de Calais in France (CEC, 1993: 12). Relaxation of the eligibility criteria for Objective 2 (declining regions) and changes to the selection process that gave the member states more control over determining eligible areas also led to a significant expansion in the number of areas receiving Objective 2 assistance in the new programming period (from 60 to 82) (CEC, 1993: 51–2; 2003: 162). In a similar fashion, changes in the eligibility criteria and selection procedures for Objective 5b (rural areas) enabled an increase in the percentage of the EU population covered by this objective, from 5 per cent in 1989–93 to 8.1 per cent in 1994–9 (CEC, 1993: 54–5; 1996: 117).

With the 1995 enlargement, a new regional objective (Objective 6) was created to benefit the sparsely populated northern regions of the two new Nordic member states, Sweden and Finland, thus ensuring that these member states would receive structural funds assistance since their regions did not fit the existing objectives of cohesion policy (CEU, 1995; Allen, 2010: 235; Katajamäki, 2002: 20). As such, the decision to create the new objective was a classic compensatory measure and a clear example of the 'something for everyone logic' in cohesion policy decision-making.

The March 1999 agreement on Agenda 2000 initiated the use of several new cohesion policy mechanisms to counter the negative effects on net balances of enlargement and the Commission's proposals for cohesion policy reform. These included the use of transitional arrangements that provided support for regions that no longer qualified for assistance, whether because of changes to eligibility criteria or the statistical effect of enlargement, as well as 'safety net' provisions, which limited the loss of cohesion policy support from one programming period to another for specific member states. Moreover, beginning with the 2006 reform, the regional architecture of cohesion policy was redesigned – first with the creation of Regional and Competitiveness and Employment regions, and then with the three-tiered regional structure introduced for 2014–20 – in a way that ensured that all regions and member states would continue to benefit from cohesion policy assistance.

The Agenda 2000 agreement also began the practice of using 'special provisions' – additional assistance packages awarded to specific member states or groups of member states at the last minute of negotiations – to address the issue of net balances and help seal budgetary deals. As Santos (2009: 4) points out, these provisions are 'purely selective and discretionary in nature' since they are additional to the funds allocated to the member states according to the established eligibility criteria for cohesion policy. Because of their high visibility and positive impact on net budgetary positions, winning such special provisions has become 'an extremely interesting option' for national governments in the financial perspective negotiations (Molle, 2007: 139). They are thus 'a clear example of side payments needed to ensure unanimous agreement' on the EU budget (Neheider and Santos, 2011: 638; Santos, 2009: 4), reflecting 'the classic "something for everyone principle" and the role of Cohesion Policy in budget negotiations to equilibrate balances' (Ujupan, 2009: 9). According to Osterloh (2010: 88), in reference to the use of special provisions, 'nowhere else, [can the] dominance of redistributive concerns of member states over the original objectives of EU regional policy … be seen so clearly'. The use of such special provisions, as well as transitional arrangements, 'safety nets' and other compensatory measures in the 1999, 2006 and 2013 budgetary negotiations is discussed more fully in the next two sections.

Cohesion policy and the EU's north–south divide

The conflict between net contributors and recipients has long been a key factor shaping intergovernmental negotiations and decision-making on the EU budget. In the negotiations on creating the ERDF, for example, the presumed main beneficiaries of EC regional policy – the UK, Ireland and Italy – favoured a larger regional fund, while the main likely contributors – Germany, the Netherlands and Denmark – wanted a smaller fund. A similar split was also present in subsequent budgetary negotiations, including those for the Delors I and II packages. However, the impact of this division was muted by the fact that Germany, the main paymaster of the EU, was in a strong economic position and willing to open its wallet to secure agreements on further integration that it supported. In the 1992 agreement on Delors II, for example, strong British opposition to increased EU spending was overcome by Germany's decision to support the demands of Spain and other poor member states for a significant expansion of the resources available for cohesion policy, a decision influenced not just by Germany's interest in keeping the EFTA enlargement on track but also the fact that Germany now comprised new beneficiary regions (the eastern *Länder*) as a result of unification in 1990 (Baun, 1996: 117; Ujupan, 2009: 6).

All this began to change after the mid-1990s, however, as the EU struggled with slow economic growth and high unemployment, the restrictive requirements for joining the common currency area (the EMU 'convergence criteria') imposed fiscal and budgetary constraints on national governments, and the German paymaster began experiencing the negative financial effects of unification and its generous support for reconstructing the eastern *Länder*. In the next decade, the costs of Eastern enlargement and the effects of the 2008 global financial crisis and the subsequent euro-zone crisis contributed to a further worsening of the economic and political context for budgetary negotiations. As a result, beginning with the negotiations on the Agenda 2000 financial perspective, EU budgetary politics have been increasingly dominated by the basic north–south divide between net contributors and recipients, with cohesion policy spending in particular becoming a major object of contention.

Agenda 2000

Negotiations on the financial perspective for 2000–06 began with the Commission's budgetary proposal, which was submitted in June 1997 as part of the Agenda 2000 report. In its proposal, because of the known opposition of net contributors such as Germany and the Netherlands to increased EU expenditure, the Commission began with the assumption that any upward revision of the existing 'own resources' ceiling (1.27 per cent of EU GNP) was not possible. It argued, however, that the challenge of Eastern enlargement could be met without exceeding the established spending limit. In fact, the Commission estimated that the actual budgetary appropriations for

2006 would amount to only 1.22 per cent of EU GNP, well under the established ceiling. Within this framework, the Commission proposed allocating ECU 275 billion for cohesion policy in 2000–06, of which ECU 45 billion would be set aside for the new member states (CEC, 1997: 61–9, 73).

The Commission's proposal received only lukewarm response from the member states, however, which were sharply divided between net budgetary contributors and recipients. Among the former, the German and Dutch governments were demanding a reduction in their EU payments and a rebalancing of national contributions, with the German government particularly vocal in demanding a fairer distribution of budgetary burdens. Arguing that it would no longer be the *Zahlmeister* ('paymaster') of Europe, the German government pointed out that, because of unification and the incorporation of its poorer eastern states, Germany had slipped down the EU list in terms of per capita GDP and now ranked in the middle of the pack (fifth in 1997, behind Luxembourg, Denmark, Austria and Belgium). It also claimed that it was unfair for Germany to continue paying 0.6 per cent of its national income to the EU, or more than half the total net contributions to the EU budget, when its GDP made up only 25 per cent of the EU total. Instead, the German government argued for linking contributions more closely to the wealth of member states, by capping them at something like 0.4 per cent of GDP (Baun, 2000: 153–4).

On the other hand, the member states that were net recipients, led by Spain, opposed any reductions of their benefits and countered the Commission's proposal by arguing that it would be difficult to pay for enlargement within the existing budgetary ceiling without 'unjust' reductions in transfers to poorer EU15 countries. Spain also rejected German government suggestions that it and other poor member states joining the euro-zone should give up their rights to Cohesion Fund assistance. The so-called cohesion countries pointed out that it was the wealthier (mainly northern European) net contributors, after all, that were more likely to benefit economically from enlargement because of their economic prowess, geographical proximity and historical ties to the candidate countries, most of whom were in Central and Eastern Europe. For the poorer member states, on the other hand, enlargement would only bring problems in the form of increased economic competition from lower-cost producers and reduced shares of EU assistance. Among the other member states, Britain rejected calls to eliminate its special budget rebate, while such relatively wealthy net recipients as Denmark, Luxembourg and Belgium strongly defended their privileged budgetary positions (Baun, 2000: 154).

Little progress on budgetary issues was made at the December 1997 Luxembourg summit or in the course of 1998, as the EU's north–south divide on budgetary issues appeared only to deepen. In addition to cohesion policy spending, other issues in the budgetary negotiations included proposals for the partial re-nationalization of the CAP (through 'co-financing', under which national governments would become responsible for a proportion, 25 per cent, of direct income payments to farmers), elimination or reduction of the British rebate, the introduction of a 'generalized correction mechanism' to address net budgetary imbalances and reform of the 'own resources' system through greater reliance on GNP-based contributions. By the end of 1998, with the rigidity of member state positions indicating that it would be difficult to achieve a compromise, interest grew in the idea of 'freezing' the budget for 2000–06 at 1999 levels, thus eliminating the small increase in spending contained in the Commission's proposal. The budget freeze (or 'stabilization') idea was supported by large net contributors and by the French and British governments, who saw it as a means of reducing pressure for actions (CAP co-financing and shrinking or eliminating the British rebate, respectively) that would be even more harmful to their interests. It was strongly opposed, however, by the net recipients, and also by the Commission, which argued that a budget freeze would hurt its plans for reforming the CAP and the structural funds (Baun, 2000: 154–6).

Heading into the March 1999 Berlin summit there was still no agreement on the budget or cohesion policy spending. Regarding the latter, Germany and other net contributors favoured a seven-year total of less than €200 billion – well below the Commission's original proposal of €230 – while Spain and other poor member states argued for a ceiling of €239 billion or above. Decisions also had to be made on the allocation of structural funds spending, including the nature of transitional arrangements for regions losing support. The Portuguese government, in fact, had announced in February that it would veto an Agenda 2000 deal unless a way was found to spare Portugal sharp cuts in regional aid. In response, the German government, which held the rotating EU presidency in the first half of 1999, expressed support for special arrangements to help Portugal and Ireland, both of whom would lose heavily under the Commission's proposals for reforming the structural funds. No agreements on these and other issues were reached at a foreign ministers' conclave on 21 March, however, meaning that final decisions would have to await the Berlin summit, which was opening three days later (Baun, 2000: 160).

On the eve of the Berlin summit, the basis for a deal on cohesion policy spending began to emerge. The Spanish government announced that it could accept an overall ceiling for structural and cohesion spending of between €210 billion and €220 billion, a figure considerably lower than what it had previously called for. For its part, the German government agreed that Spain and other poorer member states could continue receiving Cohesion Fund assistance even if they belonged to the euro-zone, provided their GNPs remained less than 90 per cent of the EU average. However, the German government also insisted upon regular reviews of Cohesion Fund eligibility beginning in 2002 (Baun, 2000: 161).

Despite the rapprochement between Germany and Spain, the Berlin summit quickly bogged down in disputes over budgetary issues, including cuts in CAP spending (opposed by France) and Britain's refusal to accept any changes to its rebate. Spain and other poor member states also rejected the German proposal to set a ceiling of €210 billion on cohesion policy spending – the lower end of the range that the Spanish government had previously said it would accept – while the Netherlands and other wealthy net contributors called for a limit of €190 billion. Finally, at dawn of the summit's third day, and after 20 hours of difficult negotiations, EU leaders reached an agreement. While keeping the ceiling for budgetary resources at 1.27 per cent of EU GDP, they decided to limit actual expenditure for 2000–06 to 1.13 per cent. Within this context, they agreed on a seven-year total of €213 billion for cohesion policy spending, with €195 billion allocated to the four structural funds and €18 billion to the Cohesion Fund, amounting to more than a third of planned EU spending for the seven-year period. This compared with CAP spending of €40.5 billion per year, or about 42 per cent of total expenditure for 2000–06. The final deal also included changes to the EU's own resources system that shifted financing from a VAT to GNP-based resource, and it allowed Britain to retain its budget rebate, although with some modification, while approving additional compensatory mechanisms for the four biggest net contributors (Austria, Germany, the Netherlands and Sweden) (Baun, 2000: 161–2; European Council, 1999).

The Agenda 2000 agreement also included changes to the design of cohesion policy that would compensate some member states for the negative effects on their net balances of structural funds reform. These included generous transitional arrangements for regions losing assistance because they no longer qualified under Objectives 1 or 2, with the European Council setting aside nearly 6 per cent of the structural budget for this purpose. It was agreed that this transitional support, amounting to a total of €11.14 billion, would be provided on the basis of an indicative breakdown per member state determined by the Commission. Also approved was a British-proposed 'safety net', which limited the loss of Objective 2 aid to one-third of the 1999 amount (European Council, 1999).

The Berlin agreement also began the use of last-minute 'special provisions' to help seal a final budgetary deal. At the Berlin summit, a total of 13 special assistance packages were agreed for 'particular situations' in various member states where regions faced the loss of EU funds. In all, 11 different member states, ranging from the wealthiest (Germany, Sweden and the Netherlands) to the poorest (Greece, Spain and Portugal) received such special provisions, funded under the heading of cohesion policy, in total amounting to €5 billion (European Council, 1999).

The 2007–13 financial perspective

Eastern enlargement significantly affected intra-EU cleavages on the budget and cohesion policy. Thus, in the negotiations on the 2007–13 financial perspective it was possible to distinguish three distinctive groups of member states. The first group consisted of the new member states that had joined in 2004 and become major net beneficiaries of cohesion policy. The second consisted of EU15 net beneficiaries of cohesion policy (Spain, Portugal and Greece) who wanted to continue benefitting from transitional support for as long as possible. These two groups worked together in order to keep the level of cohesion policy expenditure as high as possible. Known as the 'Friends of Cohesion Policy', this coalition was later joined by Belgium, Ireland, Finland and Italy as observers. The 'Friends of Cohesion' stood against the third group, consisting of six net contributors who opposed budget increases (in fact, they requested a reduction of EU expenditure to at most 1 per cent of EU GNI) and wanted to restrict cohesion policy assistance to only the poorest regions and member states (Mrak and Rant, 2007: 21-2; Ujupan, 2009: 9).

The budgetary negotiations commenced in February 2004 with publication of the Commission's financial proposals for 2007–13. In its proposal, the Commission suggested maintaining a ceiling for financial resources of 1.24 per cent of EU GNI. It also proposed allocating €336 billion for cohesion policy in the next seven-year period (CEC, 2004b). Splits between the member states appeared immediately. While Spain, Portugal, Greece, Belgium and most of the new member states backed the Commission's proposal or, in the case of the new member states, called for an increase in cohesion policy spending, Austria, France, Germany, the Netherlands, Sweden and the UK advocated limiting expenditure to 1 per cent of EU GNI. Taking an intermediate position were Finland, Ireland and Italy, which suggested a budget in the range of 1.1–1.4 per cent of GNI. There was also disagreement about the proposed division of cohesion policy funding between old and new member states, with the UK and the Netherlands opposed to giving transitional Convergence assistance to poorer EU15 countries, arguing that funding under this objective should be concentrated on the new member states. This position was rejected by Spain, which argued that the amount proposed for transitional support was an absolute minimum (Bachtler and Wishlade, 2005: 19; Wozniak Boyle, 2006: 262). Most of the new member states also opposed the Commission's proposed 4 per cent of GDP absorption cap for cohesion policy assistance, claiming that it would significantly reduce the amount of assistance they would receive; Poland, for example, argued that without the limit it would qualify for funds amounting to 8 per cent of GDP (Wozniak Boyle, 2006: 262).

Little progress in the negotiations was made in the second half of 2004 and first half of 2005, under the Dutch and Luxembourg EU presidencies respectively. Under the Luxembourg presidency, a 'negotiating box' was produced just prior to the June 2005 Brussels summit which called for a reduction of the expenditure ceiling (appropriation for payments) to 1 per cent of EU GNI, and a reduction of cohesion policy spending to a total of €306.5 billion. At the summit itself, the expenditure ceiling was revised upward to 1.06 per cent of EU GNI, and the total for cohesion policy was raised to €309.6 billion. While these figures seemed to provide the basis for an agreement, the talks foundered on disagreement between the UK and France over the British rebate and the CAP. The Luxembourg presidency had proposed reducing the British rebate as a means of limiting EU spending. However, the British government refused to accept any reduction in its rebate unless there were also cuts in CAP spending, something that was adamantly rejected by France, which in turn called for the UK rebate to be abolished. This dispute proved intractable, and at the summit the negotiations collapsed amid 'considerable rancour and mutual recrimination among EU leaders' (Bachtler and Wishlade, 2005: 19–36).

The failure of the Brussels summit placed the onus for reaching a deal on the incoming UK presidency. After spending much of the summer and fall seeking to build a consensus among the member states, the British government finally submitted a budget proposal in early December, only two weeks before the scheduled meeting of the European Council. The British proposal called for a reduced expenditure ceiling of 1.03 per cent of EU GNI; this would be achieved, among other things, by a 10 per cent cut in structural funds for the new member states, which would be accomplished through a lowering of the absorption cap for the EU10. The sting of reduced funding would be offset by a number of changes to the rules governing the implementation of cohesion policy that would apply specifically to the new member states: a more generous co-financing rate; relaxation of the automatic de-commitment rule to allow more time to use allocated funds; the eligibility of housing projects for assistance from the ERDF; and the exemption of the new member states from new rules linking cohesion policy spending to the Lisbon strategy goals. As part of the deal, the UK presidency also proposed reducing the British rebate (Bachtler *et al.*, 2007: 4).

Response to the UK proposal was overwhelmingly critical, especially on the part of the new member states. Poland's prime minister, Kazimeirz Marcinkiewicz, claimed that the British proposal did 'not abide by the principle of solidarity', and he threatened to veto any deal that was based on it. Also unhappy were the EU15 net beneficiaries, who felt the proposed reduction of the UK rebate did not go far enough (Wozniak Boyle, 2006: 265). Also reacting negatively was Commission President Barroso, who accused the British government of using 'the Sheriff of Nottingham approach', because in its proposal Britain wanted to take money from the poor new member states and give it to the rich UK. According to Barroso, 'This is not a budget for a modern, dynamic, competitive enlarged Europe. On the contrary, it lacks ambition and threatens to make Europe less united rather than more' (Parker, 2005). Budget Commissioner Dalia Grybauskaité also condemned the proposal for creating a 'two-speed' Europe and 'dividing Europe even more' (EUObserver.com, 2005).

Responding to this criticism, the UK submitted a revised proposal just before the beginning of the 15–16 December summit. The new proposal made a series of country-specific adjustments to the budget that had the effect of reducing the cuts in structural funds for the new member states while providing extra funding for some EU15 countries. There were also improvements on the revenue side of the budget for Sweden and the Netherlands, and the changes in rules governing cohesion policy for the new member states were extended to the poorest EU15 countries, Greece and Portugal (Bachtler *et al.*, 2007: 5).

At the summit itself, the UK presidency presented a third proposal which raised the expenditure ceiling to 1.045 per cent of EU GNI. Most of this new spending consisted of additional cohesion policy payments to specific countries for assistance to poor or peripheral regions. The absorption cap for the new member states was raised slightly, adding another €4.6 billion to cohesion policy spending. There were also additional country-specific payments for rural development that helped raise the total for CAP spending by €3.41 billion. On the revenue side, further reductions were made to the UK rebate, while Austria and the Netherlands won reductions to their contributions. In return for British concessions on the UK rebate, the Council asked the Commission to conduct a mid-term review of EU spending in 2008–09 that would include the CAP (Bachtler *et al.*, 2007: 6). On the basis of this proposal a final deal was reached that included a total of €308 billion for cohesion policy in 2007–13 (CEU, 2005: 8). A key role at the summit was played by German Chancellor Angela Merkel, who approved giving Poland an additional €100 million in structural funds from money that had originally been designated for eastern Germany, while she also persuaded French president Jacques Chirac to agree to a budget review that would open the door to possible reductions in CAP spending. In order to achieve a deal, Merkel also accepted a higher

EU spending ceiling than Germany had initially desired (Wozniak Boyle, 2006: 267).

Changes to the design of cohesion policy also addressed concerns about net balances and helped to achieve a budgetary agreement. The creation of the RCE objective itself was a form of 'pay back' to wealthier net contributors who were pushing for a reduction of the EU budget, since it would ensure that these member states would also benefit from cohesion policy spending (BMWS&E Regional Assemblies, 2008; Schröder, 2008: 17). Cohesion policy played a compensatory role in other ways as well, however. Once again, generous transitional arrangements, in the form of 'phasing out' and 'phasing in' assistance for the Convergence and RCE objectives respectively, were agreed. In the latter case, transitional support was given to 16 regions in eight EU15 member states that had previously qualified for Objective 1 assistance but were no longer eligible because of the statistical effect of enlargement (CEC, 2007a: 14; 2008: 8). 'Phasing in' assistance, aimed at former Objective 1 regions that had outgrown this status and were no longer eligible even after taking into account the statistical effect of enlargement, was provided to 13 regions in nine (mostly EU15) member states (CEC, 2007a: 18; 2008: 8–9). Special phasing out assistance was also given to Spain under the Cohesion Fund (CEC, 2007a: 16). As a result of these arrangements, along with the agreement to limit cohesion policy receipts to a maximum of 3.8 per cent of GDP for the very poorest member states, the EU15 continued to receive nearly half of all cohesion policy spending in 2007–13.

Also as part of the budget deal a total of 18 'additional provisions' relating to specific member states, groups of countries or single regions, amounting to €8.7 billion, were adopted (CEU, 2005: 17–20; Osterloh, 2010: 88). Of the 27 member states, 20 benefitted from one or several of these special provisions, with their impact varying significantly for individual countries. For example, while such additional measures represented only 0.6 per cent of total cohesion policy expenditures in Hungary, they made up 6.8 per cent in Spain, 8.9 per cent in Sweden and 11.5 per cent in Austria (Neheider and Santos, 2011: 638). In absolute figures, Spain was the main beneficiary of these special provisions with €2.6 billion, followed by Italy with €1.4 billion (Osterloh, 2010: 88). On the other hand, only four special provisions were designed for new member states (Ujupan, 2009: 9), indicating the primary use of these allocations to improve the net positions of wealthier countries and address the concerns of EU15 beneficiaries who are losing support.

The 2014–20 MFF

The negotiations for the 2014–20 MFF concluded in the Council in February 2013, but final agreement between the Council, Commission and the European Parliament was only reached nine months later. The MFF negotiations were once again dominated by the EU's north–south divide, in this case exacerbated by the effects of the global financial and euro-zone crises. While the economic crisis accentuated the need of less wealthy southern and CEE member states for EU structural assistance, it made the wealthier member states even more reluctant to sustain their net contributions to the EU budget, especially as they were reducing domestic spending and under severe budgetary constraints at home. The negotiations for 2014–20 were also the first MFF negotiations to take place after enactment of the Lisbon Treaty, which gave the European Parliament a more prominent role. As in previous budgetary negotiations, in the negotiations for the 2014–20 MFF, cohesion policy played a major role, both as an object of contention and through its use as a compensatory mechanism for adjusting net balances.

In the MFF negotiations, the alignment of member states once again pitted poorer net recipients against wealthier net contributors. On one side of this divide were the 'Friends of Better Spending', initially consisting of Germany, the UK, France, Italy, the Netherlands, Sweden, Austria, Finland and Denmark (with Italy and France later distancing themselves from this group after changes in political leadership that installed less conservative governments in both countries). This group demanded a freeze or reduction of EU spending, justifying this in terms of the post-2008 economic crisis and the conditions of budgetary consolidation and austerity that most member states were enduring at the national level. In particular, this group targeted cohesion policy as an area for reduced EU spending. On the other side were the 'Friends of Cohesion', which included most of the CEE countries as well as future member state, Croatia. This group demanded no cuts to EU spending, or even an increase, both to show solidarity towards poorer member states and to enable them to make continued progress in closing the economic gap with wealthier countries. Especially in the context of economic crisis and austerity, these governments argued, EU funds were needed for public investment to promote economic development and convergence. In their advocacy of more EU spending, and continued high levels of expenditure on cohesion policy, the 'Friends of Cohesion' group had the support of both the Commission and the European Parliament.

Debate on the MFF began with the presentation of the Commission's formal budgetary proposal in June 2011. In its proposal, the Commission called for €1,025 billion in total spending (commitments) for 2014–20 (updated in July 2011 to €1,033), a 4.8 per cent increase from the previous period, with budget shares for the CAP and cohesion policy remaining basically unchanged. The Commission proposed allocating a total of €336 billion for cohesion policy in the next programming period (later revised to €339 billion), with €10 billion within the Cohesion Fund ring-fenced for a new 'Connecting Europe Facility' for transport, energy and ICT. The Commission also called for a lower cap of 2.5 per cent of GDP for cohesion policy allocations to individual member states (CEC, 2011b; Vogel, 2012).

The Commission's proposal generated predictable reactions among the member states. In September 2011, the 'Friends of Better Spending' group released a paper which claimed that the Commission's proposed budget was 'too high' and 'significantly in excess of what is needed for a stabilisation of the European budget' (Euractiv.com, 2011b). Instead, they insisted that the budget should be reduced by another €100 billion or even more. The 'Friends of Cohesion' group, on the other hand, generally welcomed the Commission's proposal, although it viewed the proposed level of cohesion policy spending as insufficient and 'an absolute minimum' that must be preserved. It also opposed the lower capping limit and the use of cohesion policy funds for the Connecting Europe Facility (Kovacheva, 2012a, 2012b).

Little progress in the negotiations was made over the next year, leaving it to the Cypriot presidency to try to secure an agreement by the end of 2012. To this end, a special summit dedicated to the MFF was scheduled for 22–3 November. After broad rejection of the negotiating box produced by the Cypriot presidency in late October (Euractiv.com, 2012b), European Council President Herman Van Rompuy stepped in and took the lead in efforts to achieve a deal. In mid-November he produced a new negotiating box, which suggested €75 billion in cuts from the Commission's proposal for total spending, including €17 billion from cohesion policy. Van Rompuy's proposal also lowered the capping limit for cohesion policy receipts to 2.4 per cent of GDP and reduced the coefficients used to calculate cohesion policy allocations for different categories of member states (Euractiv.com, 2012c).

Unsurprisingly, the proposal left most member states unhappy to varying degrees. The British government felt that the cuts proposed by the European Council president did not go far enough, and it threatened to veto a budget deal if further reductions were not made. Other member states threatening to veto an agreement included France, which opposed any cuts to agricultural spending, and Denmark, which demanded its own special rebate to match those already in place for other wealthier countries. The governments of Italy, Sweden, Latvia, Austria and Romania also brandished veto threats if the final budget deal harmed their national interests (Euractiv.com, 2012d). German Chancellor Merkel, by contrast, sought to maintain a middle ground, with a foot in both camps, and play the role of broker (Euractiv.com, 2012e).

At the summit itself, the UK and other wealthy member states sought additional cuts from Van Rompuy's proposal of €30 billion or more but were rebuffed by France, Italy and other (mainly poorer) member states. Nevertheless, despite the disagreements the outlines of a final deal began to emerge. This involved the intersection of the MFF negotiations with parallel intergovernmental negotiations on creating an EU banking union, with Chancellor Merkel offering the British prime minister her support for further budget cuts in return for his agreement on the latter issue. In the end, the meeting broke up without an agreement, but with EU leaders pledging to try and reach an MFF deal early in the next year (Euractiv.com, 2012a).

Meeting on 7–8 February 2013, after 24 hours of talks, EU leaders finally agreed to a reduced budget of €960 billion for 2014–20, representing 1 per cent of EU GNI (0.95 per cent appropriation for payments). This figure amounted to a 3.5 per cent decrease in spending from the previous period, marking the first net reduction of the EU budget in history. The amount allocated for cohesion policy was €325, about 34 per cent of total spending, but almost a 9 per cent reduction from 2007–13 and €11 billion less than the Commission initially proposed (European Council, 2013: 3–20; Euractiv.com,

2013a, 2013b). Still, the final amount for cohesion policy was about €16 billion higher than what was proposed by Van Rompuy in November, indicating the extent to which cohesion policy spending was used as a compensatory mechanism in the final bargaining rounds to help achieve a deal. This increase came at the expense of spending in other areas, especially under subheading 1a – 'Competitiveness for growth and jobs', which included the Connecting Europe Facility – but not agriculture, with the final amounts for the CAP remaining basically unchanged from the November proposal (Euractiv.com, 2013b).

As part of the MFF agreement, changes to the design of cohesion policy were approved that addressed the issue of member state net balances in various ways. One was the creation of a new three-tier regional architecture for cohesion policy, consisting of less developed, transition, and more developed regions; this ensured that all member states would continue to benefit from cohesion policy spending, while the transition region category benefitted primarily Germany, France and the UK – three net contributors – as well as Spain and Greece. The agreement also included a reduced capping level of 2.35 per cent of GDP (2.59 per cent for member states with GDP growth in 2008–10 lower than -1 per cent because of the euro-zone crisis), and 'safety net' provisions that ensured: minimum levels of support for former Convergence (now transition) regions no longer eligible for assistance under the less developed category because of the statistical effect of the 2007 enlargement; a minimum total allocation of structural and cohesion funds for all member states of 55 per cent of their 2007–13 total allocation; and minimum levels of support for transition regions (European Council, 2013: 10–22).

As was by now customary, a number of additional 'special allocations' under the cohesion policy heading – totalling almost €10 billion – were part of the budget agreement with an eye towards net balances; these included additional assistance for member states particularly affected by the euro-zone crisis – Greece, Portugal, Spain, Ireland and Italy – and special allocations for the island member states Malta and Cyprus, as well as for the French overseas department of Mayotte and the North African possessions of Spain. Additional special allocations benefitted Belgium, Germany, the UK and Ireland (for the PEACE Programme), Hungary, the Czech Republic and Slovenia (European Council, 2013: 11–20).

The negotiations for the 2014–20 MFF were the first to take place after ratification of the Lisbon Treaty, meaning that the European Parliament had to give its consent to the budgetary deal. Many Members of the European Parliament (MEPs) were unhappy with various elements of the agreement, however, with many in particular demanding greater flexibility in the budget both between budget headings and in annual budget planning. As a result, on 13 March the EP voted overwhelmingly to reject the Council's MFF agreement (Euractiv.com, 2013c). The Parliament's rejection necessitated difficult negotiations between the EP and the Council to reach an inter-institutional compromise before the MFF could become law. In late June, the EP and Council finally reached an agreement which left the budgetary amounts unchanged from the Council deal but introduced the greater flexibility that the Parliament had demanded; under the terms of the agreement, unspent money in any budget year can be rolled over to the following year or be transferred to priority areas rather than being returned to national budgets, as was previously the case. The MFF agreement also shifted some funding to more future-oriented policy areas such as youth employment programmes and research, with funding for the Youth Employment Initiative, which was increased by €2 billion, now 'frontloaded' into 2014–15, and it provided for a mid-term review of the budget in 2016 (Vogel, 2013a, 2013b).

Even after the June compromise, however, a dispute over the annual budget for 2014 prevented the EP's final approval of the MFF deal. In the end, the Parliament succeeded in getting additional resources for the 2014 budget – as well as additions to the 2013 budget to avoid beginning the new year 'in the red' – over the objections of the UK, the Netherlands, Denmark and Finland, who were outvoted in the Council. As a result, on 19 November the EP voted to formally approve the 2014–20 MFF (Euractiv.com, 2013d).

'Winners' and 'losers'

As usual, the MFF agreement produced both 'winners' and 'losers' among the member states, although in this case the gains were widely enough spread that, in the words of French President François Hollande, 'all countries [were] winners'. Perhaps the main winner was the UK, since in the final bargaining Prime Minister David Cameron was able to secure additional cuts (€18 billion) beyond those proposed by European Council President Van Rompuy in November. Hence, he was widely regarded as the summit's main victor, even by others in his own eurosceptic Conservative Party. To gain this outcome, the UK had forged an alliance with other 'budget hawks', including the Netherlands, Denmark, Sweden and Germany; indeed, the German foreign minister announced his satisfaction that the agreement on reduced EU spending sent a proper signal of budget 'consolidation ... Fiscal discipline, structural reforms and solidarity', all of which were needed 'to permanently overcome the debt crisis' (Euractiv.com, 2013e). Also adding to the UK's triumph was that it managed to preserve its budget rebate unchanged, as did Germany, while the Netherlands, Sweden and Austria had to accept cuts (by almost half) to theirs. Denmark, meanwhile, was successful in securing its own budget rebate, adding to those for wealthier net contributors already in existence (Euractiv.com, 2013a).

Among the other winners in the MFF deal were some poor member states. One of these was Poland, which emerged as the largest beneficiary of cohesion policy spending, with a total allocation for 2014–20 of more than €77 billion, an increase of about €10 billion from 2007–13 (see Table 3.2 below). This outcome prompted Poland's finance minister to term the budget deal 'a unique, huge success' for his country (Euractiv.com, 2013e). Another winner in the budget negotiations was Bulgaria, which was one of only four countries that gained an increase of cohesion policy funds from the previous period, along with Poland, Romania and Slovakia. After Estonia, Slovakia also emerged as the largest per capita recipient of cohesion funding followed by Lithuania, Latvia and Hungary.

While the Czech Republic was among the member states suffering a reduction of cohesion spending from the previous programming period (by almost €5 billion), it managed to secure an additional €900 million in the final bargaining which the Czech prime minister attributed to his 'veto threat' (Euractiv.com, 2013e). Overall, while the CEE countries and other poor member states were not successful in preventing a reduction of cohesion policy spending, the new member states ended up claiming an even greater proportion of available funds, securing almost 57 per cent of cohesion policy spending in 2014–20 compared with 51 per cent in 2007–13.

TABLE 3.2 *Cohesion policy allocations for 2014–20*

Member state	Total allocation* (€ million, 2014 prices)	€ Per capita**	% GDP***
Estonia	3,590.0	2,708.99	2.94
Slovakia	13,991.7	2,588.98	2.81
Lithuania	6,823.1	2,271.61	2.96
Latvia	4,511.8	2,206.46	2.90
Hungary	21,905.9	2,205.61	3.23
Czech Republic	21,982.9	2,092.52	2.05
Portugal	21,465.0	2,036.06	1.86
Croatia	8,609.4	2,013.4	2.82
Poland	77,567.0	2,012.72	2.90
Malta	725.0	1,736.34	1.51
Slovenia	3,074.8	1,495.89	1.24
Greece	15,521.9	1,395.47	1.15
Romania	22,993.8	1,144.20	2.50
Bulgaria	7,588.4	1,035.65	2.72
Cyprus	735.6	853.35	0.59
Spain	28,559.5	610.01	2.78
Italy	32,823.0	552.63	0.30
Finland	1,465.8	271.38	0.11
Ireland	1,188.6	259.37	0.10
France	15,852.5	242.81	0.11
Germany	19,234.9	239.46	0.10
Sweden	2,105.8	222.06	0.07
Belgium	2,283.9	205.85	0.09
UK	11,839.9	186.47	0.09
Austria	1,235.6	146.95	0.06
Luxembourg	59.7	113.75	0.02
Denmark	553.4	99.17	0.03
Netherlands	1,404.3	83.94	0.03

* With additional allocation for Youth Employment Initiative; Source: CEC (2014b) © European Union.
** Total allocation for 2014–20/2012 population; Population source: Eurostat (2013b) © European Union.
*** One-year average of total cohesion policy allocation/2012 GDP (market prices), GDP source: Eurostat (2013c) © European Union.

Among the other member states, while it was disappointed with the reduced size of the EU budget, France was able to preserve a high level of CAP spending in the final deal, with cuts to direct payments to farmers largely offset by increased funding for rural development. For its part, Spain was happy that it remained a net beneficiary of the EU budget, and that, with a youth unemployment rate of nearly 60 per cent – the highest in Europe – it would get nearly a third of the money allocated for the Youth Guarantee Fund. Italy was also disappointed with the reduction of cohesion policy spending, although in late bargaining it was able to reduce its net negative balance by €3.5 billion through additional allocations for its less developed regions (Euractiv.com, 2013a, 2013e).

Among the EU institutions, the Commission was disappointed in the budget outcome, which slashed spending by €93 billion from the original Commission proposal, including more than €50 billion for cohesion policy. Nevertheless, while claiming that the final deal was insufficient for the EU's investment needs, Commission representatives also expressed relief that an agreement was finally reached and preparations for the next programming period could now go forward (Euractiv.com, 2013f). Also disappointed with the reduced level of spending was the European Parliament. However, the Parliament emerged a winner by using its new budgetary powers to force adjustments to the final MFF deal – although it was not able to change the overall amount of spending – perhaps presaging an increased influence for the EP in budgetary negotiations in the future.

Conclusion

Cohesion policy plays a very large and important role in EU budgetary politics, because of the share of EU expenditure that it accounts for, and because of its traditional role as a compensatory mechanism used to facilitate intergovernmental bargaining and agreement. In the latter case, cohesion policy spending has been used as a 'side payment' to help achieve agreements between the member states on EU widening and deepening, with increased funding used to sway the votes of poorer member states who feel they will be economically disadvantaged by enlargement or further integration. Cohesion policy spending has also been used to address the issue of net balances in budgetary negotiations, thus helping to secure intergovernmental agreement on complex multi-annual financial packages or frameworks. In either respect, the use of cohesion policy as a compensatory mechanism to facilitate intergovernmental bargaining and agreement – and thus European integration – is an important, if unstated, role of cohesion policy, existing – if uneasily, and in some case contradictorily – alongside its official purpose of promoting cohesion and economic growth and competitiveness.

The amount of cohesion policy spending and the share of the EU budget it accounts for also means that cohesion policy has become an increasingly contentious subject in EU budgetary negotiations, especially since the late 1990s in the context of slow economic growth, high unemployment and the budgetary and fiscal constraints imposed by EMU. It has become even more so because of the 2008 global financial crisis and the subsequent euro-zone crisis. For wealthier net contributors facing their own budgetary and fiscal problems, cohesion policy has been a logical target in efforts to reduce EU spending. Poorer net recipients that are also the main beneficiaries of cohesion policy, on the other hand, ardently defend expenditure on cohesion policy as more necessary than ever, both as an expression of EU solidarity and to allow them to continue making progress towards economic development and convergence in economically hard times. The division between net contributors and recipients, which has only grown as a consequence of enlargement, has dominated negotiations on the EU budget and cohesion policy spending since the late 1990s, and it is certain to do so in the future as well. The impact of this north–south divide on EU budgetary politics and its implications for the future of cohesion policy is discussed further in the final chapter of this book.

Chapter 4

Implementing Cohesion Policy

It is in the implementation phase that cohesion policy reveals its unique multi-level character. The decision-making steps examined in the previous chapters – the multi-annual agreements on the basic design of cohesion policy, including its priority objectives, programming procedures and implementation rules, and on the budgetary allocation for cohesion policy, including the distribution of funding among its various objectives and the indicative amounts for individual member states – take place predominantly at the EU level, involving proposals from the Commission and negotiations between the member states, with final intergovernmental agreements on both the MFF and the cohesion policy regulations requiring the approval of the European Parliament. The implementation phase, on the other hand, occurs at the EU, national and subnational levels and involves public actors from each: the Commission, national governments and subnational (regional and local) authorities. In accordance with the key operational principle of partnership, non-governmental and civil society actors are also supposed to be involved.

This chapter examines how cohesion policy is implemented after the basic decisions on policy design and budgetary allocation have been made. It explains the main steps or phases of the implementation process and who is involved in each. It also examines how the implementation process has changed over the years with respect to each of these steps and the reasons for these changes. Several key issues or trends are emphasized: the changing role of the Commission in the implementation process; the shift towards strategic planning in order to align cohesion policy more closely with the EU's growth, competitiveness and environmental sustainability priorities; an increased emphasis on effectiveness and performance along with evaluation and reporting; and the efforts to decentralize and simplify cohesion policy implementation. Also discussed are some key problems in the implementation process, including absorption and the misuse of EU funds. While it is touched upon in this chapter, the application of the partnership principle and its implications for multi-level governance in the EU is examined in the next chapter.

The implementation process

Prior to 1989, EC regional assistance was distributed to the member states according to a system of national quotas, with intergovernmental bargaining over national percentages having more to do with net budgetary balances than actual Community regional development needs (Leonardi, 2005: 42–3; Manzella and Mendez, 2009: 10). In this system, the member states retained the right to determine which regions would be eligible for Community support, by limiting ERDF funds to areas targeted by their own regional policies. Applications for project financing were also channelled through national governments, thereby giving them the primary role in project selection and greatly limiting the Commission's influence over the use of EC funds (Manzella and Mendez, 2009: 10). As a result, EC regional policy in its early years was managed primarily by the member states, with the Community's role consisting mainly 'of providing additional financial resources to member states for the pursuit of [national] regional development policies' (Leonardi, 2005: 42).

The 1988 reform of the structural funds introduced an entirely new implementation system for what was now EC cohesion policy. This implementation or 'delivery' system has evolved considerably over the years through successive policy reforms, but it still consists of three basic steps or phases. The first of these steps is deciding which geographical areas will receive assistance under the regional objectives of cohesion policy, or the process of 'area designation'. While the structural funds regulations establish clear criteria for which geographical areas are eligible to receive assistance under each objective, these often leave enough 'wriggle room' to allow for negotiations between the member states and the Commission over which areas should receive assistance. The opportunity for member states to influence Commission decision-making on area designation was especially good before the 2006 reform when it came to Objectives 2 and (until 1999) 5b. In the 2006 reform, however, the responsibility for designating which areas were to receive assistance under the new RCE objective was largely ceded to the member states, while the 2013 reform introduced an entirely new regional classification scheme for the allocation of EU structural funding.

The second step in the implementation process is 'programming'. In this step, the Commission and national governments, with the involvement of subnational and non-governmental partners, agree upon general plans for the use of allocated structural funds in each member state for a multi-annual period, as well as on specific operational programmes (OPs) supported by those funds. This phase also occurs at the very beginning of the programming period, usually before the first year of the period for which EU funds have been allocated. Since the 2006 reform the programming phase has also included the preparation of strategic guidelines for the use of EU funds by the Commission, in order to ensure that cohesion policy spending supports the goals of the EU's growth and competitiveness strategies.

The third step in the implementation process is 'programme management', which involves the execution of EU-funded programmes and projects ('structural operations'), including the key tasks of programme monitoring and the exercise of financial control. It also involves evaluating the effectiveness of EU-funded programmes and their contribution to the achievement of EU strategic goals, and reporting outcomes and results. This phase takes place largely at the member state level, and the key actors are national and subnational governmental authorities and the private and non-governmental partners, although the Commission also plays an important role. As with area designation and programming, the rules and procedures for programme management have changed over the years, in response to lessons drawn from experience, the demands of the member states and other policy actors, and changes to the basic goals and objectives of cohesion policy.

Key trends

The evolution of the cohesion policy implementation process has been marked by several key trends. One of these has been the Commission's changing role in the implementation process. Broadly speaking, over the years the Commission has progressively stepped back from detailed involvement in programming and programme management, thus allowing the member states greater flexibility and more control over these aspects of the implementation process. At the same time, however, the Commission has assumed a larger role in setting strategic guidelines and priorities for the use of EU funds. It has also assumed a greater role in monitoring the use of EU funds and in evaluating the performance of EU-funded programmes.

The relationship between the Commission and the member states when it comes to cohesion policy implementation has been the subject of considerable academic debate. According to the 'inter-governmentalist' perspective, the Commission's receding role in the implementation process in such areas as programming, area designation and programme monitoring, and its increased focus instead on strategic guidance and evaluation, can be viewed as the outcome of member states successfully exercising their 'gatekeeping' capacity and thus maintaining a firm grip on the implementation process. In this view, changes to the implementation process since the 1988 structural funds reform amount to a progressive 're-nationalization' of cohesion policy implementation, largely to the detriment of the Commission's influence and control (Bachtler and Mendez, 2007: 535; Pollack, 1995; Bache, 1998, 1999; Allen, 2005). Other scholars, however, including those coming from the Multi-level Governance (MLG) perspective (see next chapter), argue that the Commission retains a great amount of influence in the implementation process, even if that is exercised now in more indirect and subtle ways, and that the role of national governments relative to the Commission in cohesion policy implementation is 'exaggerated' (Bachtler and Mendez, 2007: 555–6).

A second key trend is the increasingly strategic nature of the implementation process. This trend began with the 1999 cohesion policy reform, which for the first time authorized the Commission to draft broad indicative guidelines for the use of EU assistance. The strategic approach really took hold with the 2006 reform and the new regulations for 2007–13, however. From this point, national programming has been guided by strategic documents prepared by the Commission which link cohesion policy spending to the EU's medium-term growth and competitiveness strategies – first the Lisbon strategy, and later Europe 2020. EU-funded projects are also increasingly evaluated in terms of their contribution to these strategic goals.

Another notable trend is the growing emphasis on effectiveness and performance. This emphasis has been motivated by concerns about waste and fraud in EU-funded projects, but also by increased budgetary constraints and the consequent need to demonstrate 'value for money' and the 'added value' of cohesion policy. It has led, among other things, to the increased use of measurable targets and performance indicators, as well as the increased importance of evaluation and reporting. In the 2013 cohesion policy reform, *ex ante* conditionalities were also introduced which linked the disbursal of allocated funds to the fulfilment of specific administrative and policy requirements in order to ensure that EU funds are used effectively.

Other key trends include the efforts to decentralize cohesion policy implementation, by devolving responsibilities to the member states and subnational levels in accordance with the principle of 'subsidiarity', and to simplify programming procedures and programme administrative responsibilities, to make them less onerous for national and subnational authorities. Both efforts have come in response to the demands of the member states and subnational authorities, who have consistently pushed for more control, greater flexibility and fewer burdensome restrictions in the management of cohesion policy. As discussed below, however, there is also some tension between the emphasis on effectiveness and evaluation, on the one hand, and efforts to decentralize and simplify, on the other. Each of these trends is highlighted in the remainder of this chapter, which examines the evolution of the cohesion policy implementation process since the 1988 reform with respect to each of its three basic steps.

Area designation

Before 1989 EC regional assistance was provided to the member states, which used it to finance their own regional development policies and priorities. The 1988 structural funds reform, however, introduced a new set of regional objectives for cohesion policy, with clear criteria for determining which geographical areas would be eligible for Community assistance. The new eligibility criteria were drafted by the Commission and approved at the Community level, but they nevertheless left some room for negotiation between the Commission and the member states over which regions would receive support. In successive cohesion policy reforms after 1988, however, the member states were able to gain greater influence in the selection of eligible regions, especially when it came to assistance under Objectives 2 and (before 2000) 5b. In 2006, the area designation system was overhauled completely, and an entirely new regional classification scheme was introduced in 2013. As a result of these changes, the influence and role of the Commission in the area designation process has evolved considerably.

1989–93

The 1988 reform established eligibility criteria for assistance under each of the three regional objectives of cohesion policy, Objectives 1, 2 and 5b. These criteria were drafted by the Commission and approved by the Council as part of the new regulations for cohesion policy. On the basis of these criteria, the Commission was responsible for drawing up a list of eligible geographical areas. However, each of these objectives also included provisions for 'special reasons' (Objective 1) or 'secondary criteria' (Objectives 2 and 5b) which allowed the member states the possibility of influencing the Commission's decisions.

For Objective 1, established to assist economically lagging regions, the eligibility standard was NUTS 2 regions with a GDP per capita less than 75 per cent of the EC average. However, regions whose per capita GDP was 'close to' (that is, somewhat above) this criteria could also be included 'for special reasons' (OJEC, 1988: 13). On this basis, the overseas departments of France and Northern Ireland in the UK qualified for Objective 1 assistance (CEC, 1993: 12).

To qualify for assistance under Objective 2, established to assist regions 'seriously affected by industrial decline', especially those suffering from high levels of unemployment, eligible areas had to satisfy all of the following criteria:

1. an average rate of unemployment recorded over the preceding three years above the EC average;
2. a percentage share of industrial employment in total employment equal to or exceeding the EC average in any reference year from 1975 onwards;
3. an observable fall in industrial employment compared with the reference year.

However, there was also a list of secondary criteria that allowed for assistance to be extended to other areas suffering from high unemployment as well. The list of areas eligible for Objective 2 assistance in each member state was drawn up and maintained by the Commission, on the basis of information provided by the member states (OJEC, 1988: 14–15). For the 1989–93 funding period, 60 regions in nine member states, representing a total of 16.8 per cent of the EC population, were awarded Objective 2 status (Bache, 1998: 72; CEC, 1996: 151).

Likewise for Objective 5b, created to assist the development of rural areas, especially those vulnerable to changes in the agricultural sector stemming from efforts to reform the CAP, eligible areas were selected by the Commission, but in this case with the assistance of a Management Committee composed of representatives of the member states (OJEC, 1988: 16, 18). Assistance under Objective 5b was provided to only a small number of disadvantaged regions, however, together accounting for about 5 per cent of the EC population (CEC, 1996: 145, 151).

1994–9

In the 1994–9 programming period the member states were able to exert greater influence over the designation of areas eligible to receive EU assistance. Objective 1 remained focused on economic development in regions that were lagging behind, but the list of eligible regions was expanded from the previous period, with the member states insisting that assistance be extended to more regions for 'special reasons'. In this manner, Objective 1 assistance became newly available for Merseyside and the Scottish Highlands and Islands in the UK, the Hainaut region in Belgium, Flevoland in the Netherlands and parts of Nord-Pas de Calais in France, in addition to the regions already covered in the previous programming period (CEC, 1993: 12). As a result of this 'political compromise' (in the Commission's words) between the Commission and national governments on eligibility, there was a wider distribution of Objective 1 funding, which now targeted nearly 27 per cent of the EU population, with 8 per cent of the eligible population living in regions with a GDP per capita above the 75 per cent threshold (CEC, 1996: 116, 151).

Changes were also made to the area designation procedures for Objectives 2 and 5b. Objective 2 still channelled assistance to regions seriously affected by the decline of traditional industries, such as iron and coal mining, steel, shipbuilding and textiles. Unlike in the previous period, however, when eligible areas were determined unilaterally by the Commission, in the 1994–9 programming period these areas were chosen on the basis of proposals made by the member states. Eligibility for Objective 2 assistance was still defined by the three unemployment criteria established by the 1988 regulations; however, the list of secondary criteria was expanded to include urban areas facing 'severe problems linked to the regeneration of derelict industrial sites' and industrial or urban areas negatively affected by the restructuring of the fisheries sector (OJEC, 1993: 11–12). As a result of these changes, as well as the accession of Austria, Sweden and Finland, whose industrial regions also became eligible for Objective 2 assistance, and the move towards 'zoning', or the targeting of assistance on smaller areas, the number of eligible areas in 1994–9 increased from 60 to 82, although the percentage of the EU population covered by the objective dropped slightly from the previous period to 16.4 per cent (CEC, 2003: 162; 1996: 145, 151).

Objective 5b underwent a minor change in that it now focused on the development and structural adjustment of rural areas, not only their development as in the previous period. Eligible areas had to have a low level of socio-economic development (assessed in terms of per capita GDP) and meet at least two of three additional criteria:

1.   a high share of agricultural employment;
2.   a low level of agricultural income;
3.   low population density and/or significant depopulation trends. (OJEC, 1993: 14)

However, none of these criteria were quantified, which left a lot of space for 'political' designation (Reiner, 1999: 83). In addition, eligibility could be extended to other areas not covered by Objective 1 but with a low level of development, provided they met at least one of a number of secondary criteria, including a remote location, sensitivity to trends in the agricultural sector or the restructuring of the fisheries sector, the structure of agricultural holdings and of the agricultural working population, etc. Eligible areas were also no longer designated by the Commission with the assistance of a Management Committee, but selected according to proposals submitted by the member states (OJEC, 1993: 14–15). These changes to the eligibility criteria and selection method led to an increase in the population living in eligible areas, from 5 per cent of the EU population in 1989–93 to 8.1 per cent in 1994–9 (CEC, 1996: 117, 145).

A new regional objective was also created as a result of the EU's 1995 enlargement, since it was decided that the northernmost parts of the two new Nordic member states – Sweden and Finland – should have their own tailor-made development programmes, as these areas lagged behind the EU average in several aspects, including per capita GDP and employment, but they did not fit the existing objectives of cohesion policy (Allen, 2010: 235; Katajamäki, 2002: 20). As a result, a new Objective 6 was created by the Act of Accession for Austria, Finland and Sweden to foster the development and structural adjustment of peripheral regions with an extremely low population density, defined as regions with a population density of eight persons per square kilometre or less. In addition, EU assistance could also extend to adjacent and contiguous smaller areas fulfilling the same population density criterion (CEU, 1995). Assistance under Objective 6 only ended up targeting 0.4 per cent of the EU population, however (CEC, 1996: 145, 151).

2000–06

The 1999 reform reduced the number of objectives for cohesion policy to just three, two of which, Objectives 1 and 2, had a regional focus. Eligibility for Objective 1 continued to be defined as a per capita GDP less than 75 per cent of the EU average. In keeping with the increased emphasis on 'concentration', however, the Commission was able to enforce a stricter application of this criterion than in the previous period (with the exception of the northern regions of Sweden and Finland that were previously covered by Objective 6 and were now deemed eligible for Objective 1 assistance). As a result, assistance under Objective 1 targeted only 22.2 per cent of the EU15 population in 2000–06, compared with 26.6 per cent in 1999 (CEC, 1999: 9–10). The trade-off for this stricter enforcement of the 75 per cent threshold was the decision to grant transitional assistance to regions that no longer qualified under Objective 1 but had done so previously, with the amount of this assistance gradually declining each year. These regions included

East Berlin in Germany, the Hainaut region in Belgium, Flevoland in the Netherlands, Northern Ireland and the Scottish Highlands and Islands in the UK, and Corsica and parts of Nord-Pas de Calais in France. About 6 per cent of the financial resources allocated for Objective 1 in this period were earmarked for such transitional assistance (CEC, 1999: 11, 19)

The new Objective 2 supported 'the economic and social conversion of areas facing structural difficulties', including 'areas undergoing socio-economic change in industrial and service sectors, declining rural areas, urban areas in difficulty and depressed areas dependent on fisheries' (OJEC, 1999: 7–8). Different eligibility criteria applied for each of the four types of regions, with a common theme being a high level of unemployment. Based on these criteria, member states submitted to the Commission a list of areas eligible for assistance, subject to a population ceiling for each country. It was also required that industrial and rural areas must contain at least 50 per cent of the population covered by Objective 2 in a member state (CEC, 1999: 12–13).

To achieve a greater concentration of resources, the maximum coverage rate for Objective 2 assistance was set at 18 per cent of the EU15 population, which was less than the 25 per cent rate for Objectives 2 and 5b combined in 1999. Within this limit, the following indicative breakdown was set: industrial areas – 8.5 per cent; rural areas – 5.2 per cent; urban areas – 1.9 per cent; areas dependent on fishing – 0.3 per cent; and mixed areas – 2.1 per cent. However, about 12 per cent of the resources for Objective 2 were earmarked for transitional assistance, to be given to regions that were eligible under Objective 2 or 5b in 1999 but did not qualify for assistance under the new Objective 2 (CEC, 1999: 12–13, 19; CEC, 2001a: 123–4).

2007–13

The 2006 reform replaced Objectives 1 and 2 with two new regionalized objectives. The Convergence objective essentially replicated the old Objective 1, with the same eligibility criteria. Generous transitional support was given, however, to 16 'phasing out' regions which had previously qualified for Objective 1 assistance but did not qualify under the Convergence objective because of the statistical effect of enlargement.

The main change to the area designation system came with the replacement of Objective 2 by the new Regional Competitiveness and Cooperation objective, which would target regions not qualifying for assistance under the Convergence objective. In contrast to the previous Objective 2, in which assistance was restricted to areas facing structural change, the new RCE objective was more thematic in approach, with full responsibility granted to the member states to determine the geographic areas eligible for assistance. Transitional assistance was also given to 13 'phasing in' regions, former Objective 1 regions which had outgrown this status and no longer qualified, even taking into account the statistical effect of enlargement (CEC, 2008: 8–9).

The new thematic approach to targeting EU assistance under the RCE objective entailed the transfer of responsibility for area designation to the member states. According to Bachtler and Mendez (2007: 544), this was interpreted by some as 'the culmination of a trend of increasing national influence on the spatial coverage of this objective [Objective 2/RCE] since 1993', and as a 'vindication of the renationalization [of cohesion policy] thesis'. They point out, however, that despite these changes cohesion policy spending after the 2006 reform was still decided on the basis of EU-wide criteria and indicators. Moreover, while the Commission sacrificed some control over the designation of areas in which the funds could be used, by doing so it was able to retain 'Commission influence on Cohesion policy throughout the EU' (Bachtler and Mendez, 2007: 545), the clear implication being that without this compromise, those wealthier member states favouring a true re-nationalization of cohesion policy might have succeeded in getting it limited to only the very poorest countries and regions.

The 2006 reform also included numerous 'special provisions' or allocations under the cohesion policy heading that were requested by the member states as part of the budget negotiations. These allocations only amounted to about 2 per cent of the total budget for cohesion policy. Nevertheless, they undermined somewhat the goal of concentrating assistance on the neediest regions, as well as the use of objective EU criteria to determine the spatial coverage of structural assistance and financial allocations (Bachtler and Mendez, 2007: 544).

2014–20

The 2013 reform further revised the territorial architecture for cohesion policy. In the 2014–20 programming period, support under the new 'investment for growth and jobs' goal is allocated on the basis of a new three-tier classification of EU regions: less developed regions, whose GDP per capita is less than 75 per cent of the EU average; transition regions, whose GDP per capita is between 75 and 90 per cent of the EU average; and more developed regions, whose GDP per capita is above 90 per cent of the EU average. The task of determining which NUTS 2 regions belonged to which regional category was given to the Commission, which based its decision on the GPD per capita (Purchasing Power Parity (PPP)) of each region in 2007–09 relative to the EU27 average for that period (OJEU, 2013a: 382). Following the final approval of the new cohesion policy regulations, the Commission published its list of eligible regions in February 2014 (see Table 4.1; the Commission's official map of eligible regions is available at http://ec. europa.eu/regional_policy/what/future/ eligibility/index_en.cfm).

The new regional classification scheme, and the use of an allocation methodology which directs proportionately more funding to poorer or more disadvantaged regions, is intended to meet the traditional cohesion policy goal of concentrating available resources where they are most needed. The creation of the transition region category somewhat undermines this goal, however, and was widely viewed as a concession to Germany, France, the UK and Spain, the member states in which most of the transition regions are located. It is also undermined by the safety net provisions that are part of the 2013 reform, which assure minimum levels of support for both former Convergence regions and individual member states. Finally, it is undermined by the agreement on numerous special allocations in the final budgetary negotiations, amounting to about 3 per cent of the total budget for cohesion policy, which reflect more the principles of *just retour* and 'something for everyone' rather than concentration.

Programming

Another innovation of the 1988 reform was the introduction of multi-annual programming. In the new system, the Commission,

TABLE 4.1　*Structural funds regional eligibility, 2014–20*

Category of region	Member state	Eligible regions
Less developed	Bulgaria	6 regions
	Croatia	2 regions
	Czech Republic	7 regions
	Estonia	1 region
	Greece	5 regions
	Hungary	6 regions
	France	5 regions (overseas departments)
	Italy	5 regions
	Latvia	1 region
	Lithuania	1 region
	Poland	15 regions
	Portugal	4 regions
	Romania	7 regions
	Slovenia	1 region
	Slovakia	3 regions
	Spain	1 region
	United Kingdom	2 regions
Transition	Austria	1 region
	Belgium	4 regions
	Denmark	1 region
	France	10 regions
	Germany	8 regions
	Greece	6 regions

national governments and – in accordance with the newly intro-duced principle of partnership – the subnational and non-govern-mental partners would plan for the use of allocated funds in each member state for a multi-year period. Since 1988 the programming process has evolved considerably, however, becoming both more simplified and streamlined as well as more strategic. The Commission's role in the programming process has also changed, as it has stepped back from detailed involvement in national planning and the preparation of operational programmes, leaving this more to the member states and partners, and assumed instead more of a strategic guidance role.

Category of region	Member state	Eligible regions
More developed	Italy	3 regions
	Malta	1 region
	Portugal	1 region
	Spain	5 regions
	United Kingdom	11 regions
	Austria	8 regions
	Belgium	7 regions
	Cyprus	1 region
	Czech Republic	1 region
	Denmark	4 regions
	Finland	5 regions
	France	12 regions
	Germany	31 regions
	Greece	2 regions
	Hungary	1 region
	Ireland	2 regions
	Italy	13 regions
	Luxembourg	1 region
	Netherlands	12 regions
	Poland	1 region
	Portugal	2 regions
	Romania	1 region
	Slovakia	1 region
	Slovenia	1 region
	Spain	13 regions
	Sweden	8 regions
	United Kingdom	24 regions

Source: OJEU (2014: 24–34) © European Union.

1989–93

The 1988 reform introduced a new three-stage programming process involving the Commission, national governments and the subnational partners. In the first stage, national or regional development plans were drawn up by national authorities, in partnership with relevant regional and local authorities. Regional plans concerned Objectives 1, 2 and 5b, and were 'rolling' plans covering three to five years and updated every year, while national plans concerned Objectives 3 and 4. Both types of plans were supposed to conform to the same general structure, however, consisting of:

1. an 'economic and social analysis of the region, area, sector or problem concerned';
2. a 'development strategy', including a description of the 'method and means of implementation', a plan for 'national and regional financing' [and] information about 'Community operations already under way';
3. a description of the 'development priorities to be financed';
4. 'an estimate of total funding requested, broken down by structural instruments (Funds, EIB, other instruments, etc.)'.

While regional plans normally covered one region, the poorest member states (Ireland, Greece and Portugal) were allowed to draft a single national regional development plan covering all regions. The national and regional plans were supposed to be submitted to the Commission within the first few months of the beginning of the new programming period (CEC, 1989b: 28–9).

In the second stage, the Commission developed and negotiated with the member states Community Support Frameworks (CSFs) on the basis of the national or regional development plans. Formally, the CSFs were 'the Commission's response to the needs spelt out in the plans'. According to the Commission's explanatory document, the CSFs 'map out the broad lines of the measures to be taken jointly by the Member States and the Community and provide the reference framework for the applications for assistance submitted to the Commission by the Member States'. In essence, the CSFs were a form of contract between the Commission and the member states for the allocation and use of the structural funds. CSFs were negotiated for specific regions or entire countries, depending on the regional and national plans proposed by the member states. In terms of content, the CSFs contained a statement of the main development priorities for the member state or region concerned, a multi-year plan of actions to address these priorities and a financing plan specifying financial allocations from the structural funds and other forms of assistance (CEC, 1989b: 30).

According to the new structural funds regulations, after receiving the development plans the Commission had six months to review them and approve a CSF (CEC, 1989b: 31). The CSF negotiations were often protracted, however, 'as the Commission – sometimes in the face of strong Member State resistance – sought to interpret and apply the new regulations', in some cases asking for amendments to development plans and changes to development priorities, and in others seeking the shift of 'planned expenditure away from infrastructure investment towards measures promoting direct job creation/maintenance' (Bachtler and Mendez, 2007: 548). The geographical units of the regional policy DG XVI, also had to devote considerable time to explaining the new programming procedures and correcting or redrafting programming documents (Kearney, 1997; in Bachtler and Mendez, 2007: 548). Once the changes or amendments were incorporated, the Commission adopted the CSFs.

In the third stage, the member states and regions developed the specific operational programmes through which assistance would be provided and the CSFs implemented. The OPs were of two types – programmes for specific regions (for Objectives 1, 2 and 5b) and programmes for policy areas (for example, employment policies) under Objectives 3 and 4 – and they could consist of either single projects (for example, infrastructure projects) or support schemes (for example, investment aid schemes for small and medium enterprises) (CEC, 1989b: 30–4; Tondl, 1995: 3). The regional OPs were supposed to be a 'series of consistent multiannual measures' covering 2 to 5 years. Specific regions could benefit from more than one OP, and both regional and national OPs could receive assistance from one or more of the structural funds (CEC, 1989b: 33). Once OPs were formulated they had to be approved by the Commission. The formulation and approval of the OPs was often a drawn out process, however, in many cases because the member states provided inadequate information, with some OPs not adopted until 1992 (Bachtler and Mendez, 2007: 548). As a result, there were significant delays to the start of effective spending of cohesion policy funding in first programming period (Leonardi, 2005: 53).

The new programming process gave the Commission considerable potential influence over the use of EC funds. In the negotiation of CSFs, the Commission was able to press national governments to revise development priorities and planned expenditures. The Commission could also ask member states to shift the geographical focus of CSFs, to a higher ('more aggregated') or lower ('less aggregated') level. Moreover, in addition to exerting influence over the formulation of operational programmes, the Commission could propose to member states that they develop entirely new programmes, 'comprising measures of significant interest to the Community' – 'Community Initiatives', in areas such as the environment and R&D – which were not covered in the submitted development plans (CEC, 1989b: 30, 34). However, the Commission's influence in practice was often less than it could have been. As Bachtler and Mendez (2007: 548) conclude, while the new regulations gave the Commission 'considerable powers on paper', it 'was handicapped in exercising these powers through the complexity and logistical difficulties of the process and by the inability or unwillingness of Member States to provide the requisite information'.

1994–9

The new regulations approved in 1993 modified the programming process in significant ways. To begin with, they required member states to provide additional and more detailed information in their development plans, including specific objectives, quantified where possible, an evaluation of environmental impact, more detailed financial tables and financial information to allow for the verification of additionality. Member states were also required to provide an *ex ante* evaluation of each development plan to aid the later (*ex post*) evaluation of programmes once they were completed (Bachtler and Mendez, 2007: 549; CEC, 1993: 22–6, 30).

Community Support Frameworks continued to be the key programming documents, establishing the main development priorities, plans for action and financing plans for specific regions and member states. However, for Objectives 1, 3 and 5b the CSFs were now adopted for a six-year term, to coincide with the length of the new multi-annual financial perspective agreed in December 1992 at the Edinburgh summit. In the case of Objectives 2 and 4, two three-year periods were identified, providing the possibility for CSFs to be adjusted at the end of the first phase. The programming timetable remained similar to the previous period, with development plans for Objectives 1, 3 and 4 due to the Commission no later than three months after entry into force of the new regulations, and those for Objectives 2 and 5b within three months of the adoption of the list of eligible zones, and with the Commission required to approve CSFs within six months of receiving these plans (CEC, 1993: 21–3).

A new two-stage procedure was also introduced, thus simplifying and shortening the programming process. In the new procedure, member states could draw up a Single Programming Document (SPD), which included both the development plan and the applications for assistance (the OPs) related to it. For member states which opted to submit an SPD, the Commission would adopt a single decision on both the CSFs and OPs combined, rather than two separate decisions, thus eliminating a step and saving time (CEC, 1993: 22). The new SPD procedure was used for smaller Objective 1 programmes (in Belgium, the Netherlands and the UK) and for all Objective 2 programmes except those in Spain (Bachtler and Mendez, 2007: 549).

Despite member state efforts to curtail its role, the Commission continued to exert substantial influence in the implementation of cohesion policy in the 1994–9 programming period. According to Bachtler and Mendez (2007: 549–50), in many cases the Commission provided detailed guidance to national authorities on the preparation of development plans, and it was thus able to influence national thinking and the drafting of plans before they were submitted. The new requirements for more detailed information, quantified indicators and *ex ante* appraisals also bolstered the position of the Commission in the CSF negotiations. As a result, the approved CSFs for many member states showed considerable differences from the submitted development plans, including major changes in the allocation of funds between priorities, new measures to support specific priorities and changes to the organization and format of many Objective 1 programmes. Similar changes were made to Objective 2 and 5b programmes in the negotiation of SPDs. As a consequence, and despite the limits to the Commission's influence posed by member state resistance to its requests for information or for changes to priorities and allocations, 'the 1993–94 programming process was arguably the "high water mark" of Commission influence' in the implementation of cohesion policy (Bachtler and Mendez, 2007: 550–1).

2000–06

In a major change, the new regulations adopted in 1999 gave the Commission the authority to publish broad, indicative guidelines in order to help national and regional authorities draw up development plans and carry out any later revisions. The Commission was required to produce these guidelines at the beginning of the new programming process, and subsequently before the scheduled mid-term review in 2003 (OJEC, 1999: 13–14). This change in the Commission's role foreshadowed the move to a more strategic approach in cohesion policy programming that was introduced in the subsequent (2006) reform.

Otherwise, programming continued to be a two or three-stage process, utilizing development plans, Community Support Frameworks, Single Programming Documents and Operational Programmes. SPDs, combining development plans and OPs, could be used for smaller Objective 1 allocations (less than €1 billion) and also for assistance under Objectives 2 and 3. However, for larger Objective 1 allocations the three-step process involving the adoption of a CSF followed by the submission of OPs was adhered to (CEC, 1999: 21).

The new regulations required that the SPDs contain certain elements, including:

1.   a statement of the strategy and priorities for EU-assisted actions, including an indication of how these were aligned with the Commission's indicative guidelines and other national policies, specific objectives, quantified where possible, and an environmental impact assessment;
2.   a description of planned measures to implement the identified priorities;
3.   a financial plan indicating the contribution of the structural funds and other funding sources.

However, programming procedures were also simplified and streamlined in a number of ways. For both OPs and SPDs, for instance, fewer specific details about proposed programmes – such as target groups, financial allocations or performance indicators – were now required. Instead, these could be developed and submitted later in a 'programme complement' that did not require Commission approval (OJEC, 1999: 19-20; CEC, 1999: 23). This allowed the submission of OPs and SPDs that were of a shorter and more general nature, thus facilitating more rapid adoption. Nevertheless, as in previous programming periods, in the new funding cycle significant delays in the implementation process resulted from the need to deal with inaccuracies or missing information in the development plans and OPs submitted by the national governments and regions (Leonardi, 2005: 64).

As a result of the changes introduced by the new regulations, the Commission assumed more of a strategic role in the programming process, while the member states were given more formal responsibility for programming; for instance, in the preparation of programme complements and the selection of projects. Also, in the CSF and SPD negotiations the Commission was now only able to press for changes at the priority rather than the measure or action level. Even so, the Commission retained considerable influence through the use of its new strategic role. At the beginning of the new programming period, the Commission produced a set of guidelines addressing the strategic priorities (regional competitiveness, social cohesion and employment, the development of urban and rural areas) and two horizontal principles (sustainable development and equal opportunities) for EU-assisted programmes. It also drafted a manual on the preparation of development plans and programme documents, as well as a series of working papers on various aspects of the programming and implementation process to guide the member states (Bachtler and Mendez, 2007: 551–3).

In the negotiations on the CSFs and SPDs, the Commission was determined 'that the indicative Guidelines should be followed to the greatest possible extent by the Member States' (CEC, 2001b: 11). Indeed, subsequent analyses showed that the Commission was able to secure adjustments to programme strategies and to the focus of individual priorities, and that in some cases the negotiations led to significant changes in the organization of CSFs and SPDs (Bachtler and Mendez, 2007: 552). Beyond the negotiations, Bachtler and Mendez also claim that the Commission was able to influence the content of programme complements, even though legally these were member state documents and did not have to be approved by the Commission. In this manner, they argue, the Commission was able to exercise a 'soft influence' in the programming process by means of its guidelines which complemented the 'hard influence' it exerted via specific regulatory requirements (Bachtler and Mendez, 2007: 552–3).

2007–13

The 2006 reform introduced a more strategic approach to programming linked to the goals of the Lisbon Agenda and a new, more streamlined planning framework. The number of programming instruments was reduced, with CSFs, SPDs and programming complements no longer required. Instead, a new multi-level programming process was established, involving:

1. the adoption of Community Strategic Guidelines (CSG) on Cohesion at the EU level;
2. the drafting of National Strategic Reference Frameworks (NSRFs) that are in compliance with the CSG at the national level;
3. the development of Operational Programmes on the basis of the NSRFs by the member states and regional authorities.

The OPs still had to be approved by the Commission, but the Commission could decide to approve elements of the NSRFs and OPs simultaneously, thus making programming basically a two-step process (CEC, 2007b: 28–9, 32).

The Community Strategic Guidelines identified the main priorities and principles for the use of cohesion policy assistance and determined the aims for each cohesion policy objective (House of Lords, 2008: 22; OJEU, 2006b: 42). Following the approval of the new cohesion policy regulations in July 2006, the CSG was drawn up by the Commission, in consultation with the member states, and adopted by the Council in October 2006 (OJEU, 2006c). This procedure represented a change from the previous programming period, when the indicative guidelines for cohesion policy were decided by the Commission unilaterally (CEC, 2007b: 29).

Following the approval of the CSG, over the next several months each member state developed its own National Strategic Reference Framework. The NSRF identified the main priorities and strategies for the use of cohesion policy funding that a member state was to receive in 2007–13, its main purpose being to ensure that EU assistance was consistent with the CSG, and to identify the link between EU priorities and the member state's National Reform Programme (NRP) for implementing the Lisbon strategy (OJEU, 2006b: 43). The NSRFs, therefore, enabled member states to develop a single strategy or 'overall vision' at the national level, setting out the member state's economic strengths and weaknesses and specifying how it intended to implement the priorities of EU cohesion policy (CEC, 2007b: 29; House of Lords, 2008: 22).

The NSRFs, which applied to the Convergence and RCE objectives, but also to the European Territorial Cooperation objective if the member state desired, were required to include: 'an analysis of development disparities, weaknesses and potential'; 'a strategy chosen on the basis of that analysis, including the thematic and territorial priorities'; 'a list of operational programmes for the Convergence and [RCE] objectives'; 'a description of how the expenditure for the Convergence and [RCE] objectives will contribute to the European Union priorities of promoting competitiveness and creating jobs'; and 'the indicative annual allocation from each Fund by programme' (OJEU, 2006b: 43). The member states had five months after adoption of the CSG to draft and send their NSRFs to the Commission, which then had to make a decision about 'certain elements' of the NSRFs, including the list of OPs and the indicative allocation from each fund to the programmes, after negotiations with the member states (CEC, 2007b: 28).

The operational programmes were designed by national and regional bodies of the member states in accordance with the priorities identified in the NSRFs. In the 2007–13 programming period, the OPs were 'mono-fund', meaning that their actions were supported by a single structural fund or the Cohesion Fund. In comparison to the previous programming period, the OPs for 2007–13 were more simplified and strategic in nature, containing less detail about programme management and mentioning funding amounts only at the priority rather than the action level, thus giving member states greater autonomy in implementing the programmes. The OPs were approved by the Commission after it appraised each programme and determined whether it was consistent with the priorities and objectives established in the Community Strategic Guidelines and the relevant NSRF. If not, the Commission could request additional information and revisions (CEC, 2007b: 32–3; OJEU, 2006b: 45).

The changes introduced by the 2006 reform appear to have diminished the Commission's influence in the programming process somewhat. To begin with, the indicative guidelines and priorities for cohesion policy now required the approval of the Council, rather than being decided unilaterally by the Commission as was previously the case. Moreover, while previously the main programming documents for cohesion policy – the CSFs and SPDs – were adopted by the Commission, the NSRFs were drawn up by the member states – 'in dialogue with the Commission', rather than being negotiated with it as the Commission had initially proposed – and Commission approval was required for only certain aspects of the NSRF rather than the entire document. The NSRF was also not a detailed 'management instrument', like the CSF and SPD had been, but instead more of a general policy statement that allowed the member states greater autonomy and flexibility in the implementation of cohesion policy (Bachtler and Mendez, 2007: 554). And while the OPs for 2007–13 required Commission approval, they were also more general and strategic in nature than before, with the Commission's role now largely focused on determining whether the proposed programmes fit the priorities identified in the CSG and NSRF, rather than approving the details of programme management, including decisions on specific measures and project selection.

Nevertheless, the Commission was able to exert influence in the programming process through its role in drafting the Community Strategic Guidelines, and its approval was also required for certain elements of the NSRFs. For the Convergence objective, the Commission was also required to decide whether the level of member state expenditure contained in the NSRF complied with the requirements of the additionality principle, and whether envisaged actions to reinforce member state administrative efficiency were sufficient (OJEU, 2006b: 44; CEC, 2007b: 28). Moreover, while the operational programmes sent to the Commission for approval are drafted at only a general or priority level, the Commission could request additional information and revisions of the OPs. It could also use '"soft influence" in the form of guidance ... in order to exert leverage on the design of programmes as they [were] drawn up' (Bachtler and Mendez, 2007: 555).

2014–20

The 2013 reform of cohesion policy 'reinforced' the strategic approach to programming introduced in 2006. New developments included the replacement of the CSG with a Common Strategic Framework, which would coordinate and provide 'strategic guiding principals' for all of the ESI funds so they could be better utilized to achieve EU priorities. The NSRFs were eliminated, with national cohesion policy goals now specified within the context of the National Reform Programmes, which document how member states plan to achieve the Europe 2020 goals. Instead, the primary programming document for cohesion policy in 2014–20 is the Partnership Agreement, agreed between the Commission and each member state, which elaborates specific commitments and the terms according to which the ESI funds will be used, including a number of performance indicators and conditionalities (OJEU, 2013a: 343–6).

The main purpose of the Common Strategic Framework is to provide guidance for the programming of all ESI funds and to coordinate their use in order to achieve the Europe 2020 goals of smart, sustainable and inclusive growth. In terms of content, the Common Strategic Framework establishes: the 'mechanisms for ensuring the contribution of the ESI Funds to the Union strategy for smart, sustainable and inclusive growth, and the coherence and consistency of the programming of the ESI Funds'; 'arrangements to promote an integrated use of the ESI Funds'; 'arrangements for coordination between the ESI Funds and other relevant Union policies and instruments'; 'horizontal principles' and 'cross-cutting policy objectives for the implementation of the ESI Funds'; 'arrangements to address the key territorial challenges for urban, rural, coastal and fisheries areas, the demographic challenges of regions or specific needs of geographical areas which suffer from severe or permanent natural or demographic handicaps ... and the specific challenges of outermost regions'; and 'priority areas for cooperation activities under the ESI funds, where appropriate taking account of macro-regional and sea basin strategies' (OJEU, 2013a: 344).

Unlike the CSG, the Common Strategic Framework was adopted by the Commission and did not require Council approval, although it was annexed to the general regulation for cohesion policy which was approved by the Council (OJEU, 2013a: 412–22, 'Annex I'). The Commission was empowered, however, to adopt delegated acts 'in order to supplement or amend' the sections of the Common Strategic Framework dealing with the coordination between ESI funds and other EU policies and instruments, and the priority areas for cooperation activities using the ESI funds. The Commission was also authorized to submit a proposal to review the Common

Strategic Framework, with the possibility of revising it, in the event of 'major changes in the social and economic situation in the Union' or changes to the Europe 2020 strategy (OJEU, 2013a: 344).

The Partnership Agreement becomes the major programming document for cohesion policy in 2014–20, replacing the use of NSRFs. Each member state is required to draw up a Partnership Agreement, in cooperation with subnational and non-governmental partners and 'in dialogue' with the Commission, and then submit it to the Commission. The Commission reviews the document to assess its consistency with the general regulation and relevant country-specific recommendations made by the Council in the 'European Semester', the EU's annual cycle of economic and fiscal policy coordination that has been in place since 2011. The Commission can request additional information or suggest revisions if necessary. Within four months of the submission of the Partnership Agreement, however, the Commission was required to adopt a decision to approve it, provided any Commission 'observations ... have been adequately taken into account' (OJEU, 2013a: 344–6).

In terms of content, the Partnership Agreements must include several things. First, they must set out arrangements to ensure that the use of ESI funds is properly aligned with the goals of the Europe 2020 strategy as well as the funds' own 'Treaty-based objectives' of strengthening economic, social and territorial cohesion. Among other things, this includes: an analysis of development needs and areas of growth potential, with reference to the thematic and territorial objectives of cohesion policy; a summary of the *ex ante* evaluations of the proposed operational programmes; a list of selected thematic objectives, and for each objective a summary of the main results expected for each of the ESI funds; the indicative allocations for each thematic objective from each of the ESI funds, including the amount allocated for climate change objectives; and a list of programmes supported by the ESI funds (the 2013 reform restored the multi-fund approach, allowing programmes to draw from more than one fund, in contrast to the mono-fund approach of the previous programming period), with annual indicative allocations by fund for each programme (OJEU, 2013a: 345).

The Partnership Agreements must also establish 'arrangements to ensure effective implementation of the ESI Funds', including: arrangements for ensuring coordination between the ESI funds and other EU policies; the information required for *ex ante* verification of compliance with the rules on additionality; an assessment of the fulfilment of applicable *ex ante* conditionalities or plans for fulfilling them; mechanisms to ensure the proper functioning of the performance framework (a list of measurable indicators or 'milestones' for each priority of an operational programme, agreed between the member state and the Commission); and an assessment of whether the administrative capacity of the implementing authorities needs to be bolstered and 'a summary of actions to be taken for that purpose'. Finally, the Agreements must also elaborate an 'integrated approach to territorial development supported by the ESI Funds or a summary of the integrated approaches to territorial development' in the operational programmes, including arrangements for dealing with: specific sub-regional and urban areas; 'the specific needs of geographical areas most affected by poverty or of target groups at highest risk of discrimination or exclusion'; and the needs of regions facing special demographic challenges or suffering from 'severe and permanent natural or demographic handicaps' (OJEU, 2013a: 345–6).

Operational programmes to implement the ESI Funds in accordance with the Partnership Agreements are prepared by the member states, in adherence to the partnership principle, and then submitted to the Commission (within three months of the submission of the Partnership Agreement) for review and approval. The programmes are assessed by the Commission with regard to their consistency with the cohesion policy regulations, contribution to the selected thematic objectives, and consistency with the Partnership Agreement. The Commission is required to provide its observations within three months of the submission of a programme. The Commission can also ask for further information or request revision of the programme. However, it is required to approve each programme within six months of the date of submission, providing any observations or recommendations made by the Commission have been taken into account (OJEU, 2013a: 353–4).

The 2013 reform introduced a number of new conditionality provisions to ensure the effective use of the structural funds, including both *ex ante* conditionalities, which must be fulfilled before funds are disbursed, and *ex post* conditionalities, which make the release of additional funds contingent on performance. Among the former, which are separately defined for each ESI Fund and listed in an annex (XI) to the general regulation, are conditionalities related to specific thematic objectives as well as horizontal conditions, such as the existence of appropriate policies or regulatory frameworks (OJEU, 2013a: 347, 438–56). Adequate administrative capacity is another key *ex ante* conditionality that is explicitly addressed in the Partnership Agreement. *Ex post* conditionalities, on the other hand, concern the achievement of milestones linked to Europe 2020 targets that are set out in the Partnership Agreements. The failure to achieve milestones can lead to the suspension or even cancellation of EU assistance. Member states fully achieving their milestones, however, may be rewarded with additional funding drawn from a performance reserve set aside from the national allocation of ESI funds (see below) (OJEU 2013a: 348–9).

Also provided for in the new regulations are macroeconomic conditionalities related to adherence to EU economic governance rules, concerning, for instance, maximum levels for budget deficits and public debt. The failure to adhere to these rules, or to take effective action to comply with them, could lead to the suspension of cohesion policy payments by the Commission. Payments could also be suspended if a member state failed to comply with the Commission's request to amend its Partnership Agreement to address structural weaknesses identified in the European Semester country-specific recommendations (OJEU, 2013a: 349–53).

In some ways the Commission appears to have recouped some of its influence in the programming process through the 2013 reform. The strategic guidelines for cohesion policy are once again decided by the Commission, although as a compromise with the member states and the European Parliament, which wanted the Common Strategic Framework to be approved as part of the cohesion policy regulation, the Commission agreed to include it as an annex to the regulation, rather than adopting the document as a delegated act as it had originally proposed (CEC, 2012a: 2). The Commission also must approve the Partnership Agreements, which identify the thematic objectives to be targeted by each member state and provide a list of operational programmes and the indicative allocation of EU funds. It also approves the specific operational programmes. Moreover, while the Partnership Agreement is a strategic or priority-level document, it also contains measurable indicators of progress for each programme that enable the Commission to better assess performance and ensure member state accountability in the use of EU funds, a topic which is examined further in the next section. To help guide the member states in preparing the Partnership Agreements and programmes, the Commission drafted detailed 'position papers' for each member state which set out the Commission's views on the main challenges and priorities in the new programming period. These position papers were provided to the member states in late 2012, more than a year before the April 2014 deadline for the member states to submit their Partnership Agreements to the Commission, and the Commission held an informal dialogue with most member states in 2013 to discuss funding priorities and the preparation of programming documents (CEC, 2014c; 2014h: 258).

Programme management

The 1988 reform also established new rules for the management of EC-funded programmes, including procedures for programme monitoring, financial control, evaluation and reporting. These rules have also evolved considerably over the years, with these changes reflecting several key trends: the decentralization of programme management responsibilities; the reduced role of the Commission in programme monitoring, offset by a greater Commission responsibility for financial oversight and programme evaluation; and greater emphasis on programme effectiveness and performance. Efforts have also been made to simplify programme management to reduce the administrative burdens on implementing authorities.

1989–93

In the first programming period after the 1988 reform of the structural funds, operational programmes were centrally managed by national authorities (central government departments or agencies) who were also responsible for the selection of specific projects. Member states could also designate other public (e.g. regional or local government) or non-governmental authorities to administer a programme or individual projects. To monitor EC-funded programmes, the 1988 regulations required the creation of Monitoring Committees (MCs) – consisting of national experts and Commission officials – for all CSFs and Operational Programmes. At the EC level, advisory and management committees, consisting of representatives of the member states and chaired by the Commission

– and in the case of the committee for Objectives 3 and 4 (the 'ESF Committee'), also representatives of the social partners – were also established for all five objectives and the Commission was required to submit periodic reports to these committees on the implementation of structural operations. All EC-funded operations were also subject to *ex ante* (prior) and *ex post* (after completion) assessments of their impact with respect to the priority objectives and their effectiveness in dealing with specific structural problems (OJEC, 1988: 13, 18: CEC, 1989b: 32–6, 40–1).

1994–9

The 1993 regulations retained the basic implementation rules of the previous programming period but with a stronger emphasis on monitoring. Reporting duties, as well as monitoring, evaluation and financial control requirements were also extended and clarified (Bauer, 2006: 725). Regarding *ex ante* or prior appraisal, the revised framework regulation specified that development plans for Objectives 1, 2 and 5b must include an evaluation of environmental impact (CEC, 1993: 29). It also required 'transparent project appraisal and selection systems and quantified indicators' and objectives for proposed operations to enable more effective monitoring (Bachtler and Mendez, 2007: 551). In accordance with the principle of subsidiarity (newly enshrined in the Maastricht Treaty), which calls for decision-making responsibilities to be shifted to the lowest governmental level possible, the role of MCs was strengthened and they were given the capacity to adjust procedures for granting EU financial assistance for specific programmes and projects (CEC, 1993: 30). Cohesion policy implementation also became more decentralized, as national governments made greater use of private sector and independent bodies in the management of structural operations, and as central governments devolved implementation powers to regional and local authorities, in many cases because of their increased experience with structural funds programmes after the first programming period (Ferry *et al.*, 2007: 7).

The new regulations also gave a greater role in the implementation of cohesion policy to the European Parliament, requiring the Commission to provide it with the lists of areas receiving assistance under Objectives 2 and 5b, member state development plans, the

CSFs and the texts of implementing regulations concerning monitoring and publicity. The EP was also to be notified of CIs before their adoption, so that the Commission could take note of its requests with respect to each initiative, and the Commission was required to provide it with regular and detailed information on the implementation of the structural funds (CEC, 1993: 33–4). According to Bauer (2006: 725), after 1993 both the Parliament and the Court of Auditors began to follow much more 'closely the planning and implementation of the structural funds, calling upon the Commission to fight fraudulent practice and to improve its implementation system and guarantee (and demonstrate!) good value for EU money'. Despite its limited decision-making powers in the realm of cohesion policy, he argues, the EP

> demanded sound and efficient execution and greater commitment to achieve the objectives. [It] also supported what may be called the 'societal opening' of the structural funds planning and implementation procedures, by asking for the inclusion of social and economic partners and later pushing also for the participation of environmental, gender and consumer interests in the policy networks.

2000–06

The 1999 reform brought significant changes to the procedures for programme management, with member state authorities assuming greater responsibility for basic programming decisions and programme implementation, but also becoming more accountable to the Commission for the management and delivery of structural operations (Bachtler and Mendez, 2007: 553). Among other changes, the member states were newly required to designate a Managing Authority (MA) for each operational programme. The MA would have primary responsibility for programme implementation, including the collection of financial and statistical information to be used for assessing programme performance, and for the organization of a new mid-term evaluation (see below). The MA was also required to submit to the Commission (through the monitoring committee) an annual implementation report and to meet annually with the Commission to discuss programme progress (CEC, 1999: 28; OJEC, 1999: 28–9).

The structure of the monitoring committees was also altered to give more autonomy to the member states, with the Commission giving up its previous supervisory role and becoming instead merely an *ex officio* (non-voting) member with advisory status. The role and responsibilities of the monitoring committees were also further strengthened and more clearly defined, to include approval of the programme complement, proposals for programme changes, the criteria for project selection and the annual implementation report. The MCs also assumed primary responsibility for the monitoring and evaluation of structural operations (CEC, 1999: 28; OJEC, 1999: 29–30).

On the other hand, monitoring and reporting requirements became more prescriptive and stringent than before. There was clearer specification of the kinds of physical and financial indicators required for monitoring programme progress and performance. Greater emphasis was also put on evaluation; in addition to the annual implementation report, comprehensive and rigorous *ex ante* and mid-term evaluations were now required for all programmes as well as a subsequent update of the mid-term evaluation. In the *ex ante* evaluation, the impact of structural operations on the labour market and gender equality now needed to be assessed by the member states as well as the environmental impact. The mid-term evaluation and update were both conducted by the programme MA, which was also responsible for providing the Commission with the information needed for the *ex post* evaluation, which was now carried out by an independent evaluator within three years of the end of the programming period (CEC, 1999: 29; OJEC, 1999: 30–1, 33–5).

An additional control was provided by the new 'performance reserve'. At the beginning of the programming period, 4 per cent of the allocation for each member state was held back and awarded at the mid-point of the period to programmes whose performance the Commission deemed successful, on the basis of financial, management and effectiveness performance criteria defined by the member state in consultation with the Commission (CEC, 1999: 29; OJEC, 1999: 35). Last but not least, financial management was modified by the 'automatic de-commitment' rule (also known as the '*n* + 2' rule), according to which programmes had to spend received funds within two years of their commitment or else lose them (CEC, 1999: 24; OJEC, 1999: 26). Both the performance reserve and the automatic de-commitment rule gave the Commission enhanced leverage in the implementation process and significantly increased the pressure on member states and programming authorities for the timely implementation of EU-funded programmes (Leonardi, 2005: 64).

The new regulations also gave the Commission extensive competences in the area of monitoring and financial control. For instance, after annual consultations with the managing authorities on programme implementation, the Commission could make recommendations for changes to monitoring or management procedures which the MA was required to implement (CEC, 1999: 28; OJEC, 1999: 29). The new regulations also gave the Commission the responsibility for evaluating and verifying the effectiveness of financial management systems, including the right to 'carry out on-the-spot checks … on the operations financed by the Funds and on management and control systems with a minimum of one working day's notice', and to 'require the Member State concerned to carry out an on-the-spot check to verify the correctness of one or more transactions'. After due verification, the Commission could 'suspend all or part of an interim payment if it finds that the expenditure concerned is linked to a severe irregularity which has not been corrected and that immediate action is needed' (CEC, 1999: 30; OJEC, 1999: 31–3).

2007–13

The 2006 reform of cohesion policy saw a further decentralization of programme management tasks and a reduced role in programme management for the Commission. Efforts were also made to simplify programme management procedures to make them less burdensome for implementing authorities. These changes were in response to the demands of the member states, especially EU15 member states receiving less structural funding, who complained about the onerous administrative responsibilities introduced for 2000–06. In exchange, however, the member states became more accountable for the use of EU funds, and the policy reform introduced a new layer of strategic reporting in which the Commission had a considerable influence and role (Bachtler and Mendez, 2007: 554).

In the new regulations, the basic structure of monitoring committees and managing authorities was retained along with their primary responsibilities. The main changes concerned the procedures for financial control and programme evaluation, where responsibilities were decentralized to the member states. In the new programming period, member states must establish an independent auditing authority for each operational programme to ensure the effective functioning of the programme's financial management and control system, and to ensure that proper audits of the programme's operations are carried out. The audit authority must submit an audit strategy to the Commission, as well as an annual control report and an 'opinion' on the audits carried out. However, the increased auditing responsibilities of the member states were offset by a reduction of the Commission's auditing activities, especially for programmes in which the member states were the main financial contributors (CEC, 2007b: 35; OJEU, 2006b: 54–60).

Evaluation requirements for the new programming period were also reduced and made more flexible. *Ex ante* evaluations were still required for all operational programmes under the Convergence objective, but for the RCE and ETC objectives the member states could determine, on the basis of need, whether to do *ex ante* evaluations covering all or several programmes of the objective, for each fund, for each priority or for each programme. Similarly, mid-term evaluations were no longer mandatory but would be conducted only as needed (CEC, 2007b: 34; OJEU, 2006b: 50–1).

There were also changes to the performance reserve, with the member states given the option of creating 'national performance reserves' of up to 3 per cent of the funds allocated for the Convergence and RCE objectives. The member states were also given the main responsibility for allocating these reserves midway through the programming period, based on the performance of their operational programmes. An additional 'national contingency reserve', of up to 1 per cent of the structural fund allocation for the Convergence objective and 3 per cent for the RCE objective, could be created 'to cover unforeseen local or sectoral crises linked to economic and social restructuring or to the consequences of the opening up of trade' (CEC, 2007b: 34; OJEU, 2006b: 51).

The greater flexibility given to member states when it came to programme management was summarized by the newly introduced principle of 'proportionality', which made such matters as the choice of indicators for measuring programme progress and the obligations concerning evaluation, management and reporting 'proportional to the total amount of expenditure allocated to an operational programme', meaning essentially less onerous requirements for less expensive programmes (OJEU, 2006b: 39). Moreover, for programmes under €750 million and for which the EU contribution did not exceed 40 per cent of total programme costs, the financial control and monitoring obligations of the member states were also reduced and the auditing authority was not required to submit an auditing strategy (OJEU, 2006: 39, 59–60; CEC, 2007b: 27).

The new strategic reporting requirements introduced in the 2006 reform supported the alignment of cohesion policy with the goals of the Lisbon strategy and imposed obligations on both the member states and the Commission. Each member state was now required to present an annual report on the implementation of its Lisbon National Reform Programme; among other things, this report was to include 'a concise section on the contribution of the operational programmes co-financed by the [structural and cohesion] funds towards the implementation of the national reform programme' (OJEU, 2006b: 44; CEC, 2007b: 30).

Moreover, at the latest by the end of 2009 and 2012, member states were required to provide a national strategic report, containing information on the 'contribution of the programmes co-financed by the Funds: (a) towards implementing the objectives of cohesion policy as established by the Treaty; (b) towards fulfilling the tasks of the Funds as set out in this [framework] Regulation; (c) towards implementing the priorities detailed in the Community strategic guidelines on cohesion ... (d) towards achieving the objective of promoting competitiveness and job creation and working towards meeting the objectives of the Integrated Guidelines for Growth and Jobs' (OJEU, 2006b: 44; CEC, 2007b: 30). According to the Commission, the national strategic reports were introduced in order to 'improve transparency and encourage accountability of the policy at national level in the context of the shared management of cohesion policy'; they were thus 'a key tool to monitor the implementation of the strategic commitments of the Member States to [the] delivery [of] high level EU objectives through cohesion policy' (CEC, 2010c: 2).

The 2006 reform also introduced new strategic reporting requirements for the Commission. In its Annual Progress Report, presented each spring to the European Council, the Commission was now required to include a section summarizing the member states' annual implementation reports. The Commission was also required to prepare strategic reports in 2010 and 2013 which would summarize the member states' strategic reforms (OJEU, 2006b: 44; CEC, 2007b: 30).

2014–20

The 2013 reform retained the basic structure of decentralized programme management established in 2006, featuring programme managing authorities, monitoring committees, and certifying and audit authorities. However, a significant change concerned new rules on the composition of monitoring committees, which now must include 'representatives of the partners' with voting rights, thus potentially strengthening the application of partnership in programme implementation (OJEU, 2013a: 367, 398–402).

The new regulations also retained the flexible approach to programme evaluation. While *ex ante* evaluations are once again required for all programmes, in certain cases the evaluations for more than one programme could be combined. Evaluations during the implementation of programmes are still conducted on the basis of need. Managing authorities are required to devise an evaluation plan for each programme, including evaluations by independent experts to assess programme effectiveness, efficiency and impact. At least once during the programming period, an evaluation is required to 'assess how support from the ESI Funds has contributed to the objectives for each priority'. All mid-term evaluations are sent to the Commission by way of the monitoring committees, and the Commission retains the right carry out its own evaluations of programmes at its own initiative. *Ex post* evaluations, which are to include an assessment of the programme's contribution to achievement of the Europe 2020 goals, would now be conducted either by the Commission or by the member states in close cooperation with the Commission (OJEU, 2013a: 370–1).

The new regulations established a devolved system of financial management and control under Commission supervision. Member states are required to set up management and control systems according to strict criteria, and all management and control bodies must be accredited by national authorities based on the opinion of independent auditors working in compliance with internationally accepted auditing standards. The Commission is responsible for ensuring that management and control systems comply with EU rules, and it can require changes to these systems if necessary. Moreover, the Commission is empowered to conduct 'on-the-spot' audits or checks upon giving adequate prior notice to verify the effective functioning of management and control systems and the sound financial management of structural operations or programmes (OJEU, 2013a: 379, 397–402).

The 2013 reform restored the mandatory performance reserve that had been abandoned in the previous programming period. Resources from this reserve – consisting of 6 per cent of resources allocated to the ESI funds for each member state under the 'investment for growth and jobs' goal – are allocated to better performing programmes following the 2019 performance review, by the Commission on the basis of proposals from the member states. At this time, the Commission can also reduce the funding available for poorly performing programmes (OJEU, 2013a: 348–9). Changes were also made to the automatic de-commitment rule, with de-commitment rules now different for each fund (OJEU, 2013a: 381).

Reporting requirements were also somewhat altered from the previous period. In place of the national strategic reports, member states must now submit to the Commission 'annual implementation reports' for each programme every year beginning in 2016 and ending in 2023. All implementation reports are to include an assessment of the programme's contribution to meeting the Europe 2020 goals, and the Commission can make recommendations to address issues contained in the reports. There are also now 'annual review' meetings between the Commission and the member states for each programme (one meeting can cover more than one programme) to examine programme progress and performance, taking into account the findings of the implementation report and the Commission's observations and recommendations. Additionally, member states are required to submit to the Commission – by 30 June 2017 and 30 June 2019 – a progress report on their implementation of the Partnership Agreement, followed by a performance review by the Commission of the programmes in each member state, with reference to the performance frameworks contained in the Partnership Agreement and individual programmes. The Commission, meanwhile, remains responsible for submitting annual progress reports to the European Council and strategic reports on the progress of member states in 2017 and 2019 (OJEU 2013a: 348, 368–9).

Implementation problems

Aside from ongoing tension between national governments and the Commission over who controls cohesion policy, the implementation of cohesion policy has encountered several key problems over the years. One is the difficulty some member states have had, especially those which are poorer and have a less developed institutional capacity, with absorbing and utilizing allocated funds. Indeed, it was concern over the absorption capacity of the new CEE member states that led to the EU's decision in 1999 to impose a 4 per cent of GDP cap on national cohesion policy receipts, although the desire of wealthier member states to limit EU expenditure also played a role in this decision. Since this initial decision, the capping limit has been progressively lowered to well under 3 per cent of GDP in the 2014–20 funding period.

Early indications are that these concerns were valid, although the picture is quite mixed when it comes to the performance of the CEE member states. At the end of 2012, six new member states – Romania, Bulgaria, the Czech Republic, Hungary, Slovakia and Malta – were among the seven for which the absorption rate was under the EU average of just over 40 per cent when it came to the use of allocated funds for 2007–13, the first programming period in which the 2004 and 2007 entrants were beneficiaries of cohesion policy for the entire funding cycle. In particular Romania, with an absorption rate of only about 12 per cent, was having difficulty using available EU funds, leading the Commission to propose giving it and Slovakia additional time to spend cohesion policy assistance (Romania-Insider.com, 2013). However, the remaining new member states had absorption rates at or above the EU average, and one 'old' member state, Italy, was among the poor performers when it came to the uptake of EU funds (CEC, 2013c: 10–11).

In countries and regions experiencing difficulty absorbing EU funds, key problems include limited experience with the structural funds and a lack of resources for national co-financing, especially at the regional and local levels. While the former problem should be resolved over time, the EU has sought to overcome the latter by reducing the co-financing requirement to as low as 5 per cent for some member states experiencing budgetary difficulties (CEC, 2013c: 5). Another major problem contributing to low rates of absorption, however, has been weak administrative capacity at the national and regional levels and the consequent inability to adequately plan for the use of allocated funds. To help alleviate this problem, 'enhancing institutional capacity' was made a key thematic objective for the use of ESI funds in 2014–20 (OJEU, 2013a: 343).

A second problem in the implementation of cohesion policy has been the inappropriate use of EU funds. In some cases this is the result of deliberate fraud and corruption, but for the most part it is due to inadequate knowledge of EU rules and procedures and a weak and ineffective oversight system. Some insight into the level of mismanagement in cohesion policy is provided by the annual reports on EU spending of the Court Auditors (ECA), which estimates the rate at which EU funds are spent 'in error', both as a result of honest mistakes, such as the misreading or misunderstanding of EU legislation, and of intentional fraud and corruption. In its 2010 report, the ECA estimated an error rate in cohesion policy payments in 2009 of above 5 per cent (ECA, 2010: 101), a rate that was consistent with estimates made in the previous several years. The error rate climbed to 7.7 per cent in 2010 (ECA, 2011: 108), however, but fell again to 6 per cent in 2011 (for regional policy and energy and transport policy combined; the error rate for employment and social affairs was only 2 per cent for this year) (ECA, 2012: 127, 154). In 2012, the error rate rose back to 6.8 per cent for regional policy, energy and transport policy, and 3.2 per cent for employment and social affairs (ECA, 2013:18).

The complex delivery system of cohesion policy, with its multiplicity of public actors at different governmental levels, and a weak and decentralized oversight system, is perhaps the main reason for this misuse of EU funds. This was the conclusion, at least, of an investigative report published by the *Financial Times* in November–December 2010, which found that cohesion policy had 'grown into an opaque bureaucracy that makes it extremely difficult for taxpayers to trace how their money is spent'. Moreover, according to the report, because of its 'decentralised and weak oversight system [which] rarely punishes fraud and [the] misuse' of EU funds, 'millions of euros continue to be siphoned off by organised crime syndicates despite warnings going back decades' (O'Murchu and Spiegel, 2010: 8).

While the amount of EU funds spent in error represents only a small fraction of total cohesion policy spending, and the portion of this amount attributable to fraud is even smaller – in 2009, for instance, the ECA estimated that only about 16 per cent, €109 million out of €700 million, of structural funds spent in error was due to fraud (O'Murchu and Spiegel, 2010: 8) – the amount of misspent money is also not insignificant, especially in a period of economic hard times and tight budgets. This perhaps explains why the Commission has adopted a much more proactive approach to dealing with suspected fraud and mismanagement in recent years, acting to stop payments when it simply suspects wrongdoing rather than waiting until fraud has been proven, as in the past. Thus, in the spring of 2012 the Commission suspended structural funds payments to the Czech Republic because of suspected corruption and mismanagement by both national government and regional authorities (Volynsky, 2012). Later the same year, it suspended structural funds payments to Romania because of concerns about corruption (Euractiv.com, 2012f). In January 2013, the Commission froze €890 million in funds due to Poland for road-building projects because of suspected fraud (Euractiv.com, 2013g), and in August of the same year, the Commission temporarily suspended funding to Hungary because it considered the country's financial control system to be too weak, although it had found no evidence of fraud (Euractiv.com, 2013h). Through such a tougher approach, the Commission may hope to counter negative publicity about the misuse of EU funding and the negative public perceptions of cohesion policy it helps to create, fully understanding that such perceptions are a major factor influencing the ongoing debate on the future of cohesion policy.

Two additional issues in the implementation of cohesion policy are the tensions between the principles of evaluation and simplification, on the one hand, and effectiveness and decentralization, on the other. As discussed above, the cohesion policy regulations have increasingly emphasized the need for evaluation and assessment of EU-funded programmes, to ensure they are effective and meet their stated goals. Indeed, the Commission has taken a certain amount of credit for promoting an 'evaluation culture' in the EU through the implementation system for cohesion policy (CEC, 1996: 113; 2001a, 147). However, while the Commission has been a strong advocate for better evaluation, in its efforts to strengthen evaluation norms and procedures it has also been as much 'pushed' as it is doing the pushing, since the demand for evaluation in implementation of the structural funds stems in considerable part from the desire of wealthier member states to ensure that poorer net beneficiaries are doing 'something reasonable with the money' (Bauer, 2002: 780–3).

The increased emphasis on evaluation has generated a backlash by the member states (and also regions; see Bauer, 2002), however, which have complained about overly burdensome and time-consuming administrative procedures. This was especially the case in the 2000–06 programming period, in which evaluation requirements were tightened considerably. As a result, the simplification of programme management became a major theme of the 2006 reform, with evaluation requirements both reduced and made more flexible. This more flexible approach was continued with the 2013 reform. Nevertheless, the tension between the need for rigorous evaluation and the desire for simplified programme management is inherent, and it can be expected that this will continue to be an issue as the emphasis on effectiveness and 'value for money' in cohesion policy spending will no doubt only grow.

While linked to the demand for better evaluation, the growing emphasis on effectiveness also creates an inherent tension with efforts to decentralize cohesion policy management. While for the member states the concept of decentralization may imply giving them more control of cohesion policy implementation and freedom from Commission interference, for the Commission it is clear that decentralization, viewed from the perspective of partnership and a bottom-up interpretation of the subsidiarity principle, concerns the greater involvement of regional, local and non-governmental partners in cohesion policy implementation. Decentralization in this sense creates potential problems from the perspective of effective implementation, however, including the greater amount of time needed for deliberation and decision-making involving a larger number of actors, and the increased possibilities for mismanagement discussed above.

As a result, there often seems to be a trade-off between the goals of effectiveness/efficiency and decentralization/inclusion that, given increasing pressure on public finances and accompanying demands of 'value for money', tend to be resolved in favour of the former. For instance, the performance reserve provisions of the 2013 regulations require member states to utilize available funds as efficiently as possible and meet established milestones for programmes by the mid-term review or else face the possibility of losing funding (OJEU, 2013a: 348–9). Moreover, while programming for 2014–20 was only just beginning at the time of writing, there was already ample evidence that cohesion policy will be implemented in a more centralized manner in the new programming period in some member states, such as the Czech Republic and Slovakia, the result of the economic crisis and demands for the more efficient absorption and use of EU funds, on the one hand, and corruption scandals involving regional authorities and the structural funds, on the other (Marek and Baun, 2014; CEE Bankwatch, 2013).

Conclusion

The process of cohesion policy implementation has undergone a number of changes over the years. When it comes to programming, several important trends can be identified. One is the trend towards greater simplification, with fewer steps in the programming process and fewer planning documents. Programming for 2014–20, for instance, is a fairly streamlined two-step process, compared with the more prolonged and complicated three-step process for 1989–93 that involved the drafting of national and regional development plans, the negotiation of CSFs and the development and approval of operational programmes. The trend of simplification has gone hand-in-hand with the progressive devolution of programming responsibilities to the member states, who are now chiefly responsible for designing national planning documents and operational programmes. It is also associated with the increased strategic orientation of cohesion policy and its alignment with the EU's growth and competitiveness agenda. As a consequence, the Commission has adopted more of a strategic role in setting general priorities for the use of EU funds – such as the Community Strategic Guidelines for 2007–13 and the Common Strategic Framework for 2014–20 – while the member states have been given greater responsibility for basic programming decisions.

Decentralization and simplification are also notable trends in the area of programme management, matched by a reduced role for the Commission in the management and monitoring of structural operations. At first, the decentralization of management responsibilities to the member states was accompanied by a large increase in evaluation and reporting requirements, but these requirements have been made less onerous and the member states have been given greater flexibility in meeting them since the 2006 reform. And while the

Commission has stepped back from a direct role in programme management, it has assumed a larger oversight role when it comes to ensuring member state accountability for financial management and control and assessing the performance of structural operations and their contribution to EU strategic goals. Despite these general trends, the struggle between the Commission and the member states for the control of cohesion policy implementation is certain to continue and will undoubtedly witness further ebbs and flows in the future.

Cohesion policy implementation also suffers from certain key problems, including the limited capacity of some member states to absorb and utilize allocated funds. There is also a problem, not massive but still significant, with the misuse of EU funds, largely due to the complex and multi-layered delivery system of cohesion policy and its weak and decentralized oversight mechanisms. Tensions also exist between the sometimes contradictory goals of better programme evaluation and the simplification of programme management, on the one hand, and the increased emphasis on programme effectiveness and efforts to decentralize cohesion policy implementation, on the other.

Another important feature of the implementation process for cohesion policy is the partnership principle, which requires the involvement of subnational and non-governmental actors in the planning and administration of structural programmes. While the application of the partnership principle was briefly touched upon in this chapter, the role of partnership in cohesion policy implementation, and its implications for multi-level governance in the EU more broadly, is examined more fully in the next chapter.

Chapter 5

Cohesion Policy and Multi-level Governance

A distinctive feature of cohesion policy is the partnership principle, which requires the involvement of subnational and non-governmental actors in the implementation of cohesion policy. The purpose of this requirement is to promote a participatory approach to cohesion policy implementation, which it is argued will result in greater transparency, higher quality programmes and the more effective use of EU funds. Many scholars have argued, however, that through application of the partnership principle cohesion policy also has helped to promote new modes of multi-level governance in the EU more broadly. In this manner, the promotion of multi-level governance can be regarded as an important 'side effect' or secondary objective of cohesion policy (Tarschys, 2003: 76–8).

This chapter examines the partnership principle and the impact of cohesion policy on multi-level governance in the EU. It begins with an examination of the partnership principle itself, including where it comes from and how the definition of partnership has evolved to include new types of subnational and non-governmental actors. It then looks at the actual application of the partnership principle in successive programming periods. This is followed by a discussion of the academic concept of multi-level governance and its links to cohesion policy and the partnership principle, and an examination of the impact of cohesion policy on both 'vertical' and 'horizontal' multi-level governance in the EU. In the final section, the concept of Community-led Local Development is briefly examined as a new initiative of cohesion policy with the potential to promote decentralized governance.

The partnership principle

The involvement of subnational and non-governmental actors in

Community regional policy was a goal of the Commission from the very beginning. In its first regional policy memorandum in 1965, the Commission suggested that EC-supported regional development programmes should be formulated through a participative approach, arguing that 'The active participation of interested circles in drawing up such programmes would facilitate their implementation' (CEC, 1965: 2). And in its 1973 regional policy proposal, the Commission declared that it '[attached] great importance to finding appropriate means for associating the social partners, local authorities and regional organisations with the development of Community regional policy' (CEC, 1973b: 2). The 1975 ERDF regulation contained no provisions requiring the participation of subnational and non-governmental actors in EC regional policy, however, because this idea was strongly opposed by the member states, and while the Commission sought to involve regional and local actors in the experimental integrated programmes that it initiated following the 1979 reform, it had only limited success as national governments remained firmly in control (Leonardi, 2005: 38, 45).

The Commission finally succeeded in introducing its participative approach with the 1988 structural funds reform, which made the partnership principle a key element of the delivery system for cohesion policy. Indeed, the introduction of the partnership principle was considered by some to have been the most important innovation of the 1988 reform (Paraskevopoulos, 2001: 37). Moreover, it is also clear that for the Commission partnership had more than just a 'managerial meaning' (Bauer, 2002: 772); instead, it was presented as 'the key principle underlying the [structural funds] reform' (CEC, 1989b: 14).

In the 1988 framework regulation, partnership was defined as 'close consultations between the Commission, the Member State concerned and the competent authorities designated by the latter at the national, regional, local or other level, with each party acting as a partner in pursuit of a common goal'. It was also stated that the partnership principle should apply to all aspects of the implementation process, covering 'the preparation, financing, monitoring and assessment of operations' (OJEC, 1988: 12).

The possible practical applications of the partnership principle were described further in the Commission's *Guide to the Reform of the Community's Structural Funds* that was published in 1989.

These included using the partnership approach in the negotiation of CSFs and the implementation of operational programmes. It was also suggested that beyond national, regional and local authorities, the 'various economic and social partners (chambers of commerce, industry and agriculture, trade unions, employers, etc.)' should also be involved, hinting at the future evolution of the principle to more fully embrace such private and non-state actors. However, the Commission also recognized that the nature of partnership would vary across the member states, depending on 'the institutional structures and traditions of each Member State', and that 'It [would] therefore necessarily take many forms' (CEC, 1989b: 15).

The Commission favoured the partnership approach because it believed that this would make regional programmes more efficient and effective, by 'formally including subnational actors with major knowledge of regional problems and priority needs' (Olsson, 2003: 286). According to Piattoni (2006: 62), opening the decision-making process to a variety of interests not only allows them to assert their development needs and demands, it also brings their 'ideas, expertise, resources and ultimately legitimacy to the process'; indeed 'development programmes that are widely shared and are grounded on diverse and plural knowledge are more likely to succeed than development programmes ideated in isolation by a group of technocrats'. In accordance with this logic, the Commission argued in its 1989 *Guide* that the 'quality' of partnership was 'crucial to the success or failure of the [structural funds] reform, since without a dialogue with the institutional authorities and the economic operators concerned, it would seem to be impossible to achieve the ambitious objectives the Community has set for itself'. Moreover, 'partnership arrangements should lead to some decentralization of the Community's structural action, enabling it to be geared more closely to realities in the field, both in assessing needs and in implementing measures' (CEC, 1989b: 15).

The Commission has also defended partnership as an important and practical expression of the EU principle of 'subsidiarity', according to which, as stated in the the Treaty on European Union, governmental decisions should be made 'as closely as possible to the citizen' (TEU, 1992: 4). In the Commission's view:

The notion of subsidiarity in public policy reflects a recognition of the virtues of decentralisation, involving the relevant authori-

ties at all levels in the pursuit of agreed objectives and the sharing
of responsibilities for decision-making between central and lower
tiers of government closer to the grassroots. This is important,
since it means the involvement of those nearest to the problems
for which solutions are being sought. (CEC, 1996: 114)

Both the partnership and subsidiarity principles, therefore, emphasize the value to be gained – in terms of efficiency, effectiveness, relevance and legitimacy – for public policies in general and cohesion
policy specifically if all levels of government, from the EU to local,
are involved and their efforts closely coordinated (Bailey and de
Propris, 2002a: 415). The notion of subsidiarity is thus deeply
embedded in the concept of partnership and the two principles are
closely connected (Vida, 2004: 12; CEC, 2005b: 3).

Beyond ensuring the effectiveness of Community-supported
development programmes, however, the Commission has also
promoted the partnership principle for reasons of institutional self-
interest, since the involvement of subnational and non-governmental actors would provide the Commission with potential allies in its
struggle with the member states over the implementation as well as
the future shape and direction of cohesion policy (Allen, 2005:
225–6; Bache, 1999: 35). More broadly, and speculatively, the
empowerment of subnational actors through the partnership
approach could be seen as an attempt by the Commission to
promote the emergence of an EU multi-level polity in which the
power of national governments was weakened and its own influence
correspondingly enhanced. Also indicative of these efforts is the
Commission's creation of the Consultative Committee of Local and
Regional Authorities in 1988. While this new body – a precursor to
the Committee of the Regions that was created by the Maastricht
Treaty in 1993 – had only an advisory role in cohesion policy decision-making, it was nevertheless a further attempt by the
Commission to institutionalize and enhance the role of subnational
authorities in the Community (Sutcliffe, 2000: 296).

Evolution of the partnership principle

After being introduced in 1988, the partnership principle was modified and expanded in subsequent cohesion policy reforms. In the
new regulations for 1994–9, the definition of partnership was

extended to require the inclusion of the economic and social partners (e.g. trade unions, employer and industry associations) within partnership arrangements, albeit 'within the framework of each Member State's national rules and practices' (OJEC 1993: 8). In this manner, according to Bauer (2006: 725), the Commission sought to 'enhance its link with the execution phase' of cohesion policy.

The 1999 reform further extended the partnership principle by calling for the involvement in partnership arrangements of environmental and gender equity organizations (OJEC 1999: 11–12). In a new addition to the programming process for 2000–06, the relevant partners were supposed to be consulted not only in the preparation of development plans and operational programmes but also in the drafting of programme complements (CEC, 1999: 26). The 1999 reform also strengthened the rules for partnership in programme management, requiring the member states to consult with subnational and non-governmental partners when setting up monitoring committees. The member states also had to submit plans for involving the partners in the monitoring committees to the Commission, to be approved together with the basic programming documents (the CSF-OPs or SPDs) (CEC, 1999: 26; OJEC, 1999: 18, 29). The new regulations also defined more clearly the roles of the partners in specific types of evaluations (Sutcliffe, 2000: 302).

In the 2006 reform, the partnership principle was further extended to include any appropriate non-governmental organization or 'body representing civil society'. The new regulation also strengthened the partnership approach by changing the previous wording from 'close consultation' with the relevant partners to 'close cooperation'. Moreover, it required the member states to 'involve, where appropriate, each of the relevant partners, and particularly the regions, in the different stages of programming within the time limit set for each stage', including, therefore, the drafting of NSRFs and the preparation of operational programmes to be submitted to the Commission. The new regulation also emphasized the participation of relevant partners in the implementation, monitoring and evaluation of operational programmes (OJEU 2006b: 39; CEC, 2007b: 27). In all cases, however, partnership arrangements were supposed to function 'in accordance with current national rules and practices', thus giving the member states a certain amount of flexibility and discretion in the selection of appropriate partners (OJEU, 2006b: 39).

The 2013 reform appears to further strengthen the role of subnational and non-governmental actors in cohesion policy. The new general regulation requires that, 'For the Partnership Agreement and each programme, each member state shall in accordance with its institutional and legal framework organize a partnership with the competent regional and local authorities.' Moreover, these partnerships should also include:

(a) competent urban and other public authorities;
(b) economic and social partners;
(c) relevant bodies representing civil society, including environmental partners, non-governmental organizations, and bodies responsible for promoting social inclusion, gender equality and non-discrimination. (OJEU, 2013a: 341)

The regulation further states that, 'In accordance with the multi-level governance approach, the partners ... shall be involved in the preparation of Partnership Agreements and progress reports and throughout the preparation and implementation of programmes, including through participation in the monitoring committees for programmes' (OJEU, 2013a: 341). It also specifies that Partnership Agreements must describe the actions taken to involve the partners and their role in preparation of the Agreement and the mid-term progress report, and they must specify the application of the partnership and multi-level governance principle in the implementation of EU-funded programmes, including an indicative list of partners and 'a summary of the actions taken to involve them' (OJEU, 2013a: 345). The new regulation also gives the Commission a new means to ensure the application of partnership, empowering it 'to adopt a delegated act ... to provide for a European code of conduct on partnership ... in order to support and facilitate Member States in the organisation of partnership' and to help them implement this principle (OJEU, 2013a: 341–2). Moreover, the ESF regulation contains specific provisions to strengthen partnerships and encourage the active participation of social partners and non-governmental organizations (NGOs) in ESF investments, including the use of ESF resources for 'capacity building activities' for social partners and NGOs in less developed regions (OJEU, 2013c: 476–7).

With its extension over the years to embrace private and non-governmental as well as subnational actors, it is possible to distinguish two distinct dimensions of partnership – vertical and horizontal. While vertical partnership refers to cooperation between public authorities at different territorial levels of government – the EU, national, regional and local – horizontal partnership involves the cooperation of governmental authorities with organized socio-economic groups (Dąbrowski, 2011: 2; Polverari and Michie, 2009: 1–2). The initial formulation of the partnership principle focused mainly on the vertical dimension, but since the early 1990s the Commission has steadily pushed for the greater involvement of non-governmental and private actors (Bache, 2005: 6–7; Piattoni, 2006: 62). As a result, the horizontal dimension of partnership has been strengthened over time (Dąbrowski, 2011: 4), yet the vertical dimension remains prominent because of the territorial focus of cohesion policy (Baun and Marek, 2008c: 6). The vertical dimension has also been much more researched and analysed when it comes to the question of cohesion policy's impact on multi-level governance (Polverari and Michie, 2009: 2).

Application of the partnership principle

The application of the partnership principle in cohesion policy implementation has been very uneven, across the member states, different funds and objectives, and the different stages or phases of the implementation process. Key factors affecting the application of partnership include national governmental structures and traditions, the changing partnership requirements of the cohesion policy regulations, and the role of the Commission in promoting partnership and assisting with the formation of partnership arrangements. As a result, the application of partnership is both highly differentiated and evolving. Nevertheless, after more than 25 years, partnership has become a firmly embedded aspect of the cohesion policy delivery system, with considerable spill-over potential for other policy areas and for governance norms and practices more generally. In the remainder of this section, the application of the partnership principle in successive programming periods is briefly examined.

1989–93

In the first programming period after the 1988 reform, application of the partnership principle was extremely mixed and uneven, with the role of subnational authorities varying considerably both across the member states and at different stage of the implementation process. In accordance with the partnership principle, subnational actors began playing a greater role in the drafting of regional development plans and operational programmes and in the implementation and monitoring of cohesion policy projects. They could also call for the launch of Community Initiatives and seek financial assistance from them. Nevertheless, the national governments were responsible for selecting their regional partners, and since subnational actors were not automatically guaranteed a role in cohesion policy implementation, their involvement and influence varied significantly across individual countries (Bache, 1998: 99; Bouvet and Dall'erba, 2010: 505; Sutcliffe, 2000: 296). As Bache (1998: 99) puts it, 'partnership in principle applied to all Member States, while partnership in practice was implemented unevenly'.

Indeed, not all regions were immediately able to become active partners of national governments and the Commission. In some cases, regional actors had no experience interacting with national governments in the area of regional policy, while in others regional governmental or administrative institutions did not even exist. In fact, the Commission itself was aware that only about one-third of the member states were ready to effectively implement the partnership principle (Bailey and de Propris, 2002a: 304–5; 2002b: 416–17). As a result of this regional institutional incapacity or 'vacuum', some of the Community's poorest regions were prevented from accessing and using the funds that had been allocated to them. On the other hand, established subnational authorities that were already strong at the domestic level (for example, the German *Länder*) benefitted more from the introduction of the partnership principle than subnational actors in more centralized member states (for example, the UK) (Pollack, 1995, in Sutcliffe, 2000: 296; Bache, 1998: 93–104).

As for the different stages of the implementation process, a study by Marks (1996: 406–17) concluded that subnational actors played the greatest role in the third (OP formulation) and first (drafting of national and especially regional development plans) stages, in that order, but they had relatively little influence in the second stage (the negotiation of CSFs). He found that the greatest role for subnational actors, however, was in the implementation and monitoring of OPs in the member states.

1994–9

Subnational actors were much more involved in the implementation of cohesion policy in the 1994–9 programming period, in some cases even before programming began. According to Sutcliffe (2000: 299), regional actors were much more active in lobbying to influence the shape and substance of the 1993 regulations when compared with the previous reform; this included efforts 'to influence the content of the regulations' and 'to secure specific objective status for individual regions'. Some governments also devolved implementation powers to regional and local authorities in 1994–9, in many cases because of their increased experience with structural funds programmes after the first programming period (Ferry *et al.*, 2007: 7). Nonetheless, national governments retained ultimate authority to choose their partners at the national and subnational levels, thus limiting the impact of partnership in the implementation of cohesion policy in 1994–9.

A major study of the partnership principle that was requested by the Commission and published in 1999, confirmed the still uneven application of partnership across the member states and programmes. According the study, 'The Member States continue to dominate and delimit partnership functioning through their key role in both negotiating programme content and in determining the extent of … partnership, and through their habitual roles of providing secretariats and acting as managing authorities.' However, it also found that 'Increasingly, despite initial reservations and resistance, many Member States are welcoming, encouraging or initiating more extensive and inclusive partnership strategies particularly as regards their (sometimes new found) relations with regional partners and social partners' (Kelleher *et al.*, 1999: 159–60). The study also found significant differences in the participation of partners at different stages of the implementation process, with a 'more important role for more partners at the planning and project selection stage, a variable role for different partners for various operational tasks, and a less developed role for the full formal partnership in terms of monitoring and evaluation'. Nevertheless, it concluded that 'partnership, although a relatively recent innovation, has already become deeply embedded in all stages of Structural Fund programming' (Kelleher *et al.*, 1999: 156).

Overall, however, the study confirmed the many positive benefits of the partnership approach, including more effective programme implementation, greater legitimacy and transparency in decision-making, 'greater commitment and ownership of programme outcomes', reinforced 'innovation and learning across institutional boundaries', and the development of regional and local institutional capacity, particularly in member states where it had previously been weak or non-existent. Moreover, it found that the application of partnership in cohesion policy was having an effect on the spread of multi-level governance more generally, with partnership emerging not only as 'a formal arrangement for consultation, coordination and decision making at each of the programming stages as envisaged in the Structural Fund Regulation, but also as a significant capacity for joint multi-organisational action and operations' that 'now often extends well beyond the remit of Structural Fund activities' (Kelleher *et al.*, 1999: 156).

2000–06

The regulations for cohesion policy approved in 1999 extended the horizontal dimension of partnership, putting more emphasis on the involvement of environmental and gender equity organizations, while strengthening the rules for partnership in programme management. Similar to previous programming periods, however, the involvement of subnational and non-governmental partners in the implementation of cohesion policy in 2000–06 varied considerably across the member states, with some national governments allowing more extensive involvement than others (Bachtler and McMaster, 2007: 5; Schröder, 2008: 29). This programming period also saw the initial implementation of cohesion policy in the new member states that had acceded to the EU in 2004. For the most part, the new member states were small and relatively centralized political systems, with fairly weak subnational administrative tiers and civil societies. As a result, cohesion policy was implemented in a fairly centralized fashion in these countries after they joined the EU (Baun and Marek, 2008b: 254–5).

In a mid-term evaluation of the implementation of the partnership principle, the Commission confirmed that partnership produced many positive benefits for the operation and effectiveness of the structural funds, as well as 'further benefits such as the improvement of institutional capacities at different levels (local, regional and national), better inter-institutional coordination and communication at the national level, or a better involvement of civil society'. The Commission's analysis also found 'that there have been efforts to improve the functioning of partnership' in the new programming period, including the involvement of 'a wider range of partners than ever before'. However, it also lamented that 'the involvement of partners at different stages of the programming cycle is not considered as equally necessary and sometimes is even seen as causing an additional burden on time and resources'. Moreover, it was 'not always clear whether the selection of partners is based on their specific expertise or on political preference' (CEC, 2005b: 12). To improve the functioning of partnership in the future, the Commission recommended that the member states do a better job of publicizing partnership opportunities at the beginning of the next programming period, and also of identifying potential partners and informing them how the partnership principle would be implemented in operational programmes and what the participatory rights and responsibilities of the partners were (CEC, 2005b: 13).

2007–13

The 2006 reform further extended and strengthened the partnership principle. Nevertheless, the member states retained wide discretion over the designation of appropriate partners and which partners to include in programming and implementation. As a result, the application of the partnership principle in 2007–13 continued to vary widely across the member states when it came to the role and influence of the various partners in the implementation of cohesion policy.

One notable trend in 2007–13 was the decentralization of cohesion policy implementation in some of the new CEE member states. In most cases, this was due to the increased experience of regional and subnational actors with managing EU funds that was gained in the previous programming period. Also playing a role, however, was the increased emphasis on decentralization and subsidiarity in the 2006 regulation, and the increased level of funding for the new member states in 2007–13 which made additional resources available for regional programmes. In some cases as well, such as Poland and the Czech Republic, democratically elected regional governments successfully demanded a greater role in the implementation of cohesion policy (Baun and Marek, 2008b: 255).

Another development was the Commission's effort to dissemi-nate partnership 'good practices'. This included the establishment of the 'Community of Practice on Partnership' (COP), an ESF-funded body consisting of ESF managing authorities and intermediate bodies from nine member states that was created to facilitate the exchange of experience with implementing partnership. An evalua-tion conducted in 2011 by the Tavistock Institute on Human Relations found the COP to have 'contributed to significant learn-ing and good practice exchange across EU member states' (Tavistock Institute, 2011).

2014–20

At the time of writing the implementation process for 2014–20 has only just begun, so it is impossible to assess the application of part-nership in the new programming period. However, the new regula-tions for cohesion policy approved in 2013 gave the Commission additional means for ensuring the proper application of the partner-ship principle. Most notably, it empowered the Commission to adopt a delegated act providing for a 'European code of conduct on partnership' which could be used to guide and support the member states in implementing the partnership principle (OJEU, 2013a: 341–2).

The Commission presented its new code of conduct in January 2014, together with a separate document containing a list of 'best practices' in the application of partnership (CEC, 2014d, 2014e). The former document outlined the main principles and best prac-tices for identifying and involving the relevant partners in the prepa-ration of the Partnership Agreement and ESI-funded programmes. It also set out good practices in formulating the membership rules and internal procedures of the monitoring committees, and the main principles and good practices for involving the relevant partners in the preparation of calls for proposal and progress reports and in the monitoring and evaluation of programmes. Finally, it provided a list of 'indicative areas, themes and good practices' concerning the use of ESI funds to strengthen the institutional capacity of relevant part-ners and the Commission's role in disseminating good practices. Concerning the latter, the Commission promised to set up a new cooperation mechanism – the European Community of Practice on Partnership – to facilitate the exchange of experience and the dissemination of relevant outcomes (CEC, 2014d: 5–13). The accompanying working document provided one or more examples of best practices in each of these areas, at the national and regional levels and from old as well as new member states (CEC, 2014e).

As another means for improving the implementation of the partnership principle, the ESF regulation for 2014–20 provides for the use of ESF resources for 'capacity building activities' for social partners and NGOs in less developed regions and member states. In the case of NGOs, such measures would be aimed primarily at groups active in the fields of social inclusion, gender equality and equal opportunities (OJEU, 2013c: 476–7).

By June 2014 the Commission had received the Partnership Agreements of all 28 member states, allowing it to draw some initial conclusions about the application of partnership and the Code of Conduct in formulation of the Agreements. In its *Sixth Report on Economic, Social and Territorial Cohesion*, published in July 2014, the Commission reported that the 'Partnership Agreements have largely been drafted through reasonable dialogue with partners, although there are indications that in some cases this dialogue has been insufficient, important stake-holders were not involved or [their] comments were not reflected in later versions of the documents.' The Commission promised that it would 'look very carefully at how Member States have applied the Code of Conduct on Parternship to ensure genuine participation by stakeholders' (CEC, 2014h: xxvii).

Cohesion policy and multi-level governance

Cohesion policy and the partnership principle are closely connected to the academic study of Multi-level Governance. Indeed, the 1988 reform of the structural funds acted as a 'catalyst for the popularization of the concept of multilevel governance' (Mendez, 2011: 519). Cohesion policy is the field in which the MLG concept was first theorized and tested, and it remains among the most studied examples of this phenomenon today (Piattoni, 2010: 11–18, 97–102; Bache and Flinders, 2004). According to some scholars, through the practice of partnership cohesion policy has a potentially 'far-reaching impact on the domestic administration involved in regional policy delivery', including the promotion of a 'multi-level and participative mode of governance in the member states' (Dąbrowski, 2011: 4, 7). Moreover, this impact could reach beyond the sphere of regional policy to affect other policy areas and governance norms and structures more broadly. In the view of some scholars, cohesion policy could serve as 'the leading edge of a system of *multilevel governance*' in the EU (Marks, 1993: 401–2; italics in the original).

At its core, the concept of multi-level governance describes how decision-making authority is increasingly diffused from the central state and exercised jointly by governmental and private actors at different territorial levels, with the boundaries between state and society becoming increasingly blurred as a result. In the process, the role of the state and the manner in which it exercises power is becoming transformed, with some scholars even arguing that traditional state power and control are being undermined (Marks and Hooghe, 2004: 19; Bache, 2008: 29–30). The net outcome of this process, if carried to its logical conclusion, would be the replacement of centralized, hierarchical states with a system of cooperative networks, involving public authorities and private or non-governmental actors at different territorial levels, which exercise governmental functions in different policy areas.

The initial focus of the MLG literature was on the vertical or territorial dimension of governance, with some scholars asserting that through its partnership requirement EU cohesion policy was helping to mobilize and empower regional (and supranational) actors at the expense of national governments. This was because cohesion policy required the existence of competent regional authorities that could be partners of the Commission and national governments in the administration of structural funds programmes, necessitating the creation of such bodies where they did not already exist, and their strengthening in some cases where they did. Cohesion policy also empowered subnational actors by providing them with new financial resources through access to EU funds. It also provided subnational actors with new political resources, by establishing direct links to EU institutions and encouraging the formation of transnational associations by regional and local governments, thus providing them with new means for promoting their interests. According to some scholars, in these and other ways cohesion policy was contributing to the emergence of a new system of multi-level governance in the EU, in which the power and authority of the central state was being undermined and traditional state competences were being transferred both upwards to the EU level, and downwards to subnational governments, leading to the emergence of a more complex and less state-centric 'Europe of the regions' (Marks, 1992, 1993; Jones and Keating, 1995; Hooghe, ed. 1996; Marks *et al.*, 1996; Caporaso, 1996; Kohler-Koch, 1996; Hooghe and Marks, 2001).

Other scholars disputed this assertion, however, pointing to the 'gatekeeping' capacity of national governments, and to the role of national political conditions, governance traditions and constitutional arrangements in limiting or mediating the domestic impact of cohesion policy. These assertions were supported by a number of empirical studies of cohesion policy implementation and partnership practices in various member states which revealed a high level of national differentiation in accordance with domestic structures and conditions (Pollack, 1995; Jeffery, 1997; Börzel, 1999; Benz and Eberlein, 1999; Bache, 1998, 1999; Kelleher *et. al*, 1999; Bailey and de Proporis, 2002a; Laffan, 2004). Further support for the view that cohesion policy has had only a limited and differentiated impact on multi-level governance was provided by studies of the CEE candidate states in the pre-accession period, as they adapted to EU rules and requirements for use of the structural funds (Brusis, 2001, 2002; Grabbe, 2001; Hughes *et al.* 2001, 2003, 2004; Marek and Baun, 2002; Keating, 2003; Jacoby, 2004). The MLG sceptics also looked for evidence at the EU decision-making level, pointing to the ability of the member states to claw back control of cohesion policy implementation in successive policy reforms after 1988, thus reining in and limiting the influence of the Commission in cohesion policy implementation (Bache, 1998; Allen, 2005).

Still other scholars have argued that cohesion policy does in fact have an impact on domestic governance, but this is only evident over time. According to this view, the governance effects of cohesion policy take place not just through EU pressure (i.e. formal policy requirements and the threat of sanctions for non-compliance) and incentives (i.e. funding), but also through the process of 'learning', which over time can effectively diffuse new governance norms and practices. While the initial experience with cohesion policy generally produces shallow 'strategic' adaptation (or 'thin' learning), longer-term exposure and experience generates deeper changes of interests and preferences and the internalization of EU norms (or 'thick' learning) by national and subnational actors. As a result, the multi-level governance effects of cohesion policy can best be glimpsed over an extended period of time (Kelleher *et al.*, 1999; Paraskevopoulos, 2001, 2005; Paraskevopoulos and Leonardi, 2004; Paraskevopoulos *et al.*, 2006; Leonardi, 2005; Bachtler and Taylor, 2003; Bache, 2008).

After initially focusing on territorial governance, the concept of multi-level governance was eventually refined to incorporate a separate, non-territorial dimension, reflecting the increased involvement of non-state actors in the making of cohesion policy and 'in the EU polity more generally' (Bache, 2005: 5). Thus, Marks and Hooghe (2004) define two main types of multi-level governance: 'Type I', which refers to the dispersion of decision-making authority among different territorial levels of government; and 'Type II', which refers to the exercise of public authority within 'task-specific jurisdictions' with intersecting memberships that may operate at numerous territorial levels. In other words, Type I multi-level governance concerns the vertical redistribution of power between different governmental levels (in the EU context: supranational, national, regional and local), while Type II multi-level governance concerns the horizontal transfer of state authority to functional governmental arrangements involving non-governmental or private actors.

In both types of multi-level governance, policy competences and responsibilities are shared by governmental institutions at different levels in Type I, by public and private actors in Type II – rather than monopolized by central state administrations. In both types as well, policy decisions are made and implemented in a networked fashion, featuring a high degree of coordination and cooperation between public and private actors at different levels. Especially in Type II multi-level governance, the policy process can also be considerably more 'messy' and 'disorderly' than traditional formal governance, relying on a variety of informal and sometimes ad hoc arrangements (Bache, 2008: 29). Moreover, the different political levels or arenas of a multi-level system are not isolated but interconnected. As a consequence, subnational actors are also active on both the national and supranational (i.e. EU) levels, creating their own transnational links and associations in the process (Hooghe and Marks, 2001: 3–4; Bache, 2008: 25).

Despite broad agreement on the dimensions of multi-level governance and the networked or coordinated nature of policy-making in this system, there is disagreement among scholars over what the advent of multi-level governance means for the state. One prominent view is that multi-level governance undermines the state, with its powers shifting or 'slipping away' both upward to supranational institutions (i.e. the EU) and downward to subnational levels of government (Marks and Hooghe: 2004: 19; Bache, 2008: 29–30). According to other scholars, however, multi-level governance presents the state with new means for exerting influence and power; thus, far from undermining the state, multi-level governance can enhance its capacity to project power and achieve its objectives (Jessop, 2004: 65, in Bache, 2008: 30). Regardless of whether it undermines or enhances state power, however, it is generally agreed that multi-level governance significantly transforms the nature of the state and the way it exercises power.

Another issue in the debate on multi-level governance is the distinction between 'participation' and 'governance,' with some critics of the MLG concept arguing that the former term does not imply any real influence over policy decision-making, something that is implied by the concept of governance. Thus, partnership arrangements in cohesion policy, which enable the participation of subnational and non-governmental actors, may not accord them any real influence over outcomes in practice, instead serving merely as window dressing or as a symbolic gesture. According to Bache (2008: 31), empirical studies of multi-level governance, including the partnership arrangements of cohesion policy, need to examine this question more closely.

Given these competing arguments and claims, after more than 25 years since the 1988 reform of the structural funds, and with the near completion of four programming periods (for the EU15), what evidence is there of cohesion policy's impact on territorial or vertical multi-level governance in the EU? It is to this question that we now turn.

Cohesion policy and vertical multi-level governance

It is argued that cohesion policy promotes vertical multi-level governance in two principal ways: by necessitating the creation of competent regional bodies in cases where they previously did not exist; and by empowering new and previously existing subnational authorities, by giving them a formal role in cohesion policy, access to new financial resources, and new possibilities for interest mobilization and coalition-building at the EU level – in other words, by creating a new 'opportunity structure' for subnational actors to assert their interests and exercise influence. In this manner, it is claimed, cohesion policy has promoted governmental decentralization and regionalization in the EU. Each of these claims can be examined empirically, along with the assertion that the governance effects of cohesion policy are more evident over time, as a result of the process of learning.

New regional structures

A basic precondition for receiving structural funds assistance is the existence of competent regional authorities (at the NUTS 2 level) that can serve as partners of the Commission and national governments in the administration of EU-funded programmes. However, the EU regulations do not specify the nature of these regional bodies; they can be democratically elected governments with substantial autonomy and power, or they can be purely administrative authorities appointed by central governments with very limited or no real independent power. Assuming that competent regional bodies did not already exist, therefore, the decision of what type of regional governance structure to create is wholly a matter for the member states.

Some EU15 member states already had regional governance structures that met the requirements of cohesion policy. This was the case, for instance, in federal or quasi-federal (or 'regionalized') states which had a previously existing regional tier of governance, including Germany, Belgium, Spain, Italy, Sweden and Austria. In another such state, Finland, existing regional structures were transformed to better fit the requirements of cohesion policy, with a reduction in the number of provincial governments and a corresponding reorganization of the central government's regional offices (Bache, 2008: 63–70).

In other, traditionally more centralized states, however, such as the UK, Ireland, Greece and Portugal, new regional authorities often had to be created from scratch (Piattoni, 2010: 8, 19, 166). In Greece, a new regional tier of administration had been created in 1986 in order to implement the Integrated Mediterranean Programme, which also had a partnership requirement, and thus was in place for the 1988 reform. Five new administrative regions were created for the purposes of EU cohesion policy in Portugal. In

Ireland, new regional structures were eventually created for the 2000–06 programming period, with the country divided into two NUTS 2 administrative units in an effort to retain Objective 1 funding despite Ireland's increased overall wealth, but even before this, subnational and local structures had been adapted to meet EU requirements (Bache, 2008: 58–9). New regional structures (Government Offices, in 1994, and Regional Development Agencies, in 1998) were also created in the UK to manage the structural funds and serve as the focal points for partnership arrangements at the regional level (Bache, 2008: 95–9). In contrast to the self-governing regions of federal or regionalized states, however, the new regional authorities in centralized member states were often purely administrative entities, appointed and controlled by national governments, and having very little policy-making capacity or decision-making autonomy. Nevertheless, they at least now existed, and as a result, a new 'tier of governance to activate the triangle of European Commission, national government and regional partnership' had been created (Bailey and de Propris, 2002b: 421).

The candidate states of Central and Eastern Europe were also required to establish competent regional authorities to meet the partnership requirements of the structural funds, in this case as a precondition of EU membership, and in all of the former communist countries such institutions were created in the pre-accession period. Similar to the situation of the more centralized EU15 member states, most of these countries had unitary systems and very little tradition of governmental decentralization. Also mirroring the experience of the EU15, the types of regional authorities that were created in these countries varied considerably, ranging from self-governing regions with significant powers in Poland, the Czech Republic and Slovakia, to purely administrative regions in the other candidate states, the outcome on this score being almost wholly due to nationally specific conditions, including governmental traditions and domestic politics (Brusis, 2002; Bailey and de Propris, 2002b; Baun, 2002; Hughes *et al.*, 2004).

It appears, therefore, that cohesion policy has had some impact on territorial governance in the EU, at least when it comes to the creation of new regional structures in some member states or the reform of existing institutions in others. This effect was the greatest in centralized states that did not previously have a regional administrative tier or subnational governmental institutions, such as the

UK, Ireland and Portugal among the EU15 and the CEE member states. In each of these cases, new regional structures had to be created to meet the partnership requirements of cohesion policy. Thus, according to Kelleher *et al.* (1999: 71), cohesion policy has provided a stimulus for governmental decentralization and in some cases 'the virtual invention' of a regional tier of governance, although this had taken a variety of forms in different member states

Regional empowerment and mobilization

Some proponents of the MLG thesis have argued that cohesion policy has not only led to the creation of new regional governmental institutions, it has also empowered them, by providing regional institutions with a formal role in EU policy, access to new financial resources, and an opportunity structure for projecting subnational interests and influence, including links to EU institutions and other subnational actors (Piattoni, 2010; Vida, 2004: 8). Brusis (2010: 72, 86), for instance, argues that cohesion policy has provided 'an opportunity structure for domestic political actors seeking to create regions or to increase the resources of regional government ("regionalisation"); it thus has considerably affected the power constellation between national governments and regional actors'. Similarly, Mackinnon (2001: 17) asserts that cohesion policy is framed in such a way as to 'facilitate' subnational mobilization and promote further decentralization. These and other scholars claim, in other words, that cohesion policy has created a new dynamic in relations between the central state and subnational actors that could generate new political demands and further institutional change. In this manner, according to Piattoni (2010: 98), the structural funds have become 'a battleground in the power struggle between center and periphery'.

The impact of cohesion policy on regional empowerment and mobilization appears to be highly differentiated across the member states, however, with some regional actors empowered by cohesion policy while others have not been. A key factor responsible for this differentiation is the 'national institutional set-up', which greatly affects the strength and power resources of subnational authorities and their ability to exploit the new opportunities created by cohesion policy (Piattoni, 2010: 111; Hooghe, 1996). As Piattoni (2010: 120) argues, while 'all regions try to take advantage of the new opportunities for mobilization afforded by cohesion policy ... The mobilization dynamics set in motion by cohesion policy cannot be expected to translate immediately into institutional power gains on the part of the regions nor into power gains that affect all regions equally, because not all regions start out on the same footing.' In essence, only strong regional actors have been able 'to successfully exploit the opportunities for access to new resources and influence presented by cohesion policy', while weak regional actors have been less able to do so (Baun and Marek, 2008a: 5).

Also important is the varying learning capacity of regional actors. According to Dąbrowski (2011: 23), subnational actors 'respond differently to the norms and practices promoted by EU cohesion policy, with some ... complying only superficially ... while others internalize their logic'. Furthermore:

> The 'depth' of their adjustment to the EU-imposed policy rules varies depending on their preferences and interests. It also depends on their capacity to participate in the [structural funds] programs, which is in turn determined by their financial and administrative capacity as well as their attitudes. Moreover, their responses to EU-imposed policy norms may change over time. As a consequence, the impact of the partnership principle, and more widely the EU cohesion policy and the norms it promotes, remains uneven and differentiated across the affected subnational policy actors. (Dąbrowski, 2011: 23)

In some highly centralized EU15 member states, therefore, such as France, Portugal and Greece, cohesion policy has thus far led neither to a significant empowerment of regional actors nor to governmental decentralization. This is because regional actors in these countries are fairly weak, and national governments have successfully exercised a gatekeeping role to dominate the implementation and management of cohesion policy. In the case of Greece, national administrative traditions and a statist political culture have also inhibited the capacity of regional structures to learn and adapt to the new realities of multi-level governance (Bache, 2008: 59-63).

The situation in Ireland and the UK, however, is a bit more complex. In the former, cohesion policy appears to have '[enhanced] the institutional capacity of local and regional governance' and altered 'the way in which intergovernmental relations in Ireland take place' (Bache, 2008: 58; referencing Roberts, 2003: 39 and Rees *et al.*, 2004: 39). Bache thus concludes that, while cohesion policy has not led to radical governmental decentralization in Ireland, it has nevertheless strengthened the vertical dimension of multi-level governance. This is an outcome that he attributes in part to the scale of EU funding received by the country and its perceived contribution to Ireland's economic success, which in turn helped to legitimate the EU policy approach. Moreover, he finds that the capacity of structural funds participants in Ireland for 'thick' learning in adapting to EU requirements also played an important role and enhanced the governance effect of cohesion policy (Bache, 2008: 58–9).

In the UK, Bache (2008: 155) claims that cohesion policy played a key role in 'the revival of the English regional tier [of governance] in the period 1989–1997'. He also argues that cohesion policy was an influential factor in the strengthening of English regional governance in the subsequent decade, although domestic forces (especially the policies of the Labour government, which included the formal devolution of governmental powers to Scotland and Wales in 1998) were probably more important (Bache, 2008: 128–9). Mackinnon (2001: 17) also argues that cohesion policy has had a significant effect on decentralization in the UK, claiming that the 'structural funds helped to prepare the way for the transition to devolution, training Scottish subnational authorities and other elites to take devolution in their stride'. Aside from devolution, however, governmental decentralization in the UK has only gone so far, with voters thus far rejecting plans for the creation of directly elected regional assemblies in some English regions.

In EU15 countries with federal or regionalized systems, on the other hand, cohesion policy appears to have promoted decentralization and regional empowerment to some extent. In Spain, regional governments have gained a greater role in structural funds management since 1993, although 'this did not amount to a transformation of relations with the central government' (Bache, 2008: 66). However, the Spanish regions have continued to press for more influence in the face of central government efforts to maintain control of EU policy, while many have also cultivated direct relationships with EU institutions (Bache, 2008: 65–7), suggesting that cohesion policy has had some impact on regional mobilization and that it offers the potential for further change. Cohesion policy also seems to have produced significant multi-level governance effects in Sweden, particularly in relation to the vertical dimension, with cohesion policy being assessed as 'an important driving force in the process of regional self-government' (Olsson and Astrom, 1999: 14, in Bache, 2008: 67). It also seems to have generated change in Finland, with the new regional structures established to meet the partnership requirements of cohesion policy having 'acted as a catalyst' for further reforms to strengthen the regional level of governance (Kettunen and Kungla, 2005: 370, in Bache, 2008: 69). In Italy, meanwhile, Leonardi (2005: 149) has observed learning processes at work that could increase the administrative capacity of regional governments and enable more effective multi-level governance in the future.

The situation in Germany is more complicated, despite the seemingly perfect fit between the concept of multi-level governance and German federalism. On the one hand, the federal states (*Länder*) have resisted sharing responsibility for structural funds management with sub-regional and local authorities, while on the other the federal government has resented how direct ties between Brussels and the *Länder* have undercut its traditional gatekeeping role in EU policy. The operation of partnership has improved in Germany over time, however, along both its vertical and horizontal dimensions (Bache, 2008: 63–5).

In the new member states, some analysts claim that cohesion policy has had significant effects on territorial governance and intergovernmental relations. According to Dąbrowski (2011: 4–5), implementation of the structural funds in the new member states has brought about important changes in 'center-periphery relations ... creating scope for a growing role of the regional tier and greater bottom-up regional involvement in economic development policy', even though in many cases this pressure was in conflict with long-standing traditions of centralized state administration and policy management. Bruszt (in Börzel, 2011: 16) agrees that regional and subnational actors in the new member states have utilized opportunities offered by the partnership principle to press for more resources and influence, and that cohesion policy has created a framework in these countries in which 'societal actors and subnational authorities could politicize issues of territorial decentralization and exert pressure on state reforms towards greater devolution of power'. Baun and Marek (2008b: 255–6) have also noted the increased role of regional authorities in the new member states in structural funds management over time, with cohesion policy in the 2007–13 programming period being managed in a more regionalized and decentralized manner than in 2004–06, although there are indications that cohesion policy in 2014–20 will once again be managed in a more centralized manner in the Czech Republic and some other CEE states (Marek and Baun, 2014).

The impact of cohesion policy on governmental decentralization has varied greatly in the CEE member states, however, mirroring the experience of the EU15. Once again, the varying strength and capacity of regional institutions is a major factor explaining this differentiated pattern. In the Czech Republic and Poland, self-governing regions possessing formal policy competencies in the area of regional development have managed to acquire a larger role in structural funds management, thus successfully exploiting the opportunities offered by cohesion policy to gain more influence and resources. By contrast, in more centralized states with weak regional institutions – such as Hungary, where the 'counties', the country's main administrative divisions, have only limited financial resources and no formal competencies in the area of regional development – cohesion policy does not appear to have strengthened subnational authorities in any considerable way (Baun and Marek, 2008b: 255–6).

The uneven impact of cohesion policy on vertical multi-level governance in the CEE member states also reflects the varying learning capacity of subnational actors. In Poland, for instance, Dąbrowski (2011: 21) found a mixed picture when it came to compliance with the partnership requirement, with only '"formal" and "shallow" compliance' in some areas of structural funds implementation, 'as in the case of partnership committees participating in project appraisal ([Regional Steering Committees] RSCs)'. In other areas, however, 'as for example in program formulation, partnership was keenly adopted, which suggests that this new practice can be successfully transferred to the Polish policy arena, providing that the actors involved consider it in line with their interests and preferences. The same can be said about partnership in developmental projects among local authorities, which becomes increasingly popular as officials realize its potential to generate synergies and, more importantly perhaps, to increase the chances of obtaining funding' (Dąbrowski, 2011: 21).

Another factor accounting for the differential pattern of regionalization and decentralization in EU member states is the varying strength of regional identities and demands for subnational autonomy. In some decentralizing countries, such as Spain and the devolved UK, regional mobilization from below (in Cataluña and Scotland), has played the primary role and the EU factor has mattered little (Hughes *et al.*, 2004: 174, in Brusis, 2010: 74–5). According to Brusis (2010: 77) the strength of regional actors and the nature of their representation strategies is a key determinant of whether a country regionalizes or not: 'Regionalising reforms tend to be more shallow and incremental, if functional interest representation prevails. If there are strong actors of territorial representation, regionalising reforms may result in regional self-government and a substantial devolution of power'. Indeed, in most of the member states in which there has been little decentralization and regional actors have not attempted to fully exploit the opportunity structure provided by cohesion policy, subnational identities and demands for regional autonomy are weak or non-existent.

Conclusion

Cohesion policy has had a highly variable impact on territorial governance across the member states, with a key explanatory factor being national conditions and domestic politics, while overall its impact on vertical multi-level governance in the EU has been significant but modest. While cohesion policy has led to the establishment or reform of regional governance structures in some member states, and created a new opportunity structure for subnational actors seeking to expand their influence and role, whether subnational actors are able to exploit these opportunities depends on both the capacity of regional institutions and the strength of subnational identities and demands. Subnational actors have also established an active presence in the EU arena, through membership in the Committee of the Regions, which has a formal consultative role in cohesion policy, the establishment of regional offices in Brussels and membership in transnational associations, such as the Association of European Regions, yet it is unclear just how much influence in the EU policy-making process they actually have.

Cohesion policy and horizontal multi-level governance

Scholarly analysis of the impact of cohesion policy on horizontal or

Type II multi-level governance has lagged behind the focus on territorial governance, but has grown with the increased emphasis on horizontal partnership in successive cohesion policy reforms since the late 1990s. As with vertical multi-level governance, many scholars claim that the application of the partnership principle in cohesion policy, with its requirement to involve non-governmental and private actors in partnership arrangements together with public institutions at different levels, has the potential to promote horizontal multi-level governance in the EU, with such practices eventually spreading beyond the confines of regional development policy to other policy spheres and affecting governance norms more broadly. Indeed, according to Bache (2007, 2008), the governance effect of cohesion policy can perhaps best be seen in its promotion of Type II multi-level governance in many member states, including those that have been more successful in limiting the impact of cohesion policy on territorial governance. Similar to vertical multi-level governance, the impact of cohesion policy on horizontal multi-level governance can be examined empirically, even though this dimension of partnership has a shorter history.

National conditions and variable effects

As with vertical multi-level governance, the impact of cohesion policy on horizontal multi-level governance across the member states also is highly variable. Once again, the main determining factor appears to be nationally specific conditions, in this case national governmental or administrative traditions, the strength of non-governmental and civil society groups and the learning capacity of structural funds actors.

Regarding the first of these conditions, Bache (2008: 83) draws a distinction between 'statist' and 'corporatist' political cultures, with horizontal partnership more likely to be embraced in the latter, in which traditions of public–private cooperation are strong, than in the former, in which such traditions are weak or non-existent. Another important condition is the state of civil society development, with horizontal partnership more likely to be found in countries with a strong and vibrant civil society, since well-organized economic and social groups are better able to engage with government and serve as effective partners in cohesion policy (Bache, 2008; Baun and Marek, 2008b). Learning capacity, in turn, reflects the interests and preferences of structural funds actors, their ability to participate in partnership arrangements, and such broader factors as prevailing cultural attitudes and the level and quality of social capital. Thus, we can expect the impact of cohesion policy on horizontal multi-level governance to be particularly limited in southern European countries and the formerly communist CEE member states, with their statist traditions, generally weak civil societies and high levels of social and political mistrust (Bache, 2008: 83).

A review of the member states shows this expectation to be generally confirmed. In countries with a strong tradition of inclusive policy-making and collaboration between public, private and social actors, such as Ireland, Sweden and Finland, horizontal partnership in cohesion policy has been embraced, although with varying results. In Ireland, for example, McMaster (2008: 108) argues that 'a strong basis for consultative policy was already in place', allowing the partnership principle of cohesion policy to '[build] upon pre-existing social partnership arrangements (e.g. employer/business, trade union, farming, community and voluntary interests)'. Moreover, Bache (2008: 59) found that cohesion policy has helped to 'expand this [horizontal partnership] practice', especially when it came to the increased 'involvement of the community and voluntary sectors at the local level'. Also in Ireland, through the structural funds a number of non-governmental bodies were either 'generated' or 'revitalized', and in some cases organizational cultures and social norms were changed and interests and identities reconceptualised (Rees *et al.*, 204: 401, in Bache, 2008: 59).

In both Sweden and Finland as well strong traditions of corporatism and consensual policy-making provided fertile ground for horizontal partnership, despite some misfit between the prevailing norms of economic or labour corporatism and EU-style public–private cooperation. In both countries strong institutions, a well-developed civil society and high levels of social capital also facilitated adaptation and learning. In Germany, on the other hand, despite a strong tradition of labour corporatism, there was some governmental resistance to giving the trade unions a formal role in cohesion policy decision-making. The inclusion of trade unions in partnership arrangements has also varied across the 16 *Länder*, depending on regional traditions and conditions (Bache, 2008: 63–5, 67–9).

Participatory modes of decision-making were also a part of British governance traditions, easing adaptation to the horizontal partnership requirements of cohesion policy in the UK. Bache (2008: 156) argues, however, that cohesion policy has strengthened horizontal multi-level governance in the UK, especially at the local level. 'In the longer term', he declares, 'the partnership principle helped to generate a norm of inclusion of a wide range of organizations in public decision making'; in particular, it helped to promote 'the role of the voluntary and community sector in local decision making'. Chapman (2008: 48) also reports that, in the view of the Commission itself, when it comes to horizontal partnership the UK is '"ahead of the game" as far as third sector [non-governmental] engagement is concerned'.

The situation is much different in EU15 member states with statist political cultures and little tradition of public–private partnership, however. In the case of Greece, for instance, while cohesion policy has spurred the formation of horizontal partnerships, these have generally been weak and ineffective, the result of a legacy of statist authoritarianism, a weak civil society and the lack of experience with cooperative and inclusive policy-making. These factors, combined with weak subnational institutions and a high level of political mistrust, have also inhibited the learning capacity of structural funds actors in Greece (Paraskevopoulos, 2008: 136–40; Bache, 2007: 6, 12; 2008: 60–1; Dąbrowski, 2011: 7). A similar situation exists in Portugal, Spain and France when it comes to cohesion policy and horizontal multi-level governance (Morata and Popartan, 2008: 93; Dąbrowski, 2011: 7; Bache, 2008: 61–3, 67).

The experience of the southern member states is replicated in the CEE countries, where the impact of cohesion policy on horizontal multi-level governance has been even less notable than its effect on territorial governance. This is largely due to the underdeveloped state of civil society in these countries, insufficient administrative capacity, a legacy of centralized administration and the absence of traditions of collaborative policy-making and public–private partnership (Bache, 2008: 80, 83; Baun and Marek, 2008b: 256, 265; Dąbrowski, 2011: 7–8). In Poland, for instance, research has found that horizontal partnership is impeded by 'a weak civil society, low levels of social trust and trust in political institutions, and a high level of political clientelism and corruption in a system dominated by political parties' (Bache, 2008: 75; referencing Jewtuchowicz and Czernielewska-Rutkoska, 2006: 169–71). The predominance of centralized administrative systems also works against the development of horizontal multi-level governance in these countries. Thus, according to Bruszt (in Börzel, 2011: 29), while cohesion policy has empowered subnational actors and NGOs in the CEE member states, the hierarchical governance structures of these countries 'do not offer sufficient incentives and resources to foster horizontal cooperation and power sharing in the distribution of structural funds. Rather, the shadow of hierarchy induces regional actors to build-up vertical relations', thereby reinforcing hierarchical modes of governance.

Nevertheless, some progress has been made. According to Börzel (2011: 10), despite the reluctance of central governments in the new member states to share power:

> the EU's insistence on the principle of partnership combined with diverse pre-accession assistance programs empowering diverse subnational non-state actors spurred the emergence of more or less stable partnerships among various subnational authorities, firms, and civil society organizations in the design and implementation of regional development programs.

These partnerships, she argues, have 'helped improve the absorption capacity of CEE countries by mobilizing information and resources otherwise not available, discovering new options, and improving local acceptance of governance policies', while they have also 'encouraged the creation of encompassing and inclusive development programmes by institutionalizing multi-stakeholder deliberations on the goals of development and the best ways to achieve them' (Börzel, 2011: 24). And as Baun and Marek (2008b: 256–7) suggest, improved partnership performance in the new member states can perhaps be expected in the future, 'as a result of increased experience with EU policies and governance norms, economic and social development – which should lead to stronger and better organized civil society – and learning by both the state and social actors'.

Conclusion

Similar to its impact on territorial governance, the impact of cohesion policy on horizontal or Type II multi-level governance in the member states has been highly variable, once again depending on national conditions and traditions. In member states with established traditions of collaborative or inclusive policy-making, well-developed civil societies and institutional infrastructures possessing a high capacity for learning, horizontal partnership has generally been embraced, and in these countries cohesion policy has generally reinforced or strengthened horizontal multi-level governance. For the most part, and with some variation, this has been the situation in the more economically developed member states of northern and western Europe. In the southern member states, however, and even more so in the new CEE member states, statist traditions, centralized government, limited experience with public–private partnerships and weak or underdeveloped civil societies have limited the effect of cohesion policy on horizontal multi-level governance. In these countries as well, weak public institutions, especially at the subnational level, and high levels of political mistrust and limited social capital have inhibited the learning capacity of structural funds actors, further reducing the impact of cohesion policy on horizontal multi-level governance. On the other hand, it is in these very countries, through the introduction of partnership norms and practices within the 'carrot and stick' framework of EU cohesion policy, which ties material rewards (access to EU funds) to compliance with specific operational rules (Dąbrowski, 2011: 9), that the long-term effect of cohesion policy on multi-level governance may be the most pronounced.

Community-led Local Development

While application of the partnership principle is the primary means by which the EU seeks to promote multi-level governance and a participatory approach to cohesion policy implementation, it is not the only one. The new cohesion policy regulations for 2014–20 introduced provisions for a new 'bottom-up' approach to programming, Community-led Local Development (CLLD), which could give local-level actors more input into the use of EU funds provided to member states under the Partnership Agreements.

Based on the successful experiences of the LEADER+ programme carried out under the CAP in 2007–13, and drawing on all of the ESI funds, CLLD is designed to focus on sub-regional areas with populations between 10,000 and 150,000 (although exceptions could be made for sparsely or densely populated areas or for other reasons). Within these areas, the new regulations provide for the formation of Local Action Groups (LAGs), composed of local municipalities, entrepreneurs, NGOs and active citizens, which could receive assistance from the ESI funds to support 'community-led local development strategies' that are consistent with one or more priorities of operational programmes in the Partnership Agreements. While the LAGs would be responsible for designing and implementing the strategies – including the tasks of selecting projects and operations to be funded, monitoring and evaluation – the managing authority (or authorities) would be the MA(s) for the relevant programme(s) at the national or regional level. The member states are also responsible for defining the criteria for selecting the strategies and overseeing the selection process, and for allocating ESI funds to support the strategies. The regulations specify that a first round of selection of CLLD strategies is to be completed within two years of the Partnership Agreement's date of approval, with the selection of additional strategies possible up to the end of 2017 (CEC, 2013a: 355–7).

It is thus too early to determine the success of the new CLLD instrument when it comes to promoting greater local involvement in the use of EU funds. If successful, however, CLLD could provide another valuable means for promoting bottom-up decision-making in regional development policy, while helping to realize the partnership goal of a more participatory and multi-level governance approach to the implementation of development policy.

Conclusion

The promotion of partnership and multi-level governance is an important side effect and a major secondary purpose of cohesion policy. It accomplishes this through application of the partnership principle, which requires the involvement of subnational and non-governmental actors in all stages of the implementation process. After first being introduced in the 1988 structural funds reform, the partnership principle has been progressively strengthened and extended in subsequent policy reforms to embrace new types of public and non-governmental partners. The introduction of a new Community-led Local Development instrument in 2013 could provide yet another means through which cohesion policy can promote a participatory and multi-level approach to economic development policy.

The partnership approach of cohesion policy has generated considerable academic interest in the concept of multi-level governance, with some scholars claiming that cohesion policy could serve as 'the leading edge of a new system of multilevel governance in the EU' (Marks, 1993: 401–2). In fact, cohesion policy has had a highly variable impact on both vertical and horizontal multi-level governance in the EU, with different national institutional structures, administrative traditions and political conditions being the main factors explaining this differential effect. Regarding vertical multi-level governance, while in federal or regionalized member states (such as Germany and Spain), cohesion policy may have strengthened or empowered self-governing regions which already enjoyed substantial policy competences and autonomy, in more centralized member states (in some cases newly created) administrative regions have not been empowered and central governments have managed to maintain firm control of cohesion policy implementation. In the case of horizontal multi-level governance, the key factors appear to be pre-existing traditions of inclusive or collaborative policy-making, the strength of civil society and the capacity of structural funds actors for policy learning. In member states ranking high on all of these variables (e.g. Ireland, the UK, Sweden and Finland), cohesion policy appears to have further bolstered horizontal multi-level governance. In countries ranking low on these variables, however, including the southern and CEE member states, cohesion policy seems to have had a minimal impact on the development of horizontal multi-level governance to date, although some promising signs for the future have been detected.

The governance effects of cohesion policy are thus somewhat controversial when it comes to assessing their extent or significance. Also controversial, however, are the effects of cohesion policy when it comes to achieving its main official goals or purposes. In particular, there is considerable debate over its effectiveness in promoting economic growth and convergence. It is to this debate that we now turn.

Chapter 6

The Economic Impact of Cohesion Policy

Through its alignment with the Lisbon and Europe 2020 strategies cohesion policy has been assigned the task of promoting broader EU economic growth and competitiveness, while also contributing to such goals as the fight against climate change and the promotion of social inclusion. These new tasks have been layered upon the original purpose of cohesion policy, which was the reduction of economic disparities in the EU and the promotion of convergence – or the economic catching up of poorer regions and member states with their wealthier counterparts. Convergence thus remains an official goal of cohesion policy today, even if it is now pursued in the context of cohesion policy's new growth and competitiveness mission.

The impact of cohesion policy on regional economic development and convergence has been extensively studied over the years. In fact, cohesion policy has probably been more evaluated than any other EU policy field (Mendez, 2011: 521). Despite this level of attention, however, there remains considerable debate among experts about the effectiveness of cohesion policy and its contribution to economic growth and convergence. This debate has only intensified over the years and there is a growing body of literature on the topic, some of which is discussed below. Moreover, given the budgetary and economic – not to mention institutional and political – stakes involved, the economic impact of cohesion policy is likely to remain an important topic of study and debate in the future as well.

This chapter examines the economic impact of cohesion policy. It does not offer an original analysis of the effects of cohesion policy on convergence and growth; rather, it surveys the existing literature on this topic and attempts to summarize the main issues and arguments in the debate about the economic impact of cohesion policy. Specifically, it discusses the divergence of views on two central questions: has convergence occurred in the EU since the creation of cohesion policy?

178

And, to the extent that it has, what has been the contribution of cohesion policy to convergence and economic growth in regions and member states that receive EU assistance? Before doing so, however, the chapter begins with a brief discussion of some of the problems involved with evaluating the economic impact of cohesion policy, as well as a look at different methodological approaches for doing so.

Evaluating the impact of cohesion policy

Assessing the economic impact of cohesion policy entails many methodological and operational problems making it, from a methodological perspective, 'an extremely challenging task' (Hart, 2007: 296) and 'an elusive and daunting challenge' (Santos, 2009: 6). For this reason, despite the proliferation of studies examining the impact of cohesion policy, some experts assert that the state of empirical evidence remains very limited and unsatisfactory (Barca Report, 2009: xv, xxii; Leonardi, 2011: 11). Indeed, one prominent study, the 2009 Barca Report, criticized the lack of 'any systematic attempt at EU and national/regional levels to assess whether specific interventions "work" through the use of advanced methods of impact evaluation', as well as 'a very poor use of the system of outcome indicators and targets formally built by the policy' (Barca Report, 2009: xv).

Some problems for evaluation stem from the vague or imprecise meaning of the terms 'cohesion' and 'convergence'. There is still no broad agreement on the definition of either term, and they are interpreted or understood in different ways (Faludi and Peyrony, 2011: 8; Oktayer, 2007: 116). Despite its many other possible meanings (see Tarschys, 2003: 55–67), for the purposes of EU policy 'cohesion' is commonly defined as the reduction of economic and social inequalities (including disparities in income, living standards, employment etc.) between richer and poorer regions within the EU (Bailey and de Propris, 2002a: 410; Oktayer, 2007: 116–17; Faludi and Peyrony, 2011: 8). Convergence, on the other hand, is generally understood to mean the approximation of levels of economic welfare across EU member states and regions, typically measured in terms of GDP per capita adjusted for cost of living (PPP), and it is therefore closely related to economic growth (Oktayer, 2007: 115; Tondl, 1995: 8).

Beyond this basic definitional issue, major problems arise when it comes to determining the impact of cohesion policy, especially in quantitative terms. One of these is multi-causality, or the large number of other potential determinants of a particular observed trend, creating a complex set of cause–effect relationships in which these different variables heavily influence each other (Barca Report, 2009: 46; Hart, 2007: 297; De Michelis and Monfort, 2008: 19). For example, when measuring the impact of cohesion policy on national or regional GDP, one has to take into account the fact that many other factors modify or affect the impact of EU-funded structural operations, including macroeconomic conditions, the functioning of labour and financial markets, various national policies (including regional policies and other redistributive measures) and other EU policies (for instance, competition, agriculture, energy, fishing, transport or social policies) (Hart, 2007: 299; De Michelis and Monfort, 2008: 20). Thus, assessing the impact of cohesion policy requires the evaluator to control and isolate the confounding effects of other potential determinants, for instance through the use of statistical techniques (Barca Report, 2009: xv; House of Lords, 2008: 26; De Michelis and Monfort, 2008: 19). Indeed, these problems accompany the study of any public investment policy, but it is even more vital to recognize them and to exercise care in the causal interpretation of results when it comes to cohesion policy, as it is 'by design multi-sectoral and multi-purpose' (De Michelis and Monfort, 2008: 20).

Another problem in assessing the impact of cohesion policy is that its effects are often indirect rather than direct. However, it is difficult to precisely measure the indirect effects of structural funds spending, such as, for instance, the economic impact of investments in education and lifelong learning or the impact of an infrastructure project (Oktayer, 2007: 124). As a result, due to the number and variety of potential determinants and their complex relationships, as well as the rich plurality of actors and the presence of indirect effects, some experts consider it 'very difficult, if not altogether impossible, to quantify the part of the observed regional trends that can be attributed to cohesion policy' (De Michelis and Monfort, 2008: 19).

Also complicating the task of evaluation is the difficulty of creating the 'without cohesion policy intervention scenario', in an attempt to measure what might have happened if there had been no EU support (Badea, 2011: 7; House of Lords, 2008: 25). According to Santos (2009: 6; 2008: 6), 'To really measure the impact of structural funds one needs to show that they generate benefits above and beyond what those resources would have accomplished if there were no structural funds'. As an example, Trón (2009: 161) argues that 'slow growth and the simultaneous presence of structural support [do] not necessarily signify the ineffectiveness of the aid because it can happen that in a given area the situation would have been much worse without support'. However, proving that this would have been the case is usually extremely difficult.

According to the Barca Report, when it comes to assessing the impact of cohesion policy, especially the question of 'what works':

> the most promising results are offered by a family of methods collectively defined as 'counterfactual' which are aimed at assessing the impact of an intervention by estimating what the outcome would have been had the intervention not taken place, mainly by analysing what happened in respect of a 'similar enough' population which was not targeted by the policy.

Counterfactual analyses, the report argues, tend to be more effective and accountable than any other available method (Barca Report, 2009: xxii). Unfortunately, however, because they are highly demanding and require a substantial amount of good quality information, there is a scarcity of such analyses of cohesion policy (Barca Report, 2009: xxii, 47; Sosvilla-Rivero *et al.*, 2006: 384).

An additional difficulty confronting cohesion policy evaluation is that cohesion policy interventions often take a long time to have any noticeable impact (Badea, 2011: 7; House of Lords, 2008: 26; Mohl and Hagen, 2008: 1–3; Santos, 2009: 5; Trón, 2009: 174, 178). Indeed, it may take many years for structural operations to influence a region's or member state's economic and social system in any visible way. Thus, a 2008 report by the British House of Lords (2008: 26) concluded that the four-year period since the accession of the CEE member states in May 2004 was too short to enable any meaningful evaluation of the impact of EU-funded programmes in these countries, although it was possible to evaluate the effect of cohesion policy on the EU15 cohesion countries that had benefitted from EU assistance for many years. Many evaluators also encounter problems with the low quality of structural funds data, especially at the regional level (Ederveen *et al.*, 2003: 2; Mohl and Hagen, 2008: 1, 4).

Those attempting to evaluate the impact of cohesion policy also have to be careful about generalizing their findings, since what works in one specific region or setting may not necessarily work in others. Moreover, the difficulties in assessing the impact of cohesion policy only grow as the evaluator moves from the specific to the general. As a result, it is much easier to evaluate the impact of individual projects and programmes in specific regions and member states than it is to evaluate the impact of cohesion policy as a whole (Santos, 2009: 6).

Methodological approaches

There are several different approaches used to assess the economic impact of cohesion policy. The first of these are detailed case studies of EU-funded projects, often based on the reports of the implementing authorities. Such studies are useful for evaluating the outcomes and achievements of specific projects, but not for the macro-level analysis of cohesion policy as a whole (Ederveen *et al.*, 2003: 33; Trón, 2009: 159–61, 176). Somewhat broader are the *ex post* evaluations of specific programmes and objectives conducted by independent experts as a normal part of the implementation process. These evaluations, in turn, are summarized by the Commission in its official synthesis reports for specific objectives and programming periods, for instance its 'Synthesis Report' for Objective 2 programmes in the 1994–9 period that was published in 2003 (CEC, 2003). There are also 'descriptive' assessments conducted by the Commission and others which focus on the performance of regions and member states that have been allocated cohesion policy funds. However, as Cappelen *et al.* argue, while this approach allows one to differentiate between successful and unsuccessful cases, it does not provide sufficient evidence to prove an accurate causal relationship between cohesion policy and economic and social outcomes. Moreover, this type of analysis generally utilizes a sampling of regions which is usually too small to be able to produce any general conclusions (Cappelen *et al.*, 2003: 622).

Another approach is the use of model simulations and econometric evaluations. Model simulations are appropriate for *ex ante* assessments of the impact of structural interventions and are able to calculate the potential extent of effects in an optimal political situation, but their (often positive) results are usually heavily influenced by the assumptions built into the models (Barca Report, 2009: 86; Ederveen *et al.*, 2003: 33; Trón, 2009: 161–71, 176). Moreover, the estimates produced by such studies 'are arrived at in an indirect manner (as a shift in investment, for instance), rather than as an assessment of the direct outcome of changes in specific policies or support schemes' (Cappelen *et al.*, 2003: 622). Econometric analyses, by contrast, are well-suited for *ex post* evaluations, which seek 'to match the already existing effects to some trend, detail the causes and reasons and attempt to estimate the actual effects of the supports' (Ederveen *et al.*, 2003: 33; Trón, 2009: 176). According to the Barca Report (2009: 86), however, 'beyond specific suggestions, these [econometric] studies do not offer ... a conclusive general answer on the effectiveness of cohesion policy'. Moreover, this method is used relatively rarely, owing to the lack of reliable data at the regional level (Ederveen *et al.*, 2003: 2).

Model simulations and econometric analyses utilize macroeconomic data, with GDP per head (PPP) serving as the primary indicator of the economic welfare of a country or region (Badea, 2011: 7; House of Lords, 2008: 25; Oktayer, 2007: 115). Disparities between regions and countries are then measured as the standard deviation of their GDP per capita relative to the EU average (Bailey and de Propris, 2002a: 410; De Michelis and Monfort, 2008: 15). The main advantage of this approach is the availability of reliable and consistent data across different regions (House of Lords, 2008: 25). On the other hand, according to de Michelis and Monfort (2008: 15, 20–1) cohesion policy has more varied objectives than just economic convergence, and an exclusive focus on GDP may lead to ignoring other important dimensions and effects of cohesion policy.

Another frequently used indicator when it comes to assessing convergence is the level of (un)employment (Badea, 2011: 7; Barca Report, 2009: 86; House of Lords, 2008: 25; Lóránd, 2011: 4; Oktayer, 2007: 124). There are other possible indicators of relative prosperity as well, including income per capita (either primary income, which is defined as income before taxes and transfer payments, or disposable income after taxes and benefits) that directly accrues to a region's population, and individual consumption per head, which comprises 'household final consumption expenditure (goods and services purchased by households directly) as well as the consumption of individual services, notably health and education services provided by government and non-profit organisations' (House of Lords, 2008: 25). Other alternatives include access to education and healthcare, level of social exclusion, level of innovation, quality of education, quality of the environment or the percentage of human resources in science and technology (Badea, 2011: 7; Barca Report, 2009: 86; House of Lords, 2008: 25; Lóránd, 2011: 4). Nevertheless, with the exception of in-depth analyses and case studies, few evaluations extend beyond the two main indicators of GDP per head and rate of (un)employment, particularly due to the absence of consistent and compatible cross-country statistical data (Badea, 2011: 7).

The Commission's Cohesion Reports

A major source of information about the effects of cohesion policy are the regular Reports on Economic and Social (and since 2010, Territorial) Cohesion produced by the European Commission. The 1993 Maastricht Treaty required the Commission to examine EU progress towards economic and social cohesion and the contribution of cohesion policy to achieving this goal (TEU, 1992: 26). As a consequence, the Commission has published its regular Cohesion Reports every three years beginning in 1996 (except for the five-year gap between the First and Second Cohesion Reports, with the latter published in early 2001) as well as annual Progress Reports in intervening years since 2002. While these reports provide a wealth of information and are generally considered among the most extensive analyses of the economic impact of cohesion policy (Badea, 2011: 7), the Commission's position as the EU body with the main administrative responsibility for cohesion policy creates something of a credibility problem, leading some experts to be cautious about accepting its generally positive assessments of cohesion policy at face value (Eriksson, 2005: 35; Tarschys, 2003).

In its reports, the Commission evaluates the impact of cohesion policy both at the project or programme level and also by means of an aggregative approach, using macroeconomic simulation models that estimate the growth and employment effects of cohesion policy. Regarding the former, the Commission utilizes the results of programme evaluation reports, and it cites cases of successful programmes under specific objectives and Community Initiatives to provide concrete examples. For the latter, the Commission has utilized several types of simulation models which measure how demand and output respond to cohesion policy interventions: the Beutel model, used in the First Cohesion Report in 1996, which 'attempts to capture the technical relationships between sectors of production, as well as the processes through which changes in demand affect supply, and to trace the repercussions of changes affecting one sector on other parts of the economy'; and the Quest and Hermin models, which examine 'demand and output in a less disaggregated way and [focus] on global patterns of consumption and investment behaviour and the way in which they respond and adjust after policy intervention' (CEC, 1996: 98). The latter two models also distinguish between short-term effects on demand and long-term effects on productivity and competitive strength, thus enabling an estimate of the longer term impact of cohesion policy.

In its Fourth Cohesion Report (2007) the Commission utilized a new simulation model, EcoMod, which it describes as a 'multi-sector, "recursive-dynamic" computable general equilibrium (CGE) model' that uses 'a detailed representation of the structure of the economy, notably the behaviour and interaction of different sectors, different types of economic agent (households, firms, etc.) and different types of economic behaviour (consumption, production, investment, etc.)'. According to the Commission, 'The model is therefore well-designed to capture structural shifts, trade effects and dynamic supply-side gains – a key aim of cohesion policy – but is not suitable for measuring short-term, year-on-year changes' (CEC, 2007b: 99).

Has convergence occurred?

The debate about whether or not cohesion policy has been effective in strengthening economic cohesion centres on two key questions: First, to what extent has convergence occurred in the EU since the creation of cohesion policy, both at the level of regions and of member states? Second, if there has been convergence, what has been the contribution of cohesion policy to this process? On both of these questions there are conflicting views and positions. The remainder of this section discusses the question of whether convergence has occurred, while the following section examines the impact of cohesion policy on economic growth and convergence.

The Commission's view

Among the main proponents of the view that significant convergence has occurred in the EU since the 1988 structural funds reform and the creation of cohesion policy is the Commission, although this argument has been made by independent organizations and analysts as well. A major implication of this claim is that cohesion policy has made an important contribution to the convergence process, an issue that is examined further in the next section. The Commission's assertions and findings are mainly documented in its regular Cohesion Reports, which have consistently found that convergence is occurring in the EU at both the regional and member state levels.

In its First Cohesion Report (1996), the Commission found that Objective 1 regions as a group had 'experienced convergence in terms of GDP per head, closing the gap with the rest of the EU by nearly 3 percentage points over the 5-year period 1989–93', although it also noted that the same regions suffered an increase in unemployment during this period. Unemployment also rose in Objective 2 regions in 1989–93, a period marked by recession in the early 1990s, although at a lower rate than for the EU as a whole, while average GDP per capita in these regions also fell. Objective 5b regions, on the other hand, converged with the rest of the EU in 1989–93 with regard to both unemployment and GDP per head (CEC, 1996: 95).

The Second Cohesion Report (2001) reinforced the claim that convergence was occurring in the EU. According to the Commission, between 1988 and 1998 Objective 1 regions had experienced significant convergence, with the average GDP per head of these regions improving from 63 per cent of the EU average at the beginning of this period to 70 per cent at the end, although it also noted considerable differences between individual regions. However, unemployment in the Objective 1 regions remained high and above the EU average (16.6 per cent in 1999 compared with 9.2 per cent for the EU overall), and these regions generally continued to suffer from lower rates of labour force participation and productivity levels as well, once again with considerable variation across regions. When it came to Objective 2 and 5b regions in 1994–5, while unemployment remained 'relatively low and stable in the latter', it declined by more than the EU average in Objective 2 regions (2.2 per cent compared with 1.3 per cent), even though the unemployment rate in both types of regions remained above the EU average, suggesting, according to the Commission, 'that Community assistance has been beneficial' (CEC, 2001a: 129–30).

Convergence was also happening at the member state level, with the Commission noting that since 1988 per capita GDP in the four cohesion countries as a group had risen from 68 per cent of the EU average to 79 per cent in 1999. Ireland was a particular success story, having gone from a per capita income of about 70 per cent of the EU average in the early 1990s to 14 per cent above it by 2001 (CEC, 2001a: 4). The Commission noted that convergence had occurred because annual GDP growth in the four cohesion countries outpaced the EU average in 1994–9, by almost a full percentage point in Spain and Portugal and by

6.5 per cent in Ireland, and it claimed that cohesion policy investments in these countries were a major reason for this faster growth (see below) (CEC, 2001a: 131).

The Third Cohesion Report (2004) claimed continued progress towards convergence among both countries and regions. With regard to the former, the Commission particularly noted the economic success of Ireland, where GDP per head between 1994 and 2001 had increased by almost four times the EU average (8 per cent per year, compared with just over 2 per cent per year for the entire EU) and was now 17 per cent above the EU15 average, whereas it had been 25 per cent below the EU average in the early 1990s. Claiming that cohesion policy was at least partly responsible for this success, the Commission declared that 'The Irish example demonstrates forcibly the effectiveness of Structural Funds' support if combined with growth-oriented national policies' (CEC, 2004a: 2). GDP per capita growth was also higher than the EU15 average in the other three cohesion countries in this period, by about a percentage point. As a consequence, GDP per head in the three countries combined grew to 81 per cent of the EU15 average in 2002 (more than 85 per cent in Spain, and 71 per cent in Greece and Portugal) (CEC, 2004a: 2–3).

The Commission also noted that employment growth in the four cohesion countries was above the EU average. While between 1996 and 2002 the employment rate (the proportion of people of working age, 15 to 64, in jobs) in the EU15 increased by just over 4 percentage points, in the four cohesion countries combined the increase was double this rate although with considerable national variation (Spain, almost 11 per cent; Ireland, 10 per cent; Portugal, 6.5 per cent; and Greece, 2 per cent). As a result, the average employment rate in the four countries rose to 60 per cent by 2002, just 4 per cent less than the EU15 average, and less than half the gap that existed in the mid-1990s (CEC, 2004a: 3).

In terms of convergence at the regional level, the Commission reported that Objective 1 regions collectively had grown at a faster rate than the EU as a whole (3 per cent per year, compared with 2 per cent) between 1994 and 2001, continuing the trend since 1988 whereby GDP per head in the Objective 1 regions 'has converged consistently towards the EU average'. Nevertheless, it noted that in 2001 the 29 Objective 1 regions still had an average GDP per capita that was less than two-thirds of the EU15 average. The Objective 1 regions also recorded greater increases in employment and labour productivity than the EU as a whole in this period, although with substantial differences between individual regions (CEC, 2004a: 6–7).

The Fourth Cohesion Report (2007), the first after the 2004 enlargement, reported continued progress towards economic convergence at both the member state and regional levels, with both the new member states (with the exception of Cyprus) and the four EU15 cohesion countries (except Portugal after 1999) experiencing rates of GDP per head growth in the period 1995–2005 that exceed the EU27 average (CEC, 2007b: 4–5). The Commission also reported that regional disparities had decreased in this period, with the ratio of the average GDP per head level in the wealthiest regions to that in the poorest declining from 4.1 to 3.4 per cent. Lagging regions were also catching up (experiencing higher rates of GDP growth than the EU average), including those in the new member states, with the fastest progress being made by the poorest regions (those with a GDP per capita less than 50 per cent of the EU average) (CEC, 2007b: 7–9). Most of the poorer member states and regions also experienced rates of productivity and employment growth in this period that exceeded the EU average, providing further evidence of convergence and catching up, although in most of these countries and regions unemployment levels remained well above the EU average (CEC, 2007b: 14–29).

The Fifth Cohesion Report (2010) found continued progress towards economic convergence within the EU over the previous decade, with less and moderately developed member states experiencing higher levels of GDP growth than more highly developed member states between 2000 and 2008. Almost all regions in the less developed member states, particularly the new member states, also converged towards the EU average in terms of per capita GDP. As a result, the development gap, measured in terms of GDP per capita, further narrowed between the least and most developed countries in this period, as did regional differentials (CEC, 2010b: 2, 11–13).

However, the Commission's most recent analysis, the Sixth Report on Economic, Social and Territorial Cohesion (2014), found that the 2008 economic crisis had brought this trend of growing convergence to an end, and that since 2008 regional disparities in terms of GDP per head and rates of both employment and unemployment had widened. The Commission found a considerable variation in the impact of the economic crisis on different regions, also leading to a widening of regional disparities across the EU. The economic crisis had also exacerbated regional disparities within member states, while bringing to a halt and reversing the long-term trend towards increased convergence (in terms of GDP per capita) between the member states. Nevertheless, based on the most recent economic data and forecasts, the Commission expressed optimism that this interruption was only temporary, and that the 'long-run process of convergence in the EU', assisted by productivity-enhancing investments funded under cohesion policy, would resume once the economic crisis came to an end (CEC, 2014h: 3–6).

Other analyses and studies

In addition to the Commission, other analysts and studies have argued that convergence has occurred at both at the regional and member state levels since the creation of cohesion policy. Concerning the former, a House of Lords report found that while in 1995 there were 50 underdeveloped regions in the EU15 with a per head income below 75 per cent of the EU average, by 2004, 12 of these regions had moved above 75 per cent of the EU average (House of Lords, 2008: 26). Likewise, de Michelis and Monfort (2008: 18) found that convergence was occurring among EU regions, claiming that 24 per cent of the regions with a GDP per head below 50 per cent of the EU average in 1995 had moved up to the next category (50–75 per cent) by 2005, and that upward movements of GDP per capita by EU regions were much more frequent than downward ones.

The 2009 Barca Report, prepared by an independent expert group on behalf of the Commission, also concluded that 'a strong overall regional convergence has taken place in the EU since the mid-1980s'. Moreover, this 'Overall convergence is largely associated with convergence between countries,' with faster growth especially in the new member states that joined in 2004. The report noted the particular progress of the poorest regions in converging towards the EU average since 1995, especially those in the EU15 cohesion countries and the new member states. However, it also claimed that the convergence process had been slower in the last decade (i.e. 1995–2005) and that significant regional disparities were likely to persist well into the future (Barca Report, 2009: 81–5).

Other analysts have challenged this positive view, however. Boldrin and Canova (2001: 226–7) reject the claim that significant regional convergence has occurred; in fact, they argue that more convergence took place before the late 1970s, that is, in the period before the beginning of EU regional policy. Cappelen *et al.* (2003: 621–4) also argue that the convergence of regional incomes began slowing or even stopped in the early 1980s, followed by a decade of only very limited progress. A similar argument is made by Bailey and de Propris (2002a: 413–14), who claim that a majority of EU regions (with a few exceptions, for example the East German *Länder,* Ireland or the Greek regions of Attiki and Notio Aigaio) did not experience economic convergence, in terms of GDP per capita, over the 1989–97 period.

Also questioning the extent to which convergence has occurred was the 2003 Sapir Report, prepared by a high level study group chaired by the economist André Sapir that was asked by Commission President Romano Prodi to examine the impact of EU economic policies. While the Sapir Report agreed that convergence had occurred in the period 1980–2000 both at the level of member states and six 'macro-regions' (Greece, Spain, Portugal, Ireland, the Italian *Mezzogiorno* and the six East German *Länder*), it also pointed out that across these macro-regions performance varied considerably, with much of the overall convergence driven by the fast growth of Ireland and the East German *Länder*, while Portugal, Greece and Spain grew only slightly faster than the EU average and the Italian *Mezzogiorno* showed no evidence of convergence whatsoever. Moreover, according to the report, despite the evidence of convergence at the member state and macro-region levels, at the more disaggregated level of subnational regions across the EU economic disparities appeared to be growing (Sapir Report, 2003: 59–60).

Other studies have argued that there is more convergence among member states than at the regional level, especially within countries (Cappelen *et al.*, 2003: 623; Badea, 2011: 9; Lóránd, 2011: 2). The Commission itself acknowledged in its Fourth Cohesion Report that regional disparities within member states appeared to widening, at the same time that convergence was occurring at the member state level and between regions within the EU more generally (CEC, 2004a). This trend was also noted by the Barca Report (2009: 81), which concluded that 'within-country gaps have actually widened' since the mid-1990s despite an overall pattern of convergence, and that the widening of internal disparities was particularly significant in some of the new member states. De Michelis and Monfort (2008) also draw attention to increased imbalances within many member states, particularly those that joined the EU in 2004 and 2007, while arguing that there has been a general decline of regional disparities across the EU.

In conclusion, the evidence for convergence appears somewhat mixed. While there has been an overall pattern of convergence since the creation of cohesion policy, this process appears to have lost steam since the mid-1990s, and it has been at least temporarily halted and even reversed by the 2008 economic crisis. Moreover, the convergence that has occurred has been highly variable. It has been especially strong at the member state level, with the EU15 cohesion countries and the new member states that joined in 2004 and 2007 making the most progress (at least until the onset of the economic crisis in 2008). Regional disparities across the EU (between the richest and poorest regions) also appear to have narrowed, although at a slower rate than among the member states; however, there is considerable variation in the performance of individual less developed regions, with some doing much better than others. Perhaps most interesting of all, however, has been the growth of regional imbalances within member states since the mid-1990s, particularly in the new CEE member states, even as a general (but slowing) convergence trend has continued.

The impact of cohesion policy on growth and convergence

To the extent that convergence has occurred in the EU since the late 1980s, what has been the contribution of cohesion policy to this trend? Even though the economic impact of cohesion policy has been extensively studied, there is no consensus in the existing literature on this question. While some studies have found evidence of a positive impact, others suggest a negligible or even negative effect. There are also many experts who believe that the impact of cohesion policy is simply impossible to determine given the lack of adequate data and the great variety of factors affecting economic growth and convergence, or that its impact is highly conditional based on the presence or absence of other factors. Each of these different positions is examined below beginning with the view that cohesion policy has had a positive impact on economic growth and convergence.

Positive impact

Many experts and empirical studies have concluded that cohesion policy does in fact promote economic growth and convergence in target regions and member states. Most studies supporting this view assume that cohesion policy has both a stimulus (increased demand) and supply-side effect. They also argue that by increasing investments in beneficiary regions and member states cohesion policy leads to a higher steady-state flow of capital, thereby increasing a region's or country's GDP (Hagen and Mohl, 2009a: 1).

The Commission's view

Unsurprisingly, the Commission is among the main proponents of the view that cohesion policy has had a positive economic impact. In its First Cohesion Report, the Commission found that cohesion policy had a positive effect in recipient countries and regions, especially the four cohesion countries, both by adding to demand and improving supply-side capacity and efficiency. Utilizing the Beutel simulation model, the report found that in the absence of cohesion policy funds 'GDP growth in the four cohesion countries would have been, on average, almost 1/2% a year lower during the 1989-93 programming period than it actually was', with the beneficial effect varying between countries according to the scale of support relative to GDP (greater in Portugal, Greece and Ireland, where the support ratio was higher, than in Spain, where it was lower). Much of this positive impact, the Commission asserted, was due to the contribution of EU funds to investment in human and physical capital, with structural and cohesion funds expenditure making up about 8 per cent of total capital formation in the four cohesion countries in 1989–93. The Commission also concluded that EU support helped to preserve or create jobs in the four countries, with about 2.5 per cent of their total labour force dependent on EU structural assistance in this period (CEC, 1996: 98–9).

The Commission's analysis using the Quest model showed that the beneficial impact of cohesion policy on economic growth and unemployment in 1989–93 was somewhat less than the estimates produced by the Beutel model, but it also suggested more beneficial longer term effects, with higher GDP growth (1 per cent in Spain, and 2–3 per cent in the other three countries) and lower unemployment in the four cohesion countries by the end of the 1990s than would have been the case without EU support. The estimates produced by the Hermin model found an even greater long-term effect of cohesion policy, with 'the combined contribution of demand and supply-side effects expected to lead to levels of GDP which are 9 per cent higher than they would otherwise have been in Ireland and Portugal and nearly 4 per cent higher in Spain' (CEC, 1996: 99).

The Commission also found that EU assistance had produced positive results under each of the six priority objectives of cohesion policy. Of particular note, the Commission estimated that 530,000 net additional jobs were created by Objective 2 programmes in 1989–93, helping to maintain employment in assisted areas at a level that was between 1.5 and 2.5 per cent higher than would have been the case without EU support. It also claimed that Objective 3 support for human resource development, especially for the young and long-term unemployed, had a net positive effect on the Community-wide job placement rate of 10 per cent (CEC, 1996: 105). The Commission also estimated that because of Objective 5b support for revitalizing rural economies, more than 500,000 jobs would be created or preserved in assisted areas while both population and GDP decline in these areas were being successfully arrested (CEC, 1996: 108–9).

In its Second Cohesion Report, the Commission claimed that EU structural policies 'had significant effects in boosting economic growth in the countries and regions for which analysis is possible', and thus deserved substantial credit for the convergence that had occurred in the previous decade (CEC, 2001a: 130). At the member state level, the Commission noted that in 1994–9 EU funding for Greece amounted to 3.5 per cent of that country's GDP, compared with 3.3 per cent in Portugal, 2.4 per cent in Ireland and 1.5 per cent in Spain. These EU funds provided considerable support for investment in this period, amounting to 15 per cent of total investment in Greece, 14 per cent in Portugal, 10 per cent in Ireland and 6 per cent in Spain. In the Commission's view, these transfers had a significant impact on economic growth, being a key reason why annual GDP growth outpaced the EU average in all four cohesion countries (CEC, 2001a: 122, 131).

Using estimates based on the Hermin model, the Commission claimed that because of cohesion policy, GDP growth in Greece and Spain in 1999 was higher by 9.9 and 8.5 per cent, respectively, than it would have been without EU support. For Ireland and Spain, the growth effect of cohesion policy was somewhat lower (3.7 and 3.1 per cent, respectively) but still significant. The Commission's analysis also showed lower levels of unemployment in all four countries (by 6.2 per cent in Greece, 4 per cent in Portugal, 1.6 per cent in Spain and 0.4 per cent in Ireland) as a consequence of these higher growth rates, and forecast continued positive effects on growth and unemployment because of the longer-term supply-side effects of cohesion policy in these four countries (CEC, 2001a: 130–1).

Once again, the Commission reported considerable success for EU-funded programmes under each of the priority objectives. For instance, it claimed that Objective 3 assistance had contributed to improved employability and job placement rates for the young, long-term unemployed and other disadvantaged groups, with the Commission estimating that 25–50 per cent of placement rates in the member states in 1994–9 could be 'directly attributable to the ESF' (CEC, 2001a: 138). The Commission also claimed that Objective 6 programmes since 1995 had helped increase employment in sparsely populated regions in both Finland and Sweden, with the creation of 17,500 more private sector and manufacturing jobs in Finland and 9,500 in Sweden (CEC, 2001a: 142). In another finding, the Commission concluded that structural funds support for SMEs under various objectives had generated more than 300,000 new jobs throughout the entire EU (CEC, 2001a: 133).

The Third Cohesion Report reinforced the Commission's claim that cohesion policy directly contributed to the process of economic convergence and catching up. According to its macroeconomic simulations, because of EU-funded structural interventions 'GDP in real terms in 1999 was some 2.2 per cent higher in Greece than it otherwise would have been, while in Spain, the figure was 1.4 per cent, in Ireland, 2.8 per cent and in Portugal, 4.7 per cent'. The Commission also claimed that because of the structural funds GDP growth in the East German *Länder* was 4 per cent higher in 1999 than it would have been without this support, while the effect of structural support on GDP growth in Northern Ireland was a more modest 1 per cent. Across Objective 1 regions overall, the Commission found a positive relationship between the amount of structural aid provided and the growth of GDP, with those regions receiving the most aid per person tending to experience higher rates of growth (CEC, 2004a: 147–8). It also concluded that EU structural support helped to keep GDP growth in Objective 2 and 5b areas higher than it otherwise would have been (CEC, 2004a: 151–4).

The Commission also claimed that cohesion policy was linked to increased employment in assisted countries and regions. According to the Commission, structural interventions in Objective 1 regions in the 2000–06 programming period were likely to lead to the creation of around 700,000 jobs (CEC, 2004a: 148). In Objective 2 regions, the Commission estimated that structural funds interventions led to the creation of almost 500,000 jobs in net terms in 1994–9. As a result, unemployment decreased in these areas by more than in the rest of the EU over the programming period (by 3.1 per cent on average between 1996 and 2000 compared with 2.3 per cent in the EU overall), with an especially marked decline of unemployment in areas affected by the restructuring of traditional industries (CEC, 2004a: 151). In Objective 5b regions, the Commission found that structural assistance helped arrest population decline and kept the average level of unemployment below the EU average by almost two percentage points (CEC, 2004a: 154).

At the same time, EU structural support led to increased levels of investment in assisted regions and countries, especially in infrastructure and human capital. According to the Commission, because of EU support such investment was 24 per cent higher in Portugal and 18 per cent higher in Greece in 1999. In both countries, the Commission claimed that structural assistance contributed to the growth of labour productivity at a level that was twice the increase in employment, while it noted that structural funds investments in new technologies spurred growth in employment and productivity in the new German *Länder* as well (CEC, 2004a: 148).

The Fourth Cohesion Report reiterated the claim that cohesion policy was a major contributor to the process of convergence. According to estimates generated by the Hermin model, cohesion policy in 2000–06 had a positive effect on GDP growth in all new member states, EU15 cohesion countries and the Convergence regions of Eastern Germany and the Italian *Mezzogiorno*, ranging from 0.1 per cent in Cyprus to 2.8 per cent in Greece. The model also showed cohesion policy being responsible for employment gains in all assisted countries, of between 0.1 per cent in Cyprus to 2 per cent in Greece, and for the creation of almost 570,000 new jobs by 2006 in these countries and regions. Projecting to 2015 and including cohesion policy spending for 2007–13, the same model estimated an even greater positive impact on GDP growth (ranging from 0.6 per cent in Ireland to 9.3 per cent in Latvia) and employment (0.4 per cent in Ireland to 6 per cent in Latvia), with an expectation of nearly 2 million new jobs created in these countries and regions because of EU structural operations (CEC, 2007b: 95–6).

A new simulation model, EcoMod, also predicted a highly positive impact for cohesion policy on GDP growth in all assisted countries and regions, especially in the new member states, with GDP in Slovakia,

Lithuania and Bulgaria estimated to be about 15 per cent higher by 2020 because of cohesion policy support than would have been the case without it. In the same countries and regions, the model estimated that cohesion policy would be responsible for the creation of over 2 million new jobs by 2015 and 2.5 million by 2020, leading to significant reductions in unemployment (CEC, 2007b: 96–7). The Quest simulation model, on the other hand, predicted more modest near-term gains in GDP growth and employment from cohesion policy for beneficiary countries and regions; however, it also showed that cohesion policy would 'increase the long-term productive potential of the EU as a whole, as well as assisting convergence' (CEC, 2007b: 98).

The report also cited recent evaluations of Objective 2 programmes which indicated that, in the six countries in which the evaluations were carried out (together accounting for more than 54 per cent of the allocations for Objective 2 in 2000–06), more than 450,000 jobs had been created (CEC, 2007b: 98). The Commission claimed that it was more difficult to show a direct link between the expenditure of EU funds and job creation for Objective 3 programmes; nevertheless, in its report the Commission documented support for the establishment of new firms and employment measures in various member states (CEC, 2007b: 100). It also described EU-supported programmes and projects under the various objectives and Community Initiatives that focused on key thematic priorities, including the improvement of transport infrastructure, environmental sustainability, knowledge and innovation, support for SMEs and entrepreneurship, and strengthened human capital and institutional capacity (CEC, 2007b: 100–15).

In its Fifth Cohesion Report, the Commission argued that cohesion policy remained a major contributor to the convergence process. Using estimates provided by the Hermin model, the Commission claimed that cohesion policy had increased GDP in the main beneficiary countries by an average of 1.2 per cent annually over the 2000–06 spending period. As a result, 'by 2009, GDP in these countries is estimated to have been around 11 per cent higher than it otherwise would have been' without cohesion policy (CEC, 2010b: 249–50). While the Quest model estimated the short-term growth effect of cohesion policy in these countries to be somewhat less, it projected a greater long-term effect on GDP (of two percentage points or more for some beneficiary countries in 2014) because of the supply-side benefits of cohesion policy expenditure. According to the Quest model, by 2020 the estimated return from cohesion policy was €4.2 for each euro invested in the 2000–06 programming period, and the cumulative net effect on the EU25 GDP of cohesion policy spending in this period was estimated at 4 per cent (CEC, 2010b: 250–3). Both models also predicted a significant boost to GDP in the beneficiary countries from cohesion policy expenditure in 2007–13, especially for the new member states excepting Cyprus (of 1.0–4.5 per cent over the period 2007–16, according to the Hermin model), with smaller growth effects for the EU15 cohesion countries and the Convergence regions of southern Italy and Eastern Germany (CEC, 2010b: 251).

In its report, the Commission also cited a recent independent academic study of the dynamics of regional GDP growth in the EU15 (later published as Pellegrini *et al.*, 2013) which found that regions eligible for Objective 1 assistance in the years 1995–2006 had grown at an average of 0.6–0.9 of a percentage point faster than non-eligible regions. According to the Commission, this implied 'something like an extra 10 per cent addition to GDP over the two programming periods concerned (1994–1999 and 2000–2006)' as a result of cohesion policy. Moreover, the Commission argued, 'The scale of this effect is much larger than the amount of funding involved (or the direct stimulus to demand from this) which suggests that it mostly reflects a strengthening of the supply-side of the economy in the regions concerned' (CEC, 2010b: 205).

The Commission also claimed a significant impact for cohesion policy on employment, estimating that 'in 2009, the number employed was 5.6 million higher as a result of [cohesion] policy in 2000–2006 … or an average of 560 thousand more a year than without Cohesion policy' (CEC, 2010b: 253). At the programme or project level, the Commission utilized evaluation data for the 2000–06 programming period to show the contributions of cohesion policy to the strengthening of SMEs and competitiveness, support for knowledge and innovation, improvements in the development of human capital and basic infrastructure, the integration of unemployed and disadvantaged groups into the labour market and social inclusion, interregional cooperation, local development and urban regeneration, protection of the environment and other policy objectives (CEC, 2010b: 207–43).

In July 2013, a joint paper from the DGs for Regional and Urban Policy and for Employment, Social Affairs and Inclusion – the Commission departments responsible for the ERDF and ESF respectively, and thus the main DGs involved in the administration of cohesion policy – provided an initial analysis of the impact of cohesion policy in the 2007–13 programming period. Using estimates generated by the Hermin simulation model, the paper claimed that cohesion policy expenditure in this period would increase the GDP of the main beneficiary countries by 1.2 per cent per year between 2007 and 2016. In the new members states (EU12), this growth effect would be even greater, at 2.4 per cent per year. Moreover, the model showed that cohesion policy expenditure would continue having a positive impact on economic growth for years after the end of the implementation period, with a GDP increase of 0.8 per cent in the main beneficiaries and 2.1 per cent in the EU12 in 2020 (CEC, 2013b: 8).

The positive economic impact of cohesion policy was also asserted in the Commission's Sixth Cohesion Report. Based on national reporting, the Commission claimed that by the end of 2012 ERDF-funded programmes for 2007–13 had directly created 593,954 jobs, 'suggesting that by the end of 2015 there might be close to 1.4 million new jobs as a direct result of ERDF support' (CEC, 2014h: 214). It is also claimed that around 3.3 million participants in ESF-supported programmes in this period (up to the end of 2012) had found employment 'soon afterwards' (CEC, 2014h: 219).

The report also contained further evidence of cohesion policy's effects from macroeconomic modelling. Using a version of the Quest model, the Commission analysed the impact of EU assistance provided in the 2000–06 and 2007–13 programming periods on the main beneficiaries of cohesion policy (Spain, Portugal and Italy, the EU12, and the eastern German *Länder* and southern Italy). It found that cohesion policy investments for 2000–06 potentially increased GDP in all examined member states and regions, up to 1.8 per cent a year on average in Latvia, 1.6 per cent a year in Portugal and 1.3 per cent a year in Greece. The same positive effect was estimated for assistance provided in 2007–13, with the average increase in GDP as a result of cohesion policy estimated to be 2.1 per cent a year in Latvia, 1.8 per cent a year in Lithuania and 1.7 per cent annually in Poland. The model simulations also projected an even larger medium- and long-term impact of cohesion policy investment, with 2000–06 assistance projected to increase GDP in Spain by almost 1 per cent by 2015 over what it otherwise would have been, and by almost 3 per cent in both Greece and Portugal. Similarly, 2007–13 investments were projected to increase GDP in both Lithuania and Poland in 2022 by over 4 per cent above what it would have been without these investments, and in Latvia by 5 per cent (CEC, 2014h: 231–3).

The Commission's model simulations also revealed a positive impact of cohesion policy on employment, estimating that 2000–06 programmes increased employment by around 0.5 per cent above what it otherwise would have been in Lithuania and Portugal, and by 0.3 per cent in Poland, Latvia and Spain. Similarly, 2007–13 investments were projected to increase annual employment levels by 1 per cent in Poland, 0.6 per cent in Hungary, and 0.4 per cent in Slovakia and Lithuania. Over the longer run, 2000–06 investments were projected to increase employment in 2014 in Lithuania by 1.3 per cent, and by 0.9 per cent and 0.8 per cent in Latvia and Poland respectively, while 2007–13 programmes were expected to increase employment in 2022 in Poland by 1.8 per cent and by 0.7 per cent in both Hungary and Slovakia (CEC, 2014h: 232–3).

Other analyses and studies

Aside from the Commission, other analyses and studies have argued for the positive economic impact of cohesion policy. For instance, Cappelen *et al.* (2003) have concluded that EU support has had a significant and positive impact on the growth performance of EU regions, thus contributing to greater equality in productivity and income in Europe. De Michelis and Monfort (2008: 22) assert that cohesion policy has helped to

> improve [the] standard of living and economic opportunities in regions, by supporting institutional convergence and administrative modernization; by improving accessibility to and from the regions; by establishing linkages between research institutions, universities and the business community; by improving skills and employability; [and] by providing advanced services to small and medium-sized businesses.

According to Katsaitis and Doulos (2009), the effects of the structural funds are both short-run (on demand) and long-run (on supply), as they both stimulate spending and expand the potential of the receiving economy.

Other studies finding that cohesion policy has had a positive impact on economic growth and convergence include Bouvet (2005; in Hagen and Mohl, 2009b: 24), Beugelsdijk and Eijffinger (2005), Sosvilla-Rivero *et al.* (2006) and Lima and Cardenete (2008). A positive impact is also confirmed by Becker *et al.* (2008), who conclude that €1 of

Objective 1 assistance generates €1.21 of additional GDP in eligible regions. The aforementioned House of Lords (2008: 27) report also comes to the conclusion that the structural funds have helped to reduce economic disparities in Europe. However, while acknowledging this positive impact, many studies touting the achievements of cohesion policy also note that significant regional disparities in the EU remain (Oktayer, 2007: 118, 120; Lóránd, 2011: 1; Tarschys, 2011: 4).

Some studies have focused on the four EU15 cohesion countries, each of which have made considerable progress in catching up with the EU average and the more developed member states. Ireland, in particular, stands out as a success story, and during the 1990s no other member state was able to match its growth. Before 1989, Ireland's GDP per head oscillated between 62 and 66 per cent of the EU average (Oktayer, 2007: 124). By 1996, however, it had almost reached the EU average (Bailey and de Propris, 2002a: 413). During the 1995–2005 period, moreover, Ireland grew at 4 per cent above the EU15 average, and before the 2008 global financial crisis it featured the second highest GDP per head in the EU (House of Lords, 2008: 26).

While not matching Ireland, the other three cohesion countries have also made substantial progress. Between 1995 and 2005, Spain and Greece exceeded the EU15 average growth rate by 0.7 per cent and 1.5 per cent respectively (House of Lords, 2008: 26), although Greece recorded a highly uneven level of performance between 1989 and 1995 (Oktayer, 2007: 124; Tondl, 1995: 14). Portugal, by contrast, boasted a growth rate above the EU average until 1999 (Oktayer, 2007: 124), but it has grown at a rate well below the EU average ever since (House of Lords, 2008: 26).

The success of the EU15 cohesion countries is generally presented as evidence of the positive impact of cohesion policy on economic growth and convergence (Tondl, 1995: 14; Bailey and de Propris, 2002a; Cappelen *et al.*, 2003; Beugelsdijk and Eijffinger, 2005; Oktayer, 2007). Because of this success, moreover, it is argued that cohesion policy offers significant opportunities for promoting economic development in Central and Eastern Europe and for decreasing the development gap between the new member states and Western European countries (Dąbrowski, 2011: 4). A direct causal relationship between the success of the EU15 cohesion countries and the structural funds is not necessarily clear, however. A key factor may have been the Cohesion Fund – national-level assistance available to these four countries because their per capita GDP was below 90 per cent of the EU average. According to Santos (2009: 5), regions in the cohesion countries have benefitted more from EU structural assistance than regions in non-cohesion countries, suggesting a Cohesion Fund effect. The fact that cohesion country regions suffered from the largest economic declines in 1990, recovered by 1992, and since then have gradually grown, also suggests that it was Cohesion Fund assistance after 1993 that made a difference (Bailey and de Propris, 2002a: 413).

No impact or negative effects

In contrast to the view presented above, some analysts are doubtful about the impact of cohesion policy on economic growth and convergence. A study by Boldrin and Canova (2001: 241–2), for instance, found that EU structural policies had no impact on income growth and unemployment in assisted regions, and thus on convergence, and only a marginal impact on labour productivity. As a result, they concluded that EU regional and structural policies 'have little relationship with fostering economic growth', and instead serve mostly a redistributional purpose, motivated by the nature of the political equilibria upon which the European Union is built'. Puga (2002) also concludes that cohesion policy has not been effective in reducing regional disparities within the EU, while Lóránd (2011) found little connection between the level of EU subsidies received and the growth of GDP per head and employment in European regions.

Also doubtful about the economic growth effect of cohesion policy are Ederveen *et al.* (2002, 2003, 2006), who have concluded that EU support equal to 1 per cent of GDP may yield an additional 0.18 percentage points in annual growth of GDP per capita, although in practice only a small portion of this result – about 0.04 per cent – is obtained, making the contribution of EU structural policies to GDP growth relatively insignificant (Ederveen *et al.* 2003: 46). They argue, moreover, that the positive effects of cohesion policy are highly conditional, with cohesion policy most likely to be effective in member states with open economies and the 'right' institutions (see below) (Ederveen *et al.*, 2002, 2006: 25). Similarly, Dall'erba and Le Gallo (2007) have discovered no statistically important impact of cohesion policy on regional growth patterns. A study by Puigcerver-Peñalver (2007), on the other hand, found that the structural funds had a positive impact on regional growth patterns in the 1989–93 programming period, but in the 1994–9 funding period no positive effects were to be observed.

Another study, by Barry *et al.* (2001), challenges the view that cohesion policy has been a major contributor to Ireland's impressive growth since the early 1990s, claiming that structural funds expenditures have had only a modest effect on that country's economic growth and performance.

McAleavy and de Rynck (1997) also question the effectiveness of cohesion policy in bringing about convergence, arguing that EU assistance can even be counterproductive by protecting dominant economic interests in weaker regions and inhibiting structural change. Also claiming that cohesion policy may have negative effects are Hagen and Mohl (2009a), who argue that the structural funds have no positive impact on national public investments in assisted countries, suggesting that EU funds have a 'crowding-out' effect on national spending. Midelfart-Knarvik and Overman (2002), meanwhile, claim that EU structural policies can have a negative impact on industrial location. EU assistance has actually worked against facilitating structural change, they argue, because it has distorted the location of R&D industries by attracting them into areas without the proper endowment of high-skilled workers. They also argue that cohesion policy has not prevented regional polarization, nor has it delivered economic and social cohesion (although they admit it has improved the functioning of state aid in the member states). Also arguing that EU structural policies can have detrimental effects is Tarschys (2003: 81), who claims that the selective subsidies disbursed through cohesion policy have 'distorted [regional development] priorities and skewed competition'. Others argue that cohesion policy has encouraged 'rent-seeking' behaviour and corruption among public officials, especially at the regional level. In Hungary, for instance, Horváth (2008: 197) claims that cohesion policy has led to the emergence of 'a new type of elite … based on the power to redistribute economic development resources'.

Variable or conditional impact

Other experts believe that it is impossible to conclusively determine the impact of cohesion policy on economic growth and convergence. Many also argue that cohesion policy's impact has been highly variable across the member states and regions due to a variety of factors. They argue, in other words, that cohesion policy is only conditionally effective, depending on the fulfilment of a number of key parameters.

Many analysts believe that it is simply not possible to isolate and conclusively determine the beneficial effects of cohesion policy. Tarschys (2003: 41–54), for example, claims it is difficult to disentangle the impact of cohesion policy from a number of other factors, including broader economic integration effects, the impact of national regional development policies and the redistributive effect of other national policies (taxation, entitlements, etc.), and the effects of other EU policies outside the sphere of cohesion policy. He concludes, therefore, that while EU structural policies may have contributed to the convergence that has occurred within the EU, the magnitude of this contribution 'cannot be pinned down' (Tarschys, 2003: 54).

The Sapir Report also found little evidence that EU funds had boosted the economic performance of lagging regions and promoted convergence with wealthier regions, claiming that 'there was not enough regional GDP data to distinguish the effects of cohesion polices in the absence of data on other regional characteristics, such as initial income, human capital, local industrial structures, quality of local administration, the peripheral nature of the region, and of random influences'. 'The net result', it claimed, 'is that it is not possible to establish conclusively what the relative performance of these regions would have been in the absence of EU cohesion policy and other policies' (Sapir Report, 2003: 60).

Although the Barca Report was generally supportive of cohesion policy, it also concluded that the weakness of existing macroeconomic simulation and econometric models, the absence of adequate impact evaluations for EU-funded programmes and the poor quality of quantitative targets and indicators, meant that there was insufficient 'macro and micro quantitative systematic evidence ... to produce a definitive assessment of cohesion policy' (Barca Report, 2009: 86–91). With regard to macro-level analysis in particular, it also noted the 'serious problems' for assessment that 'come from the great difficulty of isolating at macro-level the effects of cohesion policy from those of several external confounding factors, including the effects of seemingly spatially-blind policies, i.e. of building an acceptable counterfactual' (Barca Report, 2009: 87)

Other experts assert that the impact of cohesion policy is conditional on other factors, such as the existing level of development and the quality of institutions and policies at both the national and regional levels. For instance, Cappelen *et al.* (2003) argue that the positive effects of cohesion policy are much stronger in more developed environments, and they emphasize the importance of accompanying policies that improve the institutional competences of targeted areas. As the effectiveness of cohesion policy is heavily dependent on the receptiveness of the receiving environment, they argue, it tends to be least efficient where it is most needed, because poor regions usually suffer from an unfavourable industrial structure (with the prevalence of agriculture) and the lack of research and development capacities.

Similarly, de Michelis and Monfort (2008: 18) observe that the catching-up process of poor regions seems to be more pronounced in the EU15 than in the EU27, with more than 45 per cent of EU15 regions with a GDP per head below 60 per cent of the EU average in 1995 having moved up to the next category (60–75 per cent) by 2005, while only 24 per cent of EU27 regions with a GDP per head of less than 50 per cent of the EU average managed to move upward in that same period. Canova (1999; in Beugelsdijk and Eijffinger, 2005: 41) found that also within individual member states rich regions tend to grow more quickly than poor ones, although the rich regions of poor countries grow at a faster pace than similar regions in wealthier countries. Along similar lines, Santos (2008: 3) argues that cohesion policy interventions are growth-maximizing in wealthier regions of the member states where capital is most productive.

Lóránd (2011: 3), however, argues that cohesion policy can be effective in underdeveloped regions if other supportive policies on the national and regional level are present. In this vein, Tondl (1995) emphasizes the importance of macroeconomic stability for the success of structural policies. Santos (2008: 3; 2009: 5), meanwhile, contends that regional interventions are more effective when it comes to promoting growth the more coherent they are with national policies.

In their frequently cited study, Ederveen *et al.* (2002, 2006) found that the effectiveness of cohesion policy is conditional on the quality of the institutional set-up in the receiving countries, with the quality of institutions being manifested by several quantitative measures, including corruption, inflation and openness. Cohesion policy support, they argue, is more likely to be effective in member states with open economies and less likely to be effective in closed ones; this is because openness disciplines governments and leads to a more productive use of cohesion support (Ederveen *et al.* 2002). De Michelis and Monfort (2008: 20) arrive at a similar conclusion, emphasizing 'institutional thickness', which is 'increasingly recognized as decisive in determining the effectiveness of public investments at national and sub-national level and explaining difference in performance in regions with similar socioeconomic structures'.

The Sapir Report (2003: 61) also argued that the effectiveness of EU structural policies was influenced by the quality of local administration and policies as well as by national macroeconomic conditions and policies. It thus recommended that in a reformed cohesion policy convergence funding should be given only to poorer countries and focused on institution-building as well as improving human and physical capital (Sapir Report, 2003: 146-7). Similar arguments have been made by Hurst *et al.* (2000), who stress the importance of the quality of regional government for the effectiveness of development programmes, and by Katsaitis and Doulos (2009), who claim that the impact of the structural funds on foreign direct investment inflows critically depends on the receiving countries' institutional quality. Tondl (1995) also emphasizes the importance of a well-functioning and transparent institutional framework for the effective use of structural funds.

Badea (2011) agrees that a low level of institutional development – reflected in high levels of corruption, local elitism and political clientelism – inhibits innovation and growth, thereby decreasing the potential impact of cohesion policy, although Beugelsdijk and Eijffinger (2005: 50) have found that structural funds assistance can also generate economic growth in more corrupt countries. Santos (2008: 3; 2009: 5), meanwhile, stresses the importance of a region's strategic behaviour, as regions often 'implement projects that have other objectives besides growth, either to pursue rent-seeking activities or to retain their [structural funds] eligibility'. The tendency towards rent-seeking behaviour is also mentioned by Trón (2009: 161), who claims that 'regional plans are often designed to receive the structural funds' money rather than to help efficient allocation of expenditure'. Tondl (1995) highlights the fact that regions benefit more from cohesion policy if they have a good understanding of their own structural problems, while Bähr (2008) argues that cohesion policy is more effective in countries with a highly decentralized administrative structure, because regional authorities tend to have better information about regional growth needs and projects, leading to better implementation.

The argument that such factors as institutional quality and the strategic behaviour of regional governments are key determinants of the success of structural interventions highlights a major problem for cohesion policy, and that is the unequal ability of EU regions to benefit from cohesion policy assistance, with less developed regions being at a distinct disadvantage in this regard. This divergence in capacities, in turn, could result in the further marginalization of disadvantaged regions and the exacerbation of regional disparities rather than their amelioration. According to Bailey and de Propris (2002b: 409), for instance, 'the inability of the weakest regions to exploit the full potential of the Structural Funds' could have negative consequences, leaving them further 'isolated ... from the core of the EU, thereby preventing them from benefitting from the alleged efficiency gains of the Single Market, as well as threatening the political objective of cohesion, solidarity and equity'.

Finally, looking at things from a different perspective, some experts also consider the type of investment an important variable for explaining variation in cohesion policy effectiveness. Dall'erba and Le Gallo (2007: 220), for instance, observe that investment in human capital tends to reduce inequalities among member states and regions more effectively than investment in infrastructure. Similarly, Rodríguez-Pose and Fratesi (2004) found that structural spending in Objective 1 regions has a limited impact on growth overall, but that a positive effect was generated only by investments in education and human capital. Mohl and Hagen (2008), on the other hand, focus on the type of objective, concluding that while Objective 1 payments promote growth in assisted regions, Objective 2 and 3 payments actually have a negative impact on a region's growth rate.

Explaining divergent evaluations of cohesion policy

Why does the existing literature yield such mixed (if not to say, contradictory) evidence, according to which cohesion policy's impact on economic growth and convergence can be seen as both a success and failure at the same time? There are several explanations for these heterogeneous results.

One is that different studies use different methodologies and research models (Bachtler and Gorzelak, 2007: 314; Dall'erba and Le Gallo, 2007: 220; Ederveen *et al.*, 2003: 31; De Michelis and Monfort, 2008: 19; Puigcerver-Peñalver, 2004: 3; Trón, 2009: 155–6). For example, while econometric analyses, of the type used in most of the above-cited studies, focus on the actual impact of cohesion policy, model simulations, such as those used by the Commission, measure its potential effect. Consequently, obtained results from the first type of study are inevitably lower and more pessimistic than the estimates from the second method of investigation (Ederveen *et al.*, 2003: 31; Trón, 2009: 161–74, 176).

Another explanation is the different theoretical and philosophical assumptions underlying various research models (Bachtler and Gorzelak, 2007: 315; Ederveen *et al.*, 2003: 12–22; Trón, 2009: 155). For instance, the two main economic growth theories, neoclassical and endogenous growth theories, make different assumptions about the sources of economic growth and thus arrive at different conclusions when it comes to the possibilities for convergence. While neoclassical theories assume a natural tendency towards convergence in an open market because of the dynamics of comparative advantage (diminishing returns to capital in wealthier countries and higher productivity margins in poor ones) and the diffusion of capital and technology from wealthy to poor countries, endogenous theories focus on the internal sources of technological progress, such as R&D efforts and the accumulation of ideas and human capital, that can lead to permanent technological and income gaps between countries and inhibit convergence. Such divergent beliefs and underlying assumptions, in turn, lead econometric or simulation models based on these theories to produce very different results (Oktayer, 2007: 115–16).

Another factor leading to significant divergence in assessments of cohesion policy is the differing time spans under investigation, i.e. the different periods of time during which the effects are being observed (Bailey and de Propris, 2002a: 411; Dall'erba and Le Gallo, 2007: 220; Mohl and Hagen, 2008: 1–2). Divergent evaluations can be also explained by differences in the chosen sample (number and types of targeted countries or regions) (Bailey and de Propris, 2002a: 420; Dall'erba and Le Gallo, 2007: 220; Mohl and Hagen, 2008: 2) or the analysed cohesion policy objective (Mohl and Hagen, 2008). However, they may also be explained by the complexity of the process under investigation and the inadequacy of existing tools for assessing it. According to the Barca Report (2009: 87), for instance, the inconclusive results of cohesion policy evaluations thus far can be attributed to 'the complexity of the growth and convergence process and to the failure to model it over time and over different countries and regions which are characterised by very different institutional, economic and social conditions'.

Whatever the explanation, the divergent evaluations of cohesion policy and its effectiveness in promoting economic growth and convergence provide ample ammunition for both supporters and critics of cohesion policy alike. It is yet another variation on the theme of 'something for everyone' that is so associated with EU cohesion policy – as already seen when it comes to the allocation of funding and the pursuit of diverse goals and objectives, and now when it comes to assessing the economic impact of cohesion policy as well.

Conclusion

Even after nearly two decades of intensive study and analysis, the debate about the economic impact of cohesion policy remains very unsettled and unclear. There are disagreements about the extent to which convergence has occurred in the EU and differing views about the contributions of cohesion policy to this process, including its effectiveness in promoting economic growth and employment in assisted member states and regions. While the Commission adheres to a generally positive view of the impact of cohesion policy, an assessment that is also supported by numerous independent experts and studies, many other analysts are highly sceptical of the benefits of EU structural spending, with some even claiming that it has negative effects. These differing assessments are the outcome of different methodological techniques and approaches used to study the impact of cohesion policy, as well as the divergent theoretical assumptions and ideological beliefs of the investigators, with differing institutional and political interests also no doubt playing a role. At most, there appears to be a general consensus regarding both the difficulty of isolating the effects of cohesion policy from other growth and employment-affecting variables. There also appears to be a growing acknowledgement of the conditional impact of cohesion policy and the importance of other institutional and policy factors for the effective use of the structural funds, as reflected in the emphasis on institutional capacity and other *ex ante* conditionalities (for example, the implementation of certain EU policies and rules) in the new cohesion policy regulations for 2014–20. This lack of consensus about the economic impact or added value of cohesion policy plays an important role in debate about the future of cohesion policy, a topic which is examined further in the next chapter.

Chapter 7

Conclusion: The Future of Cohesion Policy

After final approval of the new regulations for cohesion policy by the Council and European Parliament in December 2013, the implementation of cohesion policy for the 2014–20 programming period officially began. Partnership Agreements for each of the member states were finalized and operational programmes formulated by national authorities in cooperation with regional, local and non-governmental partners. On the basis of these agreements and programmes, over the course of the next seven years more than €350 billion (2014 prices) will be disbursed to Managing Authorities in the member states to fund programmes aimed at developing transportation and ICT infrastructure, promoting innovation and R&D, enhancing the competitiveness of SMEs, improving energy efficiency and promoting the shift to a low-carbon economy, strengthening education and training systems, and ending discrimination and combatting poverty, all with the ultimate goal of reducing economic and social disparities in the EU while supporting the Europe 2020 strategy of 'smart, sustainable and inclusive' growth.

The direction of cohesion policy in the next seven years is thus clear, but what about the future of cohesion policy beyond the current programming period? Will cohesion policy continue to be funded at or near its current level, or will cohesion policy expenditure in the future be dramatically curtailed? Will cohesion policy continue with its present dual mission of promoting economic convergence and the reduction of regional disparities, on the one hand, *and* economic growth and competitiveness in alignment with EU strategic priorities, on the other, or will an entirely new policy mission or rationale emerge? And will cohesion policy continue to operate throughout the entire EU, with all member states and regions eligible for assistance as is currently the case, or will cohesion policy in the future be targeted at just the very poorest member

209

states and regions? Indeed, will cohesion policy as we know it today even continue to exist beyond the end of the current funding cycle?

This chapter examines these questions and the future of cohesion policy more generally. It begins by examining the economic and political context emerging from the global financial and euro-zone crises that will influence future decision-making on the EU budget and cohesion policy. Key elements of his context include continued slow economic growth, the growing dominance of Germany in the EU, the EU's accentuated north–south rift, and the growth of euroscepticism and populist nationalism and its impact on domestic politics and EU institutions. After outlining these developments, the chapter discusses their potential consequences for cohesion policy going forward, while it also seeks to answer the questions posed above.

The EU economic and political context after the euro-zone crisis

Although at the time of writing the implementation of cohesion policy for 2014–20 is just underway, it will not be long before discussion of the next policy reform, for the period beyond 2020, begins. This will take place in parallel with preliminary discussions on the next MFF, which are likely to begin soon after the 2016 mid-term review of the present budgetary framework. This discussion will be greatly influenced by the economic and political context in which it occurs, as have all previous rounds of cohesion policy reform. While it is impossible to forecast precisely what this context will be several years hence, it seems reasonably clear that it will be shaped by the experience of the euro-zone crisis and its lingering effects on the European economy and domestic and EU politics. In the remainder of this section, the economic impact of the euro-zone crisis and three key political effects – the growing dominance of Germany in the EU, the deepening north–south divide between rich and poor member states, and the growth of euroscepticism and populist nationalism – are briefly examined.

The euro-zone crisis and the EU economy

The euro-zone crisis has hit Europe hard and left a lasting imprint on its economy and politics. After more than four years of bank crises, spiking bond yields, emergency bailout packages engineered by the EU, European Central Bank (ECB) and International Monetary Fund (IMF) (the so-called troika) – for first Greece, followed by Ireland, Portugal, Greece again, and then Cyprus – accompanied by plunging rates of economic growth and soaring unemployment in heavily indebted countries, by early 2014 the economic picture finally seemed to be improving. It was reported by Eurostat, the EU's statistical agency, that in the first quarter of 2014 the EU28 had recorded a GDP growth 0.3 per cent (0.2 per cent for the 18 member states of the euro-zone) compared with the previous quarter. This marked the fourth consecutive quarter of growth for the EU economy, after more than six years (stretching back to 2008) of negative or very low growth, indicating that the EU might finally by exiting the crisis and returning to a more stable, growth-oriented pattern (Eurostat, 2014a). Perhaps most important, international bond markets had stabilized over the previous year, easing borrowing requirements for highly indebted euro-zone countries and creating breathing space for Spain and Italy, making it less likely that these two member states would also need bailout assistance. In the cautiously optimistic words of Olli Rehn, the EU Commissioner for Economic and Financial Affairs, as he presented the Commission's 'Winter 2014' economic forecast, 'the worst of the crisis may now be behind us' (CEC, 2014f).

Still, the EU economy remains very troubled, burdened by continued high levels of government debt and a weak banking sector. Unemployment also remains high, at nearly 11 per cent for the EU28 in early 2014, and much higher in the worst-affected countries, including nearly 27 per cent in Greece and 25 per cent in Spain (Eurostat, 2014b). According to some experts the EU also risked sliding into a potentially devastating deflation – a downward spiral of prices and economic activity that is difficult to pull out of, such as experienced by Japan in the early 1990s – with a near-zero (0.15) ECB interest rate and euro area inflation (in May 2014) of only 0.5 per cent (Eurostat, 2014c). Adding to the worries was the EU's slow progress in finalizing the creation of a new banking union, especially when it came to the establishment of a permanent authority and fund for closing and restructuring troubled banks (Hirst, 2014). As a result, while the worst of the euro-zone crisis might be over, the EU economy remained weak and highly vulnerable to new economic shocks, whether coming from within or externally generated.

Moreover, economic recovery is likely to be slow well into the future. In May 2014, the Commission projected EU28 economic growth of only 1.6 per cent for the year (1.2 per cent for the euro-zone), rising to 2 per cent in 2015 (1.7 per cent in the euro-zone) (CEC, 2014g: 1). While this is movement in the right direction, it is not likely to lead to a substantial reduction of unemployment, nor will it provide the kind of growth necessary to allow the highly indebted countries most affected by the crisis to significantly lower their debt and regain lost wealth and income. The EU economic climate for the foreseeable future, in other words, is likely to remain difficult, and it should continue to serve as a constraining factor on both national and EU spending.

The euro-zone crisis and the member states – the rise of Germany

While the euro-zone crisis has left its mark on the EU economy, it has also had a profound impact on EU politics and relations between the member states. In particular, the economic crisis has shifted the balance of power in the EU even more sharply in favour of Germany, the Union's most economically dominant member state. While Germany has always been a major power in the EU its behaviour was traditionally constrained by a variety of political, cultural and historical factors. While many of these constraints remain, the euro-zone crisis has accentuated Germany's relative dominance in economic terms and given rise to demands that it play a political leadership role more commensurate with its economic strength.

A greater leadership role for Germany would represent a significant change in its traditional EU behaviour, which has been based on three key facts or preferences:

1. Germany's position as Europe's leading economic and monetary power, based primarily on its manufacturing and exporting prowess, as well as the success of its supply-side and monetarist economic approach that emphasizes low inflation, sound money, a conducive regulatory framework for the operation of markets and the social-market economy ('Ordoliberalism').
2. Germany's preference for more European integration, both economic and political, both as a way to expiate past national-

ist sins and to embed growing German power in a European context, in order to hide the exercise of that power and make it less offensive or threatening to other Europeans.
3.   Germany's unwillingness to be assertive or play a leadership role, at least on its own, because of the past and the continued suspicions of German power held by others.

These three factors or preferences underpinned two key characteristics of Germany's behaviour in the EU:

1.   its role as 'paymaster' for the EU, in which Germany would make large net contributions to the EU budget in order to achieve intergovernmental consensus and more integration;
2.   its special partnership with France – the so-called Franco-German partnership – which for many years served as the primary 'motor' or engine of EU integration.

Even though Germany's economic power had long eclipsed that of France, German governments would generally let France exercise political leadership in the partnership, in deference to both French sensibilities and the wariness of other Europeans of German power. By acting as 'paymaster' and in close partnership with France, therefore, Germany could utilize its growing economic power to influence EU decision-making, but in a way that furthered European integration and consensus while not threatening or upsetting others.

By and large this pattern continued to define Germany's role in the EU even after unification in 1990, which many feared would unbalance European politics and open the window for a more assertive and nationalistic Germany. The German response to these fears, of course, was to support more integration, both economically through EMU, and politically through more cooperation on foreign policy and defence. Germany did not agree to more integration without getting anything in return, however. Instead, the bargain that Germany drove in the negotiations for the 1992 Maastricht Treaty was to give up the Deutsche Mark and German monetary dominance in return for an EMU that was organized in accordance with Germany's own stability-oriented monetary philosophy, and an ECB that essentially replicated the political independence and statutory focus on low inflation of the German central bank (the *Bundesbank*) (Baun, 1995, 1996). Increased German policy independence was exhibited in its pre-emptive decision to recognize the independence of Slovenia and Croatia in December 1991, before a common EU position could be reached, while the more nationally assertive rhetoric of Chancellor Gerhard Schröder (1998–2005) indicated that a generational change in leadership could undermine the German political elite's traditional willingness to put European interests ahead of strictly national interests (Baun, 1997). Beginning with Schröder and continuing under Merkel as well, German governments became more critical of the Commission and the negative impact on German industrial interests of EU policies. Germany's complaints about its paymaster role also date back to the late 1990s, as the negative economic impact of unification and efforts to subsidize and rebuild Eastern Germany began to take effect. For the most part, however, even after unification continuity rather than change basically defined Germany's role as an EU actor.

The euro-zone crisis, however, appears to have significantly impacted Germany's position and role in the EU. As Europe's dominant economic power, Germany has used the crisis as an opportunity to further impose a German fiscal and economic template on the EU, going beyond what already existed with EMU and the ineffective Stability and Growth Pact (SGP). Evidence of Germany's influence can be seen in the March 2012 Fiscal Compact treaty, which further tightened the EU's rules limiting member state budget deficits, as well as the 2011 'six pack' legislation, which reformed the SGP and created the basis for stricter EU oversight of member state macroeconomic policies. At the same time, the German government has firmly resisted efforts to 'communitarize' the problems of highly indebted countries through the issuance of Eurobonds or other measures that would make the EU into a 'transfer union' (Bulmer and Paterson, 2013: 1395–6). The German government has also resisted the calls of the US government, southern member states, and some economic experts to drop its insistence on austerity as a condition of EU bailout assistance and to support a more expansionary European economic policy, and it has criticized the efforts of the ECB and its president Mario Draghi to stimulate the European economy through bond purchases and other market interventions.

Germany's actions have been driven by perceptions of national interest and the ideological views of its political and economic elites. However, they are also supported by domestic popular opinion, with many Germans resentful about having to bail out 'irresponsible' debtor countries. As evidence of the unpopularity of the bailouts – to which Germany, as the euro-zone's wealthiest member state, was the main contributor – and of a growing sense of 'Europe fatigue' (*Europamüdigkeit*) among the German public, in the campaign for the September 2013 parliamentary elections, eventually won by Merkel's conservative CDU/CSU and resulting in the formation of a 'grand coalition' government with the centre-left Social Democratic Party, there was a studious avoidance of EU issues by all of the main political parties and candidates (Euractiv.com, 2013i). Another factor in Germany's EU policy is the Federal Constitutional Court (FCC), which in a series of rulings in recent years has created greater domestic political constraints on federal government decision-making, by requiring the approval of the German parliament (*Bundestag*) for any further non-treaty transfers of sovereignty to the EU, and for the contribution of additional resources to the European Stability Mechanism (ESM) bailout fund (Ewing, 2014). As a result of these developments, German governments must increasingly look back over their shoulder to gauge domestic reactions to EU policy decisions, both by the public and by independent governmental institutions such as the FCC and the *Bundesbank* (Bulmer and Paterson, 2013: 1398–1400).

Germany's increased leadership role in the EU is not only the result of how the euro-zone crisis has accentuated and emphasized its relative economic power, it is also due to the impact of the crisis on other EU countries. In particular France's economic position has been weakened by the crisis, making it a less credible partner for Germany and undermining the functional effectiveness of the Franco-German partnership. While the French government has continued to assert the need for growth-enhancing measures to balance the German-led emphasis on stability, this has not yet led to any concrete EU actions, with the exception of the repurposing of unspent structural funds to guarantee EIB loans as part of the 'Compact for Growth and Jobs' that was agreed to by EU leaders in June 2012 (European Council, 2012: 12). The euro-zone crisis has stripped bare the public fiction of Franco-German parity, in other words, and left no doubt about where real power in the EU lies, even if Germany's newfound hegemony is 'reluctant and contested', and constrained both domestically and by the hesitancy of other European countries to accept it (Bulmer and Paterson, 2013: 1401).

On the other hand, in a sign that German leadership may be desired and increasingly viewed as legitimate, the foreign minister of Poland, a country that has been historically victimized by Germany and thus has plenty of reasons to be suspicious of its growing influence, famously exclaimed in November 2011 that he feared Germany's power 'less than ... its inactivity'. Germany, he argued, must play a stronger leadership role in the EU to help it overcome its problems, especially those caused by the euro-zone crisis (Sikorski, 2011: 9).

The EU's growing north–south divide

The euro-zone crisis has not only shifted the balance of power within the EU in favour of Germany, it has also accentuated the Union's already existing north–south divide between wealthy and poor member states. This divide first began to emerge with the accession of Greece, Spain and Portugal in the 1980s, but it was papered over by the expansion of structural funds assistance and creation of the Cohesion Fund, through which the wealthier member states channelled EU funds to poorer countries to gain their acceptance of further economic integration and liberalization (the single market and EMU). It became a bigger issue in budgetary negotiations in the late 1990s, as the EU prepared for Eastern enlargement and Germany, facing economic difficulties at home, began to balk at continuing to play its traditional paymaster role, and it has been the dominant feature of EU budgetary politics ever since (see Chapter 3).

The euro-zone crisis has only deepened this intra-EU split, which pits wealthier northern European countries that are the main net contributors to the EU budget – Germany, the Netherlands, the UK, Sweden, Austria and Finland – against poorer member states from southern and Central and Eastern Europe that are net budgetary recipients and the primary beneficiaries of cohesion policy. It has done this in two key ways: by accentuating the underlying structural advantages of the wealthier member states and widening the competitive gap between them and the poorer countries, and by intensifying the struggle for resources within the EU when it comes to the budget and spending. The limited flexibility and options left to highly indebted countries within the euro-zone, and the harsh austerity and structural reform measures imposed by the contributor countries as a condition of bailout assistance, have also embittered the citizens of the bailout countries and worsened the north–south split, as has the resentment felt by the citizens of the wealthier countries at having to rescue 'irresponsible' debtors.

In structural terms, the crisis has exposed the basically uncompetitive position (high labour costs, over-regulation, bloated and inefficient public sectors, etc.) of southern euro-zone members – Greece, Portugal, Italy and Spain – which for more than a decade was hidden by the low borrowing costs resulting from euro-zone membership. Once the ability to borrow cheaply was cut off after 2009, the fundamental weakness of these economies was laid bare. Some of the CEE member states have also been hit hard by the global financial and euro-zone crises, especially Hungary and Latvia, although the latter has since recovered and even joined the euro area, and Cyprus, which required its own bailout in early 2013 after the collapse of its banking sector. Other CEE countries, including Poland, the Czech Republic and Slovakia, have not suffered as much, in large part because of their economic ties to Germany. However, these former communist countries remain relatively less developed and economically disadvantaged, and despite the considerable progress they have made since the 1990s they are still struggling to catch up economically with their wealthier northern and western European counterparts.

While the non-euro area CEE countries retain the option, theoretically at least, of restoring competitiveness by allowing a devaluation of their currencies, this is not a possibility for countries using the euro. Instead, their choices are limited to basically two: either leave the euro-zone, or restore competitiveness via 'internal devaluation', which means the adoption of harsh austerity measures and brutal structural reforms in order to lower the domestic costs of production. Since the former option is unpalatable for many reasons and could have untold negative consequences for the exiting country and for EMU and the EU overall, and thus it is not favoured by either the debtor countries or other euro-zone members, the remaining option is to accept EU/IMF bailout assistance in return for the harsh conditionalities of austerity and structural reform.

There is, however, a third option for dealing with the EU's competitiveness gap, and that is for wealthier 'surplus' countries – those enjoying a consistently positive structural trade balance – to intentionally reduce their competitive edge, by allowing wages to rise and stimulating their economies through more government spending, for instance. In this manner, the competitiveness advantage of the surplus countries would be reduced, and larger markets for the exports of the 'deficit' countries would be created. In practice, this option concerns mainly Germany, which is not only the EU's largest economy but also among its most competitive after undergoing its own difficult structural reforms in the late 1990s and early 2000s. As a consequence, Germany consistently runs a large annual surplus in intra-EU (and also external) trade at the expense of poorer deficit countries (Eurostat, 2013d). Indeed, it is this competitive imbalance that many experts feel is at the root of the euro-zone crisis (Kirkegaard, 2011). However, asking Germany to voluntarily reduce its competitiveness – as some in the EU and the US government indeed have done – means asking it to negate the sacrifices made more than a decade ago, while such actions would also contradict the dominant stability-oriented consensus of German political and economic elites and the broader populace. It has thus not been seriously considered by Germany as a solution to Europe's economic problems.

The widened north–south economic split has inevitably translated into a north–south political divide when it comes to debate on EU policies and the budget. The economic crisis has bolstered the demands of wealthier member states that have called for reduced EU spending, both as a way of limiting their own net contributions, which they argue is justified by domestic fiscal and budgetary constraints, and as a proper reflection at the EU level of the budget-cutting and austerity measures being undertaken by member states at the national level. These demands are opposed by poorer net recipients, who argue that EU spending that shifts resources from wealthier to poorer member states is necessary to honour the Union's fundamental commitment to solidarity, especially at a time of economic crisis. The poor member states also assert the practical economic need for EU structural spending, as a source of growth-inducing public investment at a time of national budgetary consolidation. In making this case they are supported by the Commission, which claims that together with the co-financing provided by the member states, cohesion policy represented more than 50 per cent of total public investment in 10 EU countries in 2010–12, all of them but Portugal new member states; in some countries, such as Romania, Hungary and Bulgaria, this figure exceeded 80 per cent (CEC, 2013b: 4).

Finally, in making the case for EU spending, on cohesion policy in particular, the poor member states also appeal to the economic self-interest of the wealthier countries, arguing that they are ultimately major beneficiaries of cohesion policy assistance since much of this money ends up in the hands of their own companies. In March 2012, for example, the Polish government released the results of a study sponsored by its regional development ministry which found that every euro paid into cohesion policy by Germany since 2004 had generated €1.25 in revenues from German exports to four CEE countries: Poland, Hungary, the Czech Republic and Slovakia. The study also found that the EU15 member states will earn a total of €74.69 billion in exports from cohesion policy expenditure over the period 2004–15 (Expatica.com, 2012).

In the end, the EU's north–south split is not a permanent division that precludes either upward or downward mobility. A good case in point is Ireland, which after decades as one of the EU's 'poor four' experienced explosive economic growth in the 1990s that elevated it above the EU per capita GDP average, only to slide back again after the 2010 banking collapse to become one of the ignominious 'PIGS' (Portugal, Ireland, Greece and Spain) – the four highly indebted member states most affected by the euro-zone crisis. Similarly, better performing CEE member states such as Poland and the Czech Republic aspire to one day join the more developed and economically prosperous 'north', while France for a brief period in 2012 risked being sucked into the maul of international bond market speculation, a development which could have cost Paris its coveted position in the euro-zone core. What is certain, however, is that for the foreseeable future the north–south divide will be at the centre of intra-EU politics, with major consequences for decision-making on the EU budget and cohesion policy.

Rising euroscepticism and populist nationalism

The euro-zone crisis has also exacerbated another pre-existing problem with potentially serious consequences for cohesion policy, and that is the rise of euroscepticism and populist nationalism throughout the EU. The growth of eurosceptism is reflected in numerous surveys of public opinion. A spring 2013 Eurobarometer survey, for instance, found that public confidence in the EU had plunged to record lows. In the survey, only 31 per cent of those questioned replied that they 'tended to trust' the EU, a drop from the nearly 60 per cent of respondents who expressed confidence in the EU in a spring 2007 Eurobarometer poll. The percentage of respondents holding a 'positive' image of the EU also continued to hover near record lows, at 30 per cent; this compared with more than 50 per cent in 2007, before the onset of the euro-zone crisis. Respondents holding a 'negative' image of the EU, on the other hand, was up from only 15 per cent six years before, to 29 per cent (CEC, 2013d: 9–10).

The growth of euroscepticism is reflected not only in public opinion surveys but also in the growing electoral success of national-populist and eurosceptic political parties (Grabow and Hartleb, 2013). At the national level, this is perhaps best seen in the rise of the UK Independence Party (UKIP), which calls for Britain's complete withdrawal from the EU. While UKIP is unlikely to win many seats in the upcoming British parliamentary elections given the nature of Britain's first-past-the-post electoral system, the popularity of its anti-Europe and anti-immigration message is exerting considerable pressure on the main parties, particularly Prime Minister David Cameron's Conservative Party. Indeed, this pressure was a key reason for Cameron's risky decision to schedule a referendum on EU membership in 2017, provided his government is returned to power in 2015. Eurosceptic parties have also made gains in other member states, including the True Finns party in Finland, the Dutch Party for Freedom in the Netherlands, the Vlaams Belang in Belgium, the Northern League in Italy, the Sweden Democrats in Sweden, the National Front in France and the Freedom Party and Team Stronach in Austria.

Not only have eurosceptic and nationalist parties been increasingly successful at the national level, unhappiness with the economic crisis and the national and EU responses to it also led to a surge of support for anti-EU parties in the May 2014 European Parliament elections (BBC.com, 2014). As a result, the EP, which has traditionally been a strong advocate of further integration, could become a more critical and less cooperative partner in the EU legislative process in the future. It could also become less supportive of EU spending and cohesion policy specifically, unlike in the past, thus depriving the Commission and poorer member states of a critical ally in the EU policy-making process.

Reflecting both the growth of popular euroscepticism and the success of anti-EU parties, national governments, especially those of the wealthier member states, have taken an increasingly tougher stance on EU issues, including the budget and the transfer of further policy competences to Brussels. Beyond budgetary negotiations, this mood of national retrenchment is perhaps best indicated by the halting response of EU governments to the euro-zone crisis, with prolonged debate and negotiations required to approve even small steps towards the further centralization of EU economic governance, such as the creation of a banking union. Ironically, the willingness of member states to support further integration has eroded even further as the crisis has waned, and the sense of urgency it generated has dissipated.

The stronger assertion of national interests within the EU is taking place against the backdrop of an in increasingly poisonous popular discourse in the member states as well, with the citizens of countries receiving EU bailout assistance directing vitriolic attacks at the wealthier member states, especially Germany, because of the strict austerity measures and structural reforms they have imposed as a condition of assistance. This discourse reached such low points as the depiction by Greek protestors of Chancellor Merkel with a Hitler moustache, and the comparison of German-mandated austerity measures with Nazi atrocities during the occupation of Greece in the Second World War. In Germany, meanwhile, Greeks and other southern Europeans are commonly depicted as corrupt, lazy and undeserving of German and EU assistance. Reflecting on these unfortunate developments, in April 2013 Commission President Barroso warned of 'political extremes and populism tearing apart the political support and the social fabric' of Europe, leading him to call for more unity and solidarity instead (Euractiv.com, 2013j).

If it continues, the growth of euroscepticism and populist nationalism could have significant implications for the future of cohesion policy. As its very name suggests, cohesion policy seeks to promote a sense of community within the EU while it is also dependent upon a spirit of solidarity between rich and poor member states. Especially in wealthier countries that are net contributors to the EU budget, however, the domestic politics of EU spending and net budgetary balances is difficult and makes continued support for cohesion policy a 'hard sell'. While this is the case in any circumstances, it is particularly so in tough economic times which have fed the growth of euroscepticsm and populist nationalism.

The future of cohesion policy

It is impossible to know exactly what the economic and political situation will be several years hence, as the discussion over the next MFF and cohesion policy reform begins. Economic developments are unpredictable, as are politics; elections happen and the partisan composition of national governments can change. Nevertheless, given the current situation and existing trends, and extrapolating from recent developments in the evolution of cohesion policy, we can attempt to answer the questions about the future of cohesion policy posed at the beginning of this chapter.

Cohesion policy expenditure

Since the late 1990s cohesion policy has accounted for roughly a third of the total EU budget. From 1989 until 1999 cohesion policy expenditure rose steadily as a percentage of EU GDP, but it declined and stabilized after that point until 2013, although it continued to grow in absolute terms (see Figure 2.1). In the MFF for 2014–20, however, the EU budget and cohesion policy will both experience a net reduction for the first time ever. This outcome is the result of domestic budgetary constraints and the insistence on reduced EU spending of wealthier net contributors, who argue that the EU budget should reflect the budgetary decisions being made by national governments in a period of economic crisis and austerity.

Given the likely scenario of continued slow economic growth and pressures for budgetary consolidation at the national level, it can be expected that the demands for EU budgetary consolidation will continue as well. It is difficult to imagine wealthier net contributors acceding to a real increase in EU spending in the next MFF. At best, a zero net increase will be agreed, but a freeze or additional net reductions are very possible. In this scenario, cohesion policy will not go unscathed and will have to absorb its share of any further reductions in expenditure. The poorer member states will undoubtedly wage a fierce struggle to preserve current levels of spending or perhaps even gain a slight increase. In doing so, they will continue to make a three-pronged argument that cohesion policy expenditure is:

1. a moral and political imperative, deriving from the EU's commitment to the value of solidarity and the objective of

economic and social cohesion, both of which are firmly established in the EU treaties;

2. an economic necessity, given the constraints on national
   budgets and the lack of other sources of growth-inducing and
   competitiveness-enhancing public investment;

3. in the economic self-interest of the wealthier countries themselves, both because it promotes EU economic growth overall,
   from which the wealthier countries benefit, and because a large
   percentage of cohesion policy spending ends up in the pockets
   of their own companies and exporters.

The forthcoming negotiations on the next MFF, including cohesion
policy's share of the EU budget and the size of national allocations,
will once again take place along the EU's north–south divide. That
much is certain, at least, as is the likelihood that these negotiations
will be difficult and prolonged. Unless the economic situation in the
EU improves dramatically in the meantime, a further stabilization of
cohesion policy expenditure, and perhaps another small reduction,
is a likely outcome.

Goals and purposes

The official goals and objectives of cohesion policy have also
evolved over the years. The strengthening of economic and social
(and now territorial) cohesion in the EU, defined mainly as
economic convergence and the reduction of regional disparities, was
the original goal and purpose of cohesion policy, and it remains the
official EU treaty-based objective of the structural funds today.
Since the 2006 policy reform, however, cohesion policy has also
been assigned the task of supporting the EU's growth, competitiveness and environmental sustainability agenda, as defined in the
Lisbon and Europe 2020 strategies. As a result, cohesion policy
today is formally entrusted with a dual mission, entailing the simultaneous promotion of both cohesion/convergence and economic
growth and competitiveness.

This dual mission for cohesion policy is likely to be retained in the
future, as the EU seeks to honour its commitment to solidarity and
the treaty-based cohesion objective while also addressing its strategic
growth and competitiveness priorities. While the promotion of
convergence addresses moral and political imperatives deriving from

the EU commitment to solidarity and the redistributionist logic of EU politics, support for innovation, SMEs and the development of a low-carbon economy demonstrates the continued relevance and added value of cohesion policy, which is necessary to ensure both its continued existence as an EU-wide policy and a high level of funding. The Europe 2020 strategy runs until the end of the current programming period, and the spending priorities for cohesion policy in the next funding period beyond 2020 are likely to be closely linked to whatever medium-term EU economic strategy succeeds it.

Cohesion policy in the future is also likely to play an increased role as an instrument of EU economic governance. The regulations approved in 2013 introduced new conditionality provisions that allow cohesion policy funds to be used as leverage to promote a variety of economic governance objectives. These include both *ex ante* conditionalities, which make the disbursal of allocated funds conditional on the existence of adequate institutional and administrative capacity and the implementation of specific EU rules and policies, and macroeconomic conditionalities, which allow for the suspension of allocated funds if member states fail to adhere to EU rules pertaining to fiscal and budgetary discipline, or to respond adequately to the Council's country-specific recommendations made in the 'European Semester' process. The new conditionality provisions are aimed primarily at the economically weaker member states and are thus highly controversial, but they are an important part of the new cohesion policy bargain, in which wealthier member states continue to support the transfer of resources to poorer member states but only in return for increased assurances that the money will not be wasted and the beneficiary countries use them effectively. In step with the increased centralization of EU economic governance as a result of the euro-zone crisis, it is likely that cohesion policy in the future will continue to utilize such conditionality provisions, also as a means of promoting structural reforms in the poorer member states to make them economically stronger and more competitive.

Finally, cohesion policy in the future is likely to play an increasingly important role as an instrument of EU economic policy, especially when it comes to crisis management. With only a very limited budget (about 1 per cent of EU GDP) and no capacity to borrow, the EU has few fiscal tools at its disposal for dealing with economic crises and shocks, as became amply apparent when confronted by the global financial and euro-zone crises. Despite its relatively limited resources and flexibility, cohesion policy is the closest thing to such a fiscal instrument that the EU has (Jacoby, 2014:65–6). Thus, the advanced payment of allocated structural funds formed an important part of the €400 billion economic stimulus package approved by the EU in March 2009 as a response to the global financial crisis. Changes were also made to cohesion policy implementation rules to make it easier to use allocated funds, and unspent funds were repurposed to support new EIB lending and measures to combat youth unemployment in member states strongly affected by the euro-zone crisis. The availability of cohesion policy as a fiscal instrument for dealing with economic shocks and crises is yet another argument in its favour when it comes to decision-making on EU expenditure, therefore, and it could prompt efforts to make cohesion policy spending even more flexible in the future to allow for its use in this manner.

The increased use of cohesion policy as an instrument of EU economic governance and crisis management would only add to its multiplicity of purposes and objectives, however, thus creating additional confusion about the rationale for cohesion policy and raising further concerns about its effectiveness. As has been the case throughout its history, however, the broadening of cohesion policy and its accumulation of different functions is a response to changing political and economic conditions, and thus it is both a reflection of those conditions and a requirement for cohesion policy's survival.

Coverage

A third question concerning the future of cohesion policy is whether it will remain what it has been, an EU-wide policy that applies to all member states and regions, or whether its coverage will be narrowed to focus on just the poorest member states and regions. Since its creation cohesion policy assistance has been concentrated on the neediest member states and regions, in accordance with the policy's redistributive (cohesion and convergence) goals. Nevertheless, in its first three programming periods (1989–93, 1994–9 and 2000–06), all member states and regions were eligible for EU assistance to fund horizontal or non-regional objectives such as employment and social cohesion. With the new focus of cohesion policy after 2006 on thematic priorities related to the Lisbon and Europe 2020 strategies, this EU-wide approach made even more sense, since these were priorities that applied to all member states and regions, not just the poorest. Indeed, the Commission's decision to link cohesion policy to the EU's strategic priorities in its reform proposals was in part made to counter the efforts of wealthy net contributors to 'renationalize' and downsize cohesion policy, by limiting its coverage to the Union's poorest member states and regions. As a result, the new regional architectures for cohesion policy approved in the 2006 (Convergence and RCE regions) and 2013 (less developed, transition and more developed regions) reforms ensure that all EU regions are eligible for structural funds assistance, although in accordance with EU criteria and indicators and for programmes that address EU thematic priorities.

Whether cohesion policy continues to be an EU-wide policy in the future thus seems to depend on whether it remains linked to the Union's broader economic strategy, and whether its supporters can show that it provides demonstrable added value when it comes to addressing the EU's strategic priorities. To the extent that cohesion policy is de-linked from this strategic agenda, or that its interventions are shown to be ineffective, the argument for re-nationalization is strengthened.

Yet another reason for maintaining cohesion policy as an EU-wide policy is its traditional unofficial role as a compensatory mechanism, which in recent rounds of budgetary negotiations has been used mainly for the purpose of addressing concerns about national net balances. If cohesion policy is limited to only the poorest member states and regions, it will no longer be able to play this role, and another means of equilibrating net balances and making 'side payments' as part of broader package deals will have to be found. Cohesion policy's politically useful (if not officially acknowledged) role in this regard also makes it likely, therefore, that an EU-wide approach will be continued in the future.

Conclusion

For more than 25 years cohesion policy has been a major EU policy, accounting for about a third of all EU spending and funding economic development operations in all of the EU's member states and regions. Over this period of time there have been changes to the basic goals and objectives of cohesion policy, and also to its implementation rules and procedures. These changes have reflected shifting economic and political circumstances, and the new challenges, opportunities and constraints these have created for European policy makers. As a consequence, cohesion policy has developed into an increasingly complex and multi-layered policy, with multiple objectives, roles and purposes. This complexity and multi-functionality is at once a weakness of cohesion policy, generating confusion about its basic purpose and raising questions about its effectiveness, and a strength, making it flexible and capable of adapting to new challenges and priorities.

Cohesion policy is also a highly contested policy, with considerable disagreement about its basic goals and objectives, about how much money it should be allocated and how those funds should be distributed among different member states and objectives, about how it operates and is implemented, and about whether it is effective or even necessary. As such, for almost three decades cohesion policy has been at the centre of debate about the EU budget, as well as debate about what the EU is or should be, and what it should do or not do.

This book has attempted to explain the complexity and multifaceted nature of cohesion policy and also why it is so contested. It has argued that the evolution of cohesion policy has been shaped by changing economic and political circumstances and the different coalitions of interest among national and EU policy makers that these create. As this chapter has argued, this is likely to be the case in the future as well. While the future of cohesion policy may be unclear, it is likely to remain a major EU policy, and also one that is extremely complex and highly contested. In this regard, it is not unlike the EU itself.

References

Allen, David (2000) 'Cohesion and the Structural Funds: Transfers and Trade-Offs', in Helen Wallace and William Wallace (eds), *Policy-Making in the European Union*, 4th edn, Oxford: Oxford University Press, pp. 243–65.

—— (2005) 'Cohesion and the Structural Funds: Competing Pressures for Reform?', in Helen Wallace, William Wallace and Mark A. Pollack (eds), *Policy-Making in the European Union*, 5th edn, Oxford: Oxford University Press, pp. 213–51.

—— (2010) 'The Structural Funds and Cohesion Policy: Extending the Bargain to Meet New Challenges', in Helen Wallace, Mark A. Pollack and Alasdair R. Young (eds), *Policy-Making in the European Union*, 6th edn, Oxford: Oxford University Press, pp. 229–52.

Bache, Ian (1998) *The Politics of European Union Regional Policy: Multi-level Governance or Flexible Gatekeeping?* Sheffield: Sheffield Academic Press.

—— (1999) 'The Extended Gatekeeper: Central Government and the Implementation of EU Regional Policy in the UK', *Journal of European Public Policy*, 6 (1): 28–45.

—— (2005) 'Europeanization and Britain: Towards Multi-level Governance?' Paper prepared for the EUSA 9th Biennial Conference in Austin, Texas, 31 March–2 April, available at: http://aei.pitt.edu/ 3158/2/Bache.doc (accessed 9 September 2011).

—— (2007) 'Cohesion Policy', in P. Graziano and M. Vink (eds), *Europeanization: New Research Agendas*, Basingstoke: Palgrave, pp. 239–52.

—— (2008) *Europeanization and Multilevel Governance: Cohesion Policy in the European Union and Britain*, Lanham: Rowman & Littlefield.

Bache, I. and Flinders, M. (eds) (2004) *Multi-Level Governance*, Oxford: Oxford University Press.

Bachtler, John and Gorzelak, Grzegorz (2007) 'Reforming EU Cohesion Policy: A Reappraisal of the Performance of the Structural Funds', *Policy Studies*, 28 (4): 309–26.

Bachtler, John and McMaster, Irene (2007) 'EU Cohesion Policy and the Role of the Regions: Investigating the Influence of Structural Funds in the New Member States', *Environment and Planning C: Government and Policy*, 26 (2): 398–427.

Bachtler, John and Mendez, Carlos (2007) 'Who Governs EU Cohesion

Policy? Deconstructing the Reforms of the Structural Funds', *Journal of Common Market Studies*, 45 (3): 535–64.

Bachtler, J. and Taylor, S. (2003) *The Added Value of the Structural Funds: A Regional Perspective*, IQ-net report on the reform of the Structural Funds, University of Strathclyde, June.

Bachtler, John and Wishlade, Fiona (2005) *From Building Blocks to Negotiating Boxes: The Reform of EU Cohesion Policy*, European Policy Research Paper No. 57, European Policies Research Centre, University of Strathclyde, November.

Bachtler, John, Wishlade, Fiona and Mendez, Carlos (2007) *New Budget, New Regulations, New Strategies: The 2006 Reform of EU Cohesion Policy*, European Policy Research Paper No. 63, European Policies Research Centre, University of Strathclyde, October.

Badea, Andrei Sebastian (2011) 'Perspectives on Improving Cohesion Policy Spending', CES Working Papers, 3 (1): 6–12.

Bähr, C. (2008) 'How Does Sub-national Autonomy Affect the Effectiveness of Structural Funds?', *Kyklos*, 61(1): 3–18.

Bailey, David and de Propris, Lisa (2002a) 'The 1988 Reform of the European Structural Funds: Entitlement or Empowerment?', *Journal of European Public Policy*, 9 (3): 408–28.

—— (2002b) 'EU Structural Funds, Regional Capabilities and Enlargement: Towards Multi-Level Governance?', *European Integration*, 24 (4): 303–24.

Balchin, Paul, Sýkora, Luděk and Bull, Gregory (1999) *Regional Policy and Planning in Europe*, London: Routledge.

Barca Report (2009) *An Agenda for a Reformed Cohesion Policy: A Place-based Approach for Meeting European Union Challenges and Expectations*, Independent Report prepared at the request of Danuta Hübner, Commissioner for Regional Policy, by Fabrizio Barca, April.

Barry, Frank, Bradley, John and Hannan, Aoife (2001) *The Single Market, The Structural Funds and Ireland's Recent Economic Growth*, Trinity College Dublin, May, available at: http://tcd.ie/business/staff/fbarry/papers/papers/jcms.PDF (accessed 21 September 2011).

Bauer, Michael W. (2002) 'The EU "Partnership Principle": Still a Sustainable Governance Device Across Multiple Administrative Arenas?', *Public Administration*, 80 (4): 769–89.

—— (2006) 'Co-managing Programme Implementation: Conceptualizing the European Commission's Role in Policy Execution', *Journal of European Public Policy*, 13 (5): 717–35.

Baun, Michael (1995) 'The Maastricht Treaty as High Politics: Germany, France, and European Integration after the Cold War', *Political Science Quarterly*, 110 (4): 605–24.

—— (1996) *An Imperfect Union: The Maastricht Treaty and the New Politics of European Integration*, Boulder: Westview Press.

—— (1997) 'The SPD and EMU: An End to Germany's All-Party Consensus on European Integration?', *German Politics and Society*, 15 (3): 1–23.

—— (2000) *A Wider Europe: The Process and Politics of European Union Enlargement*, Lanham: Rowman & Littlefield.

—— (2002) 'EU Regional Policy and the Candidate States: Poland and the Czech Republic', *European Integration*, 24 (3): 261–80.

Baun, Michael and Marek, Dan (eds) (2008a) 'Introduction', in Michael Baun and Dan Marek (eds), *EU Cohesion Policy after Enlargement*, Basingstoke: Palgrave Macmillan, pp. 1–14.

—— (2008b) *EU Cohesion Policy After Enlargement*. Basingstoke: Palgrave Macmillan.

—— (2008c) 'EU Cohesion Policy and Sub-National Authorities in the New Member States', *Contemporary European Studies*, 2 (2): 5–20.

BBC.com (2014) 'Eurosceptic "earthquake" rocks EU elections', available at: http://www.bbc.com/news/world-europe-27559714 (accessed 25 June 2014).

Becker, S., Egger, P., von Ehrlich, M. and Fenge, R. (2008) 'Going NUTS: The Effect of EU Structural Funds on Regional Performance', CESifo Working Paper, 2495.

Begg, Iain (1999) 'Reform of the Structural Funds after 1999', *European Policy Paper Series*, 5.

—— (2009) *The Future of Cohesion Policy in Richer Regions*, European Commission, Directorate-General for Regional Policy, Working Papers No. 3, available at: http://ec.europa.eu/regional_policy/sources/docgener/work/2009_03_richer.pdf (accessed 10 August 2010).

—— (2010) 'Cohesion or Confusion: A Policy Searching for Objectives', *Journal of European Integration*, 32 (1): 77–96.

Behrens, Petra and Smyrl, Marc (1997) 'EU Regional Policy in Theory and Practice', Bi-annual conference of the European Community Studies Association, 31 May.

Benz, A. and Eberlein, B. (1999) 'The Europeanization of Regional Policies: Patterns of Multi-level Governance', *Journal of European Public Policy*, 6 (2): 329–48.

Beugelsdijk, Maaike and Eijffinger, Sylvester C.W. (2005) 'The Effectiveness of Structural Policy in the European Union: An Empirical Analysis for the EU-15 in 1995–2001', *Journal of Common Market Studies*, 43 (1): 37–51.

Boldrin, Michele and Canova, Fabio (2001) 'Inequality and Convergence in Europe's Regions: Reconsidering European Regional Policies', *Economic Policy*, 16 (32): 205–53.

—— (2003) 'Regional Policies and EU Enlargement', in Bernard Funck and Lodovico Pizzati (eds), *European Integration, Regional Policy, and Growth*, Washington: The World Bank, pp. 33–93.

BMWS&E (Border, Midland and Western and Southern and Eastern Regional Assemblies) (2008) *Submission on the Future of EU Cohesion Policy*, November, available at: http://bmwassembly.ie/news/publications/Future%20of%20EU%20Cohesion%20Policy.pdf (accessed 3 May 2010).

Börzel, T. (1999) 'Towards Convergence in Europe? Institutional Adaptation and Europeanization in Germany and Spain', *Journal of Common Market Studies*, 37 (4): 573–96.

—— (2011) *Move Closer! New Modes of Governance and Accession to the European Union*. Working Paper Series, Institute for European Integration Research, January.

Bouvet, Florence (2005) 'European Union Regional Policy: Allocation Determinants and Effects on Regional Economic Growth', mimeo.

Bouvet, Florence and Dall'erba, Sandy (2010) 'European Regional Structural Funds: How Large is the Influence of Politics on the Allocation Process?', *Journal of Common Market Studies*, 48 (3): 501–28.

Brusis, M. (2001) 'Institution Building for Regional Development: A Comparison of the Czech Republic, Estonia, Hungary, Poland and Slovakia', in J. Beyer, J. Wielgohs, and H. Wiesenthal (eds), *Successful Transitions: Political Factors of Socio-Economic Progress in Post-socialist Countries*, Baden-Baden: Nomos, pp. 223–42.

—— (2002) 'Between EU Requirements, Competitive Politics, and National Traditions: Re-creating Regions in the Accession Countries of Central and Eastern Europe', *Governance*, 15 (4): 531–59.

—— (2010) 'European Union Incentives and Regional Interest Representation in Central and East European Countries', *Acta Politologica*, 45 (1): 70–89.

Bulletin of the European Community (1972) 'Declaration', Meetings of the Heads of State or Government, Paris, 19–21 October 1972, *Bulletin of the European Communities*, No. 10, 14–23.

Bulmer, Simon, and William E. Paterson (2013) 'Germany as the EU's Reluctant Hegemon? Of Economic Strength and Political Constraints', *Journal of European Public Policy*, 20 (10): 1387–405.

Canova, Fabio (1999) 'Testing for Convergence Clubs in Income per Capita: A Predictive Density Approach', CEPR Discussion Paper No. 2201, London: CEPR.

Caporaso, J. (1996) 'The European Union and Forms of the State: Westphalian, Regulatory or Post-Modern?', *Journal of Common Market Studies*, 34 (1): 29–52.

Cappelen, Aadne, Castellacci, Fulvio, Fagerberg, Jan and Verspagen, Bert (2003) 'The Impact of EU Regional Support on Growth and Convergence in the European Union', *Journal of Common Market Studies*, 41 (4): 621–44.

CEC (Commission of the European Communities) (1957) *Treaty of Rome*, 25 March, available at: http://ec.europa.eu/economy_finance/emu_history/documents/treaties/rometreaty2.pdf (accessed 17 September 2012).

—— (1965) *First Communication of the European Commission on Regional Policy in the European Community*, SEC (65) 1170 def., Brussels.

—— (1969) *A Regional Policy for the Community*, COM (69) 950, Brussels, 15 October.

—— (1973a) *Report on the Regional Problems in the Enlarged Community*, COM (73) 550 final, 3 May, available at: http://aei.pitt.edu/5888/ (accessed 5 October 2012).

—— (1973b) *Regional Policy: Commission Proposal to the Council*, Information Memo P-41/73, Brussels, 26 July.

—— (1973c) *Regional Policy: Commission Proposals Regarding Lists of Regions and Areas Eligible for Benefits under the Guidance Section of EAGGF and the Regional Development Fund*, Information Memo P-50/73, Brussels, October.

—— (1985) 'Programme of the Commission for 1985', *Bulletin of the European Communities*, Supplement 4/85, point 15.

—— (1987) 'The Single Act: A New Frontier for Europe,' Communication from the Commission to the Council (COM (87) 100), 15 February, *Bulletin of the European Communities*, Supplement 1/87, 1–23.

—— (1989a) *The Integrated Mediterranean Programmes*, European File 7/89, May, available at: http://aei.pitt.edu/4624/ (accessed 13 September 2013).

—— (1989b) *Guide to the Reform of the Community's Structural Funds*, Luxembourg: Office for Official Publications of the European Communities.

—— (1993) *Community Structural Funds 1994–1999 – Revised Regulations and Comments*, Brussels, August.

—— (1996) *First Cohesion Report*, available at: http://ec.europa.eu/regional_policy/sources/docoffic/official/reports/repco_en.htm (accessed 5 November 2012).

—— (1997) *Agenda 2000: For a Stronger and Wider Europe*, Document drawn up on the basis of COM(97) 2000 final, *Bulletin of the European Union*, Supplement 5/97.

—— (1998) *Proposals for a Council Regulation (EC) Laying Down General Provisions on the Structural Funds*, COM (1998) 131 final, Brussels, 18 March.

—— (1999) *Reform of the Structural Funds 2000–2006: Comparative Analysis*. Brussels, June.

—— (2001a) *Second Report on Economic and Social Cohesion. Unity, Solidarity, Diversity for Europe, its People and its Territory*, 31 January.

—— (2001b) 'Communication from the Commission to the Council, the European Parliament, the Economic and Social Committee and the Committee of the Regions. The Results of the programming of the Structural Funds for 2000–06 (Objective 1)', COM(2001)378 final, Brussels.

—— (2003) *Ex Post Evaluation of 1994–99 Objective 2 Programmes. Synthesis Report.* Brussels: European Commission, Directorate-General for Regional Policy, June, available at: http://ec.europa.eu/regional_policy/sources/docgener/evaluation/pdf/synth_objective2_94_99_en.pdf (accessed 23 January 2011).

—— (2004a) *Third Report on Economic and Social Cohesion. A New Partnership for Cohesion Convergence Competitiveness Cooperation,* February, available at: http://ec.europa.eu/regional_policy/sources/docoffic/official/reports/cohesion3/cohesion3_en.htm (accessed 20 November 2012).

—— (2004b) *Building our Common Future: Policy Challenges and Budgetary Means of the Enlarged Union 2007–2013,* Communication from the Commission to the Council and the European Parliament, COM(2004) 101 final/2, Brussels, 26 February.

—— (2005a) *Working Together for Growth and Jobs: A New Start for the Lisbon Strategy,* Communication to the Spring European Council, COM(2005) 24 final, 2 February.

—— (2005b) 'Partnership in the 2000–06 Programming Period: Analysis of the Implementation of the Partnership Principle', Discussion Paper of DG Regio, November.

—— (2007a) *Cohesion Policy 2007–13.* Commentaries and official texts, Luxembourg: Office for Official Publications of the European Communities, available at: http://ec.europa.eu/regional_policy/ sources/docoffic/official/regulation/pdf/2007/publications/guide2007_en.pdf (accessed 7 March 2013).

—— (2007b) *Growing Regions, Growing Europe: Fourth Report on Economic and Social Cohesion.* Brussels, May.

—— (2008) *Working for the Regions: EU Regional Policy 2007–2013.* Brussels: Commission of the European Communities, Directorate-General for Regional Policy, January, available at: http://ec.europa.eu/regional_policy/sources/docgener/presenta/working2008/work_en.pdf (accessed 7 March 2013).

—— (2009) *EU Budget 2008: Financial Report,* Annex 2: 'Expenditures 1958–2008 by Heading', available at: http://ec.europa.eu/budget/library/biblio/publications/2008/fin_report/fin_report_08_en.pdf (accessed 15 October 2012).

—— (2010a) *The EU Budget Review,* Communication from the Commission to the European Parliament, the Council, the European

Economic and Social Committee, the Committee of the Regions and the National Parliaments, SEC(2010) 7000, Brussels.

—— (2010b) *Investing in Europe's Future: Fifth Report on Economic, Social and Territorial Cohesion*, November, available at: http://ec. europa.eu/regional_policy/sources/docoffic/official/reports/cohesion5/ pdf/5cr_en.pdf (accessed 2 December 2010).

—— (2010c) *Communication from the Commission to the European Parliament, the Council, the European Economic and Social Committee and the Committee of the Regions: Cohesion Policy: Strategic Report 2010 on the Implementation of the Programmes 2007–2013*, COM(2010)110 final, Brussels, available at: http://ec.europa.eu/ regional_policy/sources/docoffic/official/communic/reporting2010/ com_2010_110_en.pdf (accessed 2 May 2013).

—— (2011a) *Cohesion Policy 2014–2020: Investing in Growth and Jobs*, Directorate-General for Regional Policy, Brussels.

—— (2011b) *A Budget for Europe 2020*, Communication from the Commission to the European Parliament, the Council, the European Economic and Social Committee and the Committee of the Regions, COM(2011) 500 final, Part I, Brussels, 29 June.

—— (2012a) *Amended Proposal for a Regulation of the European Parliament and of the Council Laying Down Common Provisions on the European Regional Development Fund, the European Social Fund, the Cohesion Fund, the European Agricultural Fund for Rural Development and the European Maritime and Fisheries Fund Covered by the Common Strategic Framework and Laying Down General Provisions on the European Regional Development Fund, the European Social Fund and the Cohesion Fund and Repealing Council Regulation (EC) No 1083/2006*, COM(2012) 496 final/2, Brussels 11 September.

—— (2012b) *Amended Proposal for a Council Regulation Laying Down the Multiannual Financial Framework for the Years 2014–2020*, COM (2012) 388 final, Brussels, 6 July.

—— (2013a) 'Youth Opportunities Initiative', Employment, Social Affairs and Inclusion, available at: http://ec.europa.eu/social/main.jsp?catId= 1006 (accessed 6 September 2013).

—— (2013b) *EU Cohesion Policy Contributing to Employment and Growth in Europe*, Joint Paper from the Directorates-General for Regional & Urban Policy and Employment, Social Affairs & Inclusion, Brussels, July.

—— (2013c) 'Cohesion Policy: Strategic Report 2013 on Programme Implementation 2007–13', Report from the Commission to the European Parliament, the Council, the European Economic and Social Committee and the Committee of the Regions, COM(2013) 210 final, Brussels, 18 April.

—— (2013d) *Standard Eurobarometer 79, Spring 2013: Public Opinion in the European Union – First Results*, Brussels, July, available at: http://ec. europa.eu/public_opinion/archives/eb/eb79/eb79_first_en.pdf (accessed 4 October 2013).

—— (2014a) 'EU Expenditure and Revenue', available at: http://ec.europa. eu/budget/figures/interactive/index_en.cfm (accessed 10 February 2014).

—— (2014b) 'Total allocations of Cohesion Policy 2014–2020', available at: http://ec.europa.eu/regional_policy/what/future/eligibility/index_en. cfm (accessed 6 August 2014).

—— (2014c) 'Cohesion Policy 2014–2020: Programming Process', Regional Policy – Inforegio, available at: http://ec.europa.eu/regional_ policy/what/future/program/index_en.cfm (accessed 28 February 2014).

—— (2014d) 'Commission Delegated Regulation (EU) No 240/2014 of 7.1.2014 on the European Code of Conduct on Partnership in the Framework of the European Structural and Investment Funds' C(2013) 9651 final, Brussels, 7 January.

—— (2014e) 'Commission Staff Working Document: Best Practices as Regards Implementation of the Partnership Principle in the European Structural and Investment Funds' Programmes. Accompanying the Document Commission Delegated Regulation on the European Code of Conduct on Partnership in the Framework of the European Structural and Investment Funds', SWD(2013) 540 final, Brussels, 7 January.

—— (2014f) 'Press Conference Opening Remarks by Olli Rehn, Vice-President of the EC in charge of Economic and Monetary Affairs and the Euro', available at: http://ec.europa.eu/avservices/video/player.cfm?ref= 95914 (accessed 17 March 2014).

—— (2014g) *European Economic Forecast. Spring 2014*, European Economy 3/2014, Directorate-General for Economic and Financial Affairs, May.

—— (2014h) *Investment for Jobs and Growth: Promoting Development and Good Governance in EU Regions and Cities: Sixth Report on Economic, Social and Territorial Cohesion*, Brussels, July.

CEE Bankwatch (2013) 'Democratising cohesion policy – Slovakia not ready to put EU funds spending in citizens' hands', available at http://blogactiv.eu, 10 July (accessed 12 July 2013).

Chapman, Rachel (2008) 'The United Kingdom', in Michael Baun and Dan Marek (eds) *EU Cohesion Policy After Enlargement*. Basingstoke: Palgrave Macmillan, pp. 34–61.

CEU (Council of the European Union) (1995) *Decision of the Council of the European Union of 1 January 1995 Adjusting the Instruments Concerning the Accession of New Member States to the European Union*, 95/1/EC, Euratom, ECSC, available at: http://eur-lex.europa.eu/ LexUriServ/LexUriServ.do?uri=CELEX:31995D0001:en:NOT (accessed 12 November 2012).

—— (2005) Note from the Presidency to the European Council on the Financial Perspective for 2007–2013, CADREFIN 268 (15915/05), Brussels, 19 December.

Dąbrowski, Marcin (2011) *Partnership in Implementation of the Structural Funds in Poland: 'Shallow' Adjustment or Internalization of the European Mode of Cooperative Governance?'* Institute for European Integration Research, EIF Working Paper No. 05/2011, June, available at: http://eif.univie.ac.at/downloads/workingpapers/wp2011-05.pdf (accessed 25 September 2013).

Dall'erba, Sandy and Le Gallo, Julie (2007) 'Regional Convergence and the Impact of European Structural Funds over 1989–1999: A Spatial Econometric Analysis', *Papers in Regional Science*, 87 (2): 219–44.

DG Regio (2013) 'Regional policy – Inforegio: Project examples', available at: http://ec.europa.eu/regional_policy/projects/stories/index_en.cfm (accessed 4 October 2013).

Dhéret, Claire (2011) 'What next for EU Cohesion Policy? Going "beyond GDP" to deliver greater well-being', European Policy Centre, Policy Brief, March, available at: http://epc.eu/documents/uploads/pub_1243_what_next_for_eu_cohesion_policy.pdf (accessed 29 August 2011).

Dinan, Desmond (2010) *Ever Closer Union: An Introduction to European Integration*, 4th edn, Boulder: Lynne Rienner.

—— (2012) 'The Single European Act: Revitalising European Integration', in Finn Laursen (ed.), *Designing the European Union: From Paris to Lisbon*, Basingstoke: Palgrave Macmillan, pp. 124–46.

Ederveen, Sjef, Gorter, Joeri, de Mooij, Ruud and Nahuis, Richard (2003) *Funds and Games: The Economics of European Cohesion Policy*, European Network of Economic Policy Research Institutes, Occasional Paper No. 3/October.

Ederveen, Sjef, de Groot, Henri L. F. and Nahuis, Richard (2002) 'Fertile Soil for Structural Funds?', *CPB Discussion Paper* No. 10, August.

—— (2006) 'Fertile Soil for Structural Funds? A Panel Data Analysis of the Conditional Effectiveness of European Cohesion Policy', *KYKLOS*, 59 (1): 17–42.

Eriksson, Jonas (2005) 'Cohesion Policy – Retrospect and Prospect', in Jonas Erikson, Bengt O. Karlsson and Daniel Tarschys (eds), *From Policy Takers to Policy Makers: Adapting EU Cohesion Policy to the Needs of the New Member States*, Swedish Institute for European Policy Studies (SIEPS), 5 (September): 25–42.

Euractiv.com (2003) 'UK wants to renationalise EU's regional policy', 10 March, available at: http://euractiv.com/enlargement/uk-wants-renationalise-eu-regional-policy/article-112591 (accessed 18 January 2013).

—— (2011a) 'Hahn defends proposal for regional aid "sanctions"', 12

October, available at: http://euractiv.com/regional-policy/hahn-defends-proposal-regional-aid-sanctions-news-508276 (accessed 13 October 2011).

—— (2011b) 'Nine EU countries call for slim EU budget', 12 September, available at: http://euractiv.com/euro-finance/eu-countries-call-slim-eu-budget-news-507532 (accessed 12 September 2011).

—— (2012a) 'Positions still "quite far apart" at EU budget summit', 23 November, available at: http://euractiv.com/euro-finance/positions-quite-far-apart-budget-news-516229 (accessed 23 November 2012).

—— (2012b) 'Cyprus' EU budget deal rejected by Commission, Parliament', 31 October, available at: http://euractiv.com/specialreport-budget/cyprus-presidency-budget-proposa-news-515784 (accessed 31 October 2012).

—— (2012c) 'Van Rompuy tables €950-billion budget proposal', 15 November, available at: http://euractiv.com/euro-finance/van-rompuy-tables-950-budget-pro-news-516056 (accessed 16 November 2012).

—— (2012d) 'Latvia, Italy join club threatening to veto the budget', 22 November, available at: http://euractiv.com/euro-finance/latvia-joins-club-countries-thre-news-516207 (accessed 26 November 2012).

—— (2012e) 'EU budget delay keeps pressure on UK over banking union', 23 November, available at: http://euractiv.com/priorities/eu-leaders-close-budget-deal-news-516246 (accessed 26 November 2012).

—— (2012f) 'Clock is ticking for Romania suspended funds', 26 October, available at: http://euractiv.com/regional-policy/clock-ticking-romania-suspended-news-515710 (accessed 29 November 2012).

——(2013a) 'EU budget hawks succeed in €960-billion cap', 8 February, available at: http://euractiv.com/specialreport-budget/eu-budget-hawks-succeed-cap-960-news-517677 (accessed 8 February 2013).

—— (2013b) 'The EU's 2014-2020 budget in figures', 12 February, available at: http://euractiv.com/priorities/2014-2020-budget-figures-news-517725 (accessed 12 February 2013).

—— (2013c) 'Parliament defies EU leaders with vote against long-term budget', 14 March, available at: http://euractiv.com/priorities/parliament-shows-teeth-eu-leader-news-518476 (accessed 14 March 2013).

—— (2013d) 'Parliament gives final approval to EU long-term budget', 20 November, available at: http://euractiv.com/priorities/eu-budget-gets-massive-approval-news-531817 (accessed 20 November 2013).

—— (2013e) 'EU budget summit aftermath: "Everyone's a winner"', 15 February, available at: http://euractiv.com/priorities/budget-summit-winner-news-517825 (accessed 15 February 2013).

—— (2013f) 'Commissioners on EU budget: "A deal is better than no deal"', 11 February, available at: http://euractiv.com/priorities/

commissioners-eu-budget-deal-bet-news-517708 (accessed 12 February 2013).

—— (2013g) 'EU suspends €890m for Polish roads pending fraud probe,' 31 January, available at: http://euractiv.com/regional-policy/eu-suspends-890-polish-roads-pen-news-517464 (accessed 2 September 2013).

—— (2013h) 'EU suspends funding to Hungary over weak controls', 15 August, available at: http://euractiv.com/central-europe/eu-suspends-funding-hungary-weak-news-529822 (accessed 23 August 2013).

—— (2013i) 'German elections 2013: Don't mention Europe', 6 August, available at: http://euractiv.com/elections/german-elections-2013-Europe-linksdossier-529661 (accessed 6 August 2013).

—— (2013j) 'Record 60% of Europeans "tend not to trust" EU', 25 July, available at: http://euractiv.com/elections/record-60-europeans-tend-trust-e-news-529566 (accessed 25 July 2013).

EUObserver.com (2005) 'Press review,' 2 December.

European Council (1985) *Texts Resulting from the European Council in Luxembourg, 2 and 3 December 1985.*

—— (1988) *Note from the Presidency: Making a Success of the Single European Act – Consolidated Conclusions of the European Council*, 19 February.

—— (1992) *European Council in Edinburgh, 11–12 December, 1992 – Conclusions of the Presidency*, available at: http://european-council.europa.eu/council-meetings/conclusions/archives-1992–1975 (accessed 2 November 2011).

—— (1997) *Extraordinary European Council Meeting on Employment, Luxembourg, 20 and 21 November 1997 – Presidency Conclusions*, available at; http://consilium.europa.eu/uedocs/cms_data/docs/press-data/en/ec/00300.htm (accessed 3 November 2012).

—— (1999) *Berlin European Council – Presidency Conclusions, 24 and 25 March*, available at: http://europarl.europa.eu/summits/ber1_en.htm (accessed 7 November 2012).

—— (2000) *Lisbon European Council – Presidency Conclusions, 23 and 24 March*, available at: http://consilium.europa.eu/uedocs/cms_data/docs/pressdata/en/ec/00100-r1.en0.htm (accessed 13 December 2012).

—— (2001) *Göteborg European Council – Presidency Conclusions, 15 and 16 June*, available at: http://consilium.europa.eu/press/press-releases/european-council?target=2002&infotarget=before&bid=76&lang=en (accessed 13 December 2012).

—— (2002) *Barcelona European Council – Presidency Conclusions, 15 and 16 March*, available at: http://consilium.europa.eu/uedocs/cms_data/docs/pressdata/en/ec/71025.pdf (accessed 13 December 2012)

—— (2005) *Brussels European Council – Presidency Conclusions, 22 and*

23 March, Brussels, 23 March, available at: http://consilium.europa.eu/uedocs/cms_data/docs/pressdata/en/ec/84335.pdf (accessed 13 December 2012).

—— (2009) *Brussels European Council – Presidency Conclusions 19/20 March 2009*. Revised version, Brussels, 29 April, available at: http://consilium.europa.eu/uedocs/cms_data/docs/pressdata/en/ec/106809.pdf (accessed 11 March 2013).

—— (2010) *Conclusions – European Council 25/26 March 2010*, Brussels, 26 March, available at: http://consilium.europa.eu/ueDocs/cms_Data/docs/pressData/en/ec/113591.pdf (accessed 11 March 2013).

—— (2012) *Conclusions – European Council 28/29 June 2012*, Brussels, 29 June, available at: http://consilium.europa.eu/uedocs/cms_Data/docs/pressdata/en/ec/131388.pdf (accessed 11 March 2013).

—— (2013) *Conclusions (Multiannual Financial Framework) – European Council 7/8 February 2013*, EUCO37/13, CO EUR 5 CONCL 3, Brussels, 8 February, available at: https://consilium.europa.eu/uedocs/cms_data/docs/pressdata/en/ec/135324.pdf (accessed 12 March 2013).

ECA (European Court of Auditors) (2010) 'Annual Report on the Implementation of the Budget' (2010/C 303/01), *Official Journal of the European Union*, 9 November, pp. 1–242.

—— (2011) 'Annual Report on the Implementation of the Budget' (2011/C 326/01), *Official Journal of the European Union*, 10 November, pp. 1–249.

—— (2012) 'Annual Report on the Implementation of the Budget' (2012/C 344/01), *Official Journal of the European Union*, 12 November, pp. 1–241.

—— (2013) 'Annual Report on the Implementation of the Budget' (2013/C 331/01), *Official Journal of the European Union*, 14 November, pp. 1–259.

Eurostat (2007) 'Regional GDP per inhabitant in the EU27', *Eurostat News Release*, 23/2007, 19 February.

—— (2013a) 'Nomenclature of territorial units for statistics: Introduction', available at: http://epp.eurostat.ec.europa.eu/portal/page/portal/nuts_nomenclature/introduction (accessed 4 October 2013).

—— (2013b) 'Population on 1 January', available at; http://epp.eurostat.ec.europa.eu/tgm/table.do?tab=table&language=en&pcode=tps00001&tableSelection=1&footnotes=yes&labeling=labels&plugin=1 (accessed 23 August 2013).

—— (2013c) 'GDP and main components – Current prices', available at: http://appsso.eurostat.ec.europa.eu/nui/show.do?dataset=nama_gdp_c&lang=en (accessed 21 August 2013).

—— (2013d) 'Intra and extra-EU trade by member state and by product group', last updated 18/7/2013, available at: http://appsso.eurostat.ec. europa.eu/nui/submitViewTableAction.do (accessed 18 March 2014).

—— (2014a) "Second estimate for the first quarter of 2014. Euro area GDP up by 0.2%, EU28 up by 0.3%, +0.9% and +1.4% respectively compared with the first quarter of 2013', *News Release. Euro Indicators*, 84/2014, 4 June (accessed 25 June 2014).

—— (2014b) 'April 2014. Euro area unemployment rate at 11.7%, EU28 at 10.4%', *News Release. Euro Indicators*, 83/2014, 3 June (accessed 25 June 2014).

—— (2014c) 'Flash estimate – May 2014. Euro area annual inflation down to 0.5%', *News Release. Euro Indicators*, 82/2014, 3 June (accessed 25 June 2014).

Ewing, Jack (2014) 'Germany's euro zone aid cleared by court', *New York Times*, 19 March, p. B3.

Expatica.com (2012) 'Germany top indirect beneficiary of EU cohesion funds: Study', 1 March, available at: http://expatica.com/de/news/ german-news/germany-top-indirect-beneficiary-of-eu-cohesion-funds-study_211963.html# (accessed 1 March 2012).

Faludi, Andreas and Jean Peyrony (2011) 'Cohesion Policy Contributing to Territorial Cohesion – Scenarios', *European Journal of Spatial Development*, No. 43 (September).

Ferry, Martin, Gross, Frederike, Bachtler, John and McMaster, Irene (2007) *Turning Strategies into Projects: The Implementation of 2007–13 Structural Funds Programmes*, IQ-Net Thematic Paper No. 20 (2), European Policies Research Centre, University of Strathclyde, June.

Funck, Bernard , Pizzati, Lodovico and Bruncko, Martin (2003) 'Overview', in Bernard Funck and Lodovico Pizzati (eds), *European Integration, Regional Policy, and Growth*, Washington: The World Bank:, pp. 1–17.

Giannoulis, Karafillis (2013) 'Easier access to EU funds for crisis-hit countries', *New Europe*, 22 May, available at: http://neurope.eu/article/ easier-access-eu-funds-crisis-hit-countries (accessed 23 May 2013).

Grabbe, H. (2001) 'How Does Europeanization Affect CEE Governance? Conditionality, Diffusion and Diversity?', *Journal of European Public Policy*, 8 (6): 1013–31.

Grabow, Karsten and Hartleb, Florian (eds) (2013) *Exposing the Demagogues: Right-wing and National Populist Parties in Europe*, Brussels: Konrad Adenauer Stiftung and Centre for European Studies.

Hagen, Tobias and Mohl, Philipp (2009a) *How Does EU Cohesion Policy Work? Evaluating its Effects on Fiscal Outcome Variables*, Discussion Paper No. 09-051, Zentrum für Europäische Wirtschaftsforschung.

—— (2009b) *Econometric Evaluation of EU Cohesion Policy – A Survey*, Discussion Paper No. 09-052, Zentrum für Europäische Wirtschaftsforschung.

Hart, Mark (2007) 'Evaluating EU Regional Policy. How Might We Understand the Causal Connections Between Interventions and Outcomes More Effectively?', *Policy Studies*, 28 (4): 295–308.

Hirst, Nicholas (2014) 'Deal reached on banking union', *European Voice*, 20 March, available at: http://europeanvoice.com/article/2014/march/deal-reached-on-banking-union/80162.aspx (accessed 20 March 2014).

Hooghe, Liesbet (ed.) (1996) *Cohesion Policy and European Integration: Building Multi-Level Governance*, Oxford: Oxford University Press.

—— (1996) 'Introduction: Reconciling EU-Wide Policy and National Diversity', in Liesbet Hooghe (ed.), *European Integration, Cohesion Policy and Subnational Mobilisation*. Oxford: Oxford University Press, pp. 1–26.

Hooghe, L. and Marks, G. (2001) *Multi-Level Governance and European Integration*, Lanham, MD: Rowman & Littlefield.

Horváth, Gyula (2008) 'Hungary', in Michael Baun and Dan Marek (eds) *EU Cohesion Policy After Enlargement*, Basingstoke: Palgrave Macmillan, pp. 187–204.

House of Lords (2008) *The Future of EU Regional Policy*, European Union Committee, 19th Report of Session 2007-08, 16 July.

Hübner, Danuta (2006) 'Delivering Lisbon through Cohesion Policy. Committee of the Regions – Territorial Dialogue', Brussels, 1 March, available at: http://europa.eu/rapid/pressReleasesAction.do?reference=SPEECH/06/138&format=HTML&aged=0&language=EN&guiLanguage=en (accessed 19 December 2012)

Hughes, J. Sasse, G. and Gordon, C. (2001) 'Enlargement and Regionalization: The Europeanization of Local and Regional Governance in CEE States', in H. Wallace (ed.), *Interlocking Dimensions of European Integration*, Basingstoke: Palgrave, pp. 145–78.

—— (2003) 'EU Enlargement, Europeanisation and the Dynamics of Regionalization in the CEECs', in M. Keating and J. Hughes (eds), *The Regional Challenge in Central and Eastern Europe: Territorial Restructuring and European Integration*, Brussels: P.I.E-Peter Lang, pp. 69–88.

—— (2004) *Europeanization and Regionalization in the EU's Enlargement to Central and Eastern Europe: The Myth of Conditionality*, Basingstoke: Palgrave.

Hurst, Christopher, Thisse, Jacques François and Vanhoudt, Patrick (2000) 'What Diagnosis for Europe's Ailing Regions?', *EIB Papers*, 5 (1): 9–29.

Jacoby, Wade (2004) *The Enlargement of the European Union and NATO: Ordering from the Menu in Central Europe*, Cambridge: Cambridge University Press.

—— (2014) 'The EU Factor in Fat Times and in Lean: Did the EU Amplify the Boom and Soften the Bust?' *Journal of Common Market Studies*, 52 (1): 52–70.

Jeffery, C. (ed.) (1997) *The Regional Dimension of the European Union: Towards a Third Level in Europe?* London: Frank Cass.

Jessop, B. (2004) 'Multi-level Governance and Multi-level Metagovernance', in I. Bache and M. Flinders (eds) (2004) *Multi-Level Governance*, Oxford: Oxford University Press, 49–74.

Jewtuchowicz, A. and M. Czernielewska-Rutkoska (2006) 'Between Institutional Legacies and the Challenges of Europeanisation: Governance and Learning in Regional and Environmental Policies in Poland', in C. Paraskevopoulos, P. Getemis, and N. Rees (eds), *Adapting to Multi-level Governance: Regional and Environmental Policies in Cohesion and CEE Countries*, Ashgate: Aldershot.

Jones, B. J. and Keating, M. (eds) (1995) *The European Union and the Regions*, Oxford: Oxford University Press.

Katajamäki, Hannu (2002) *Ex Post Evaluation of Objective 6 Programmes in Finland and Sweden for the Period 1995-99. Synthesis Report*, University of Vaasa, December, available at: http://ec.europa.eu/regional_policy/sources/docgener/evaluation/doc/obj6/obj6synthesis.pdf (accessed 10 May 2011).

Katsaitis, Odysseas and Doulos, Dimitris (2009) 'The Impact of EU Structural Funds on FDI', *KYKLOS*, 62 (4): 563–78.

Kearney, C. (1997) 'Development Programming, Negotiation and Evaluation: Lessons for the Future', in John Bachtler and I. Turok (eds), *The Coherence of EU Regional Policy: Contrasting Perspectives on the Structural Funds*, London: Jessica Kingsley Publishers, pp. 305–21.

Keating, Michael (1995) 'Europeanism and Regionalism', in Barry Jones and Michael Keating (eds), *The European Union and the Regions*, Oxford: Clarendon Press, pp. 1–23.

—— (2003) 'Regionalization in Central and Eastern Europe: The Diffusion of a Western Model?' in M. Keating and J. Hughes (eds), *The Regional Challenge in Central and Eastern Europe: Territorial Restructuring and European Integration*, Brussels: P.I.E-Peter Lang, pp. 51–67.

Kelleher, J., Batterbury, S. and Stern, E. (1999) *The Thematic Evaluation of the Partnership Principle: Final Synthesis Report*, London: The Tavistock Institute Evaluation Development and Review Unit.

Kengyel, Ákos (2000) *The EU's Regional Policy and Its Extension to the New Members*, Zentrum für Europäische Integrationsforschung, Discussion paper C 76.

Kettunen, P. and Kungla, T. (2005) 'Europeanization of Sub-national Governance in Unitary States: Estonia and Finland', *Regional and Federal Studies*, 15(3): 353–78.

Kirkegaard, Jacob Funk (2011) 'The Euro Area Crisis: Origin, Current

Status, and European and US Responses', Testimony before the US House Committee on Foreign Affairs Subcommittee on Europe and Eurasia, 27 October.

Kohler-Koch, B. (1996) 'Catching up with Change: The Transformation of Governance in the European Union', *Journal of European Public Policy*, 3 (3): 359–80.

Kok Report (2004) *Facing the Challenge: The Lisbon Strategy for Growth and Employment*, Report of the High Level Group Chaired by Wim Kok, November, Luxembourg: Office for Official Publications of the European Communities.

Kovacheva, Ralitsa (2012a) 'New member states and the EU 2014–2020 budget,' euinside.eu, 30 March, available at: http://euinside.eu/en/news/new-member-states-and-the-eu-budget-2014-2020#ixzz1quOmPmUV (accessed 1 April 2012).

—— (2012b) 'Friendly fire during the negotiations on the EU 2014-2020 budget', euinside.eu, 26 April, available at: http://euinside.eu/en/analyses/friendly-fire-in-the-negotiations-on-the-eu-2014-2020-budget#ixzz1tXxXx8wQL (accessed 28 April 2012).

Laffan, B. (2004) *Multi-level Governance: The Dynamics of EU Cohesion Policy: A Comparative Analysis*, OEUE Phase II Occasional Paper 3–9 April, Dublin European Institute University College, Dublin.

Laffan, Brigid and Lindner, Johannes (2005) 'The Budget: Who Gets What, When and How?', in Helen Wallace, William Wallace and Mark A. Pollack (eds), *Policy-Making in the European Union*, Oxford: Oxford University Press, pp. 207–28.

Lefebvre, Maxim (2005) 'The European Budget at the Test of Enlargement', in Maxim Lefebvre (ed.), *What Kind of European Budget for 2013? Means and Policies of an Enlarged Union*, Paris: Institut français des relations internationales, pp. 13–45, available at: http://ifri.org/files/TetR_budget_europeen_GB.pdf (accessed 6 June 2011).

Leonardi, Robert (2005) *Cohesion Policy in the European Union: The Building of Europe*, London: Palgrave Macmillan.

—— (2011) *The Future of Cohesion Policy in 2014–2020: Can Cohesion Policy Be Merged with the Europe 2020 Programme?* Regional Studies Association, 'What Future for Cohesion Policy?' 16–18 March, Bled, Slovenia.

Lima, M. C. and M. A. Cardenete (2008) 'The Impact of European Structural Funds in the South of Spain', *European Planning Studies*, 16 (10): 1445–57.

Lóránd, Balázs (2011) *Performance and Effectiveness of the Cohesion Policy – Evaluation of the Allocation Mechanisms*, University of Pécs, Faculty of Business and Economics.

Mackinnon, Patricia (2001) 'EU Regional Policy and Sub-national

Authorities: Gateway to the Future or Blind Alley?' *European Consortium for Political Research*, Grenoble, 6–10 April.

Manzella, Gian Paolo and Mendez, Carlos (2009) *The Turning Points of EU Cohesion Policy*, Report Working Paper, European Policies Research Centre, University of Strathclyde, UK, January.

Marek, Dan and Baun, Michael (2002) 'The EU as a Regional Actor: The Case of the Czech Republic', *Journal of Common Market Studies*, 40 (5): 895–919.

—— (2014) 'The Limits of Regionalization: The Role of EU Structural Funds in the Czech Republic' (unpublished manuscript).

Marks, Gary (1992) 'Structural Policy in the European Community', in A. Sbragia (ed.), *Euro-Politics: Institutions and Policymaking in the 'New' European Community*, Washington, DC: Brookings Institution, pp. 191–224.

—— (1993) 'Structural Policy and Multilevel Governance in the EC', in A. W. Cafruny and G. Rosenthal, G. (eds), *The State of the European Community, Vol 2: The Maastricht Debates and Beyond*, Boulder, CO: Lynne Rienner, pp. 391–411.

—— (1996) 'Exploring and Explaining Variation in EU Cohesion Policy', in Liesbet Hooghe (ed.), *European Integration, Cohesion Policy and Subnational Mobilisation*, Oxford: Oxford University Press, pp. 388–422.

Marks, G. and Hooghe, L. (2004) 'Contrasting Visions of Multi-level Governance', in I. Bache and M. Flinders (eds), *Multi-Level Governance*, Oxford: Oxford University Press, pp. 15–30.

Marks, G., Nielsen, F., Ray, L. and Salk, J. (1996) 'Competencies, Cracks and Conflicts: Regional Mobilization in the European Union', in G. Marks, F. W. Scharpf, P. C. Schmitter and W. Streeck (eds), *Governance in the European Union*, London: Sage, pp. 40–63.

McAleavey, Paul and de Rynck, Stefaan (1997) *Regional or Local? The EU's Future Partners in Cohesion Policy*, ESCA conference in Seattle, May.

McMaster, Irene (2008) 'Ireland', in Michael Baun and Dan Marek (eds) *EU Cohesion Policy After Enlargement*, Basingstoke: Palgrave Macmillan, pp. 96–120.

Mendez, Carlos (2011) 'The Lisbonization of EU Cohesion Policy: A Successful Case of Experimentalist Governance?', *European Planning Studies*, 19 (3): 519–35.

—— (2012) 'Clouds, Clocks and Policy Dynamics: A Path-(inter)dependent Analysis of EU Cohesion Policy', *Policy & Politics*, 40 (2): 153–70.

Mendez, Carlos, Wishlade, Fiona and Bachtler, John (2013) 'Negotiation Boxes and Blocks: Crafting a Deal on the EU Budget and Cohesion Policy', EoRPA Paper 12/4, *European Policies Research Centre*, University of Strathclyde, UK, January.

Michelis, N. de and Monfort, P. (2008) 'Some Reflections Concerning GDP, Regional Convergence and European Cohesion Policy', *Regional Science Policy & Practice*, 1 (1): 15–22.

Midelfart-Knarvik, K. H. and Overman, H. G. (2002) 'Delocation and European Integration: Is Structural Spending Justified?' *Economic Policy* (October): 323–59.

Mohl, Philipp and Hagen, Tobias (2008) *Does EU Cohesion Policy Promote Growth? Evidence from Regional Data and Alternative Econometric Approaches*, ZEW Discussion Paper No. 08-086, 30 October, available at: ftp://ftp.zew.de/pub/zew-docs/dp/dp08086.pdf (accessed 17 July 2013).

Molle, Willem (2007) *European Cohesion Policy*, London: Routledge.

Morata, Francesc and Popartan, Lucia (2008) 'Spain', in Michael Baun and Dan Marek (eds) *EU Cohesion Policy After Enlargement*, Basingstoke: Palgrave Macmillan, pp. 73–95.

Moravcsik, Andrew (1991) 'Negotiating the Single European Act', in Robert Keohane and Stanley Hoffmann (eds), *The New European Community: Decision-making and Institutional Change*, Boulder: Westview, pp. 41–84.

—— (1998) *The Choice for Europe: Social Purpose and State Power from Messina to Maastricht*, Ithaca: Cornell University Press.

Mrak, Mojmir and Rant, Vasja (2007) *Financial Perspective 2007–2013: Domination of National Interests*, EU-CONSENT, EU-Budget Working Paper No. 1, July, available at: http://eu-consent.net/library/papers/EU-Budget_wp1.pdf (accessed 6 June 2011).

Neheider, Susanne and Santos, Indhira (2011) 'Reframing the EU Budget Decision-Making Process', *Journal of Common Market Studies*, 49 (3): 631–51.

Nugent, Neill (2010) *The Government and Politics of the European Union*, 7th edn, Basingstoke: Palgrave Macmillan.

OJEC (1975) Regulation (EEC) No. 724/75 of the Council of 18 March 1975 establishing a European Regional Development Fund, *Official Journal of the European Communities* (L 73), 21 March.

—— (1979) Council Regulation (EEC) No. 214/79 of 6 February 1979 amending Regulation (EEC) No. 724/75, *Official Journal of the European Communities* (L 35), 9 February.

—— (1984) Council Regulation (EEC) No. 1787/84 of 19 June 1984 on the European Regional Development Fund, *Official Journal of the European Communities* (L 169), 28 June.

—— (1988) Council Regulation (EEC) No. 2052/88 of 24 June 1988 on the tasks of the Structural Funds and their effectiveness and on coordination of their activities between themselves and with the operations of the European Investment Bank and the other existing financial instruments, *Official Journal of the European Communities* (L 185), 15 July.

—— (1993) Council Regulation (EEC) No. 2081/93 of 20 July 1993 amending regulation No. 2052/88 on the tasks of the Structural Funds and their effectiveness and on coordination of their activities between themselves and with the operations of the European Investment Bank and the other existing financial instruments, *Official Journal of the European Communities* (L 193), 31 July.

—— (1999) Council Regulation (EC) No. 1260/1999 of 21 June 1999 Laying Down General Provisions on the Structural Funds, *Official Journal of the European Communities*, (L 161), 26 June.

OJEU (2006a) 'Interinstitutional Agreement between the European Parliament, the Council and the Commission on Budgetary Discipline and Sound Financial Management', *Official Journal of the European Union* (C 139), 14 June.

—— (2006b) 'Council Regulation (EC) No. 1083/2006 of 11 July 2006 Laying Down General Provisions on the European Regional Development Fund, the European Social Fund and the Cohesion Fund and Repealing Regulation (EC) No. 1260/1999', *Official Journal of the European Union* (L 210), 31 July.

—— (2006c) 'Council Regulation (EC) No. 702/2006 of 6 October 2006, on Community Strategic Guidelines on Cohesion', *Official Journal of the European Union* (L 291), 21 October.

—— (2007) 'Treaty of Lisbon amending the Treaty on European Union and the Treaty establishing the European Community, signed at Lisbon, 13 December 2007', *Official Journal of the European Union* (C 306).

—— (2013a) 'Regulation (EU) No. 1303/2013 of the European Parliament and of the Council of 17 December 2013 laying down common provisions on the European Regional Development Fund, the European Social Fund, the Cohesion Fund, the European Agricultural Fund for Rural Development and the European Maritime and Fisheries Fund and laying down general provisions on the European Regional Development Fund, the European Social Fund, the Cohesion Fund and the European Maritime and Fisheries Fund and repealing Council Regulation (EC) No 1083/2006', *Official Journal of the European Union* (L 347), 20 December.

—— (2013b) 'Regulation (EU) No. 1301/2013 of the European Parliament and of the Council of 17 December 2013 on the European Regional Development Fund and on Specific Provisions Concerning the Investment for Growth and Jobs Goal and Repealing Regulation (EC) No. 1080/ 2006', *Official Journal of the European Union* (L 347), 20 December, pp. 289–302.

—— (2013c) 'Regulation (EU) No. 1304/2013 of the European Parliament and of the Council of 17 December 2013 on the European Social Fund and Repealing Regulation (EC) No. 1081/ 2006', *Official Journal of the European Union* (L 347), 20 December, pp. 470–86.

—— (2013d) 'Regulation (EU) No. 1300/2013 of the European Parliament and of the Council of 17 December 2013 on the Cohesion Fund and Repealing Regulation (EC) No. 1084/2006', *Official Journal of the European Union* (L 347), 20 December, pp. 281–8.

—— (2013e) 'Regulation (EU) No. 1299/2013 of the European Parliament and of the Council of 17 December 2013 on Specific Provisions for the Support from the European Regional Development Fund to the European Territorial Cooperation Goal', *Official Journal of the European Union* (L 347), 20 December, pp. 259–80.

—— (2014) 'Commission Implementing Decision of 18 February 2014 Setting out the List of Regions Eligible for Funding from the European Regional Development Fund and the European Social Fund and of Member States Eligible for Funding from the Cohesion Fund for the Period 2014–2020', *Official Journal of the European Union* (L 50), 20 February, pp. 22–34.

Oktayer, Nagihan (2007) 'Regional Policy and Structural Funds in the European Union: The Problem of Effectiveness', *Ankara Review of European Studies*, 7 (1): 113–30.

Olsson, Jan (2003) 'Democracy Paradoxes in Multi-level Governance: Theorizing on Structural Fund System Research', *Journal of European Public Policy*, 10 (2): 283–300.

Olsson, J. and Astrom, J. (1999) 'Europeanization and Regionalism in Sweden', Paper presented at the 27th ECPR Joint Session of Workshops, University of Mannheim, Germany.

O'Murchu, Cynthia and Spiegel, Peter (2010) 'Grand vision loses focus in opaque system', *Financial Times*, 30 November, p. 8.

Osterloh, Steffen (2010) *The Fiscal Consequences of EU Cohesion Policy after 2013*. Mannheim: Centre for European Economic Research, available at: http://ief.es/documentos/recursos/publicaciones/revistas/presu_gasto_publico/57_04.pdf (accessed 6 June 2011).

Paraskevopoulos, Christos J. (2001) *Interpreting Convergence in the European Union: Patterns of Collective Action, Social Learning and Europeanization*, New York: Palgrave Macmillan.

—— (2005) 'Developing Infrastructure as a Learning Process in Greece', in K. Featherstone (ed.), 'The Challenge of Modernisation: Politics and Policy in Greece', *West European Politics*, Special Issue, 28 (2): 445–70.

—— (2008) 'Greece', in Michael Baun and Dan Marek (eds) *EU Cohesion Policy After Enlargement*, Basingstoke: Palgrave Macmillan, pp. 121–40.

Paraskevopoulos, C. J. and Leonardi, R. (2004) 'Introduction: Adaptational Pressures and Social Learning in European Regional Policy: Cohesion (Greece, Ireland and Portugal) vs. CEE (Hungary, Poland) Countries', *Regional and Federal Studies*, 14 (3): 315–54.

Paraskevopoulos, C. J., Panagiotes, G. and Rees, N. (eds) (2006) *Adapting to EU Multi-Level Governance: Regional and Environmental Policies in Cohesion and CEE Countries*, Aldershot: Ashgate.

Parker, George (2005) 'Funding feud displays inertia and shrunken ambitions', *Financial Times*, 13 December.

Pellegrini, Guido, Terribile, Flavia, Tarola, Ornella, Muccigrosso, Teo and Busillo, Frederica (2013) 'Measuring the Effects of European Regional Policy on Economic Growth: A Regression Discontinuity Approach', *Papers in Regional Science*, 92 (1) (March): 217–33.

Piattoni, Simona (2006) 'Informal Governance in Structural Policy?', *Perspectives on European Politics and Society*, 7 (1): 56–74.

—— (2010) The Theory of Multi-level Governance: Conceptual, Empirical, and Normative Challenges, Oxford: Oxford University Press.

Pollack, Mark (1995) 'Regional Actors in an Intergovernmental Play', in Carolyn Rhodes and Sonia Mazey (eds), *The State of the European Union III: Building a European Polity?* Boulder: Lynne Rienner, pp. 361–90.

Polverari, Laura and Michie, Rona (2009) 'New Partnership Dynamics in a Changing Cohesion Context', IQ-Net Thematic Paper No. 25 (2), available at: http://eprc.strath.ac.uk/iqnet/downloads/IQ-Net_Reports (Public)/ThematicPaper25(2) Final.pdf (accessed 24 October 2012).

Puga, Diego (2002) 'European Regional Policies in Light of Recent Location Theories', *Journal of Economic Geography*, 2 (4): 373–406.

Puigcerver-Peñalver, Mari-Carmen (2007) 'The Impact of Structural Funds Policy on European Regions' Growth. A Theoretical and Empirical Approach', *The European Journal of Comparative Economics*, 4 (2): 179–208.

Rees, N., Quinn, B. and Connaughton, B. (2004) 'Ireland's Pragmatic Adaptation to Regionalization: The Mid-West Region', *Regional and Federal Studies*, 14 (3): 379–404.

Reiner, Martin (1999) *The Regional Dimension in European Public Policy: Convergence or Divergence?* Basingstoke: Macmillan.

Roberts, P. (2003) 'Partnerships, Programmes and the Promotion of Regional Development: An Evaluation of the Operation of the Structural Funds Regional Programmes', *Progress in Planning*, 59: 1–69.

Rodríguez-Pose, A. and Fratesi, U. (2004) 'Between Development and Social Policies: The Impact of European Structural Funds in Objective 1 Regions', *Regional Studies*, 38(1): 97–113.

Romania-Insider.com (2013) 'Romania could get extra time to spend EU money', available at: http://.romania-insider.com/romania-could-get-extra-time-to-spend-eu-money/99823/ (accessed 23 May 2013).

Ross, George (1995) *Jacques Delors and European Integration*, Oxford: Oxford University Press.

Rumford, Chris (2000) *European Cohesion? Contradictions in EU Integration*, London: Macmillan.

Rynck, Stefaan de and McAleavey, Paul (2001) 'The Cohesion Deficit in Structural Fund Policy', *Journal of European Public Policy*, 8 (4): 541–57.

Santos, Indhira (2008) 'Is Structural Spending on Solid Foundations?', in *Bruegel Policy Brief*, Issue 2 (February): 1–8.

—— (2009) 'EU Cohesion Policy: Some Fundamental Questions', in *Bruegel Policy Brief*, Issue 7 (May): 1–10.

Sapir Report (2003) *An Agenda for a Growing Europe: Making the EU Economic System Deliver*, Report of an independent high-level study group established on the initiative of the president of the European Commission, July.

Schneider, Christina (2009) *Conflict, Negotiation and European Union Enlargement*, Cambridge: Cambridge University Press.

Schröder, Sonja (2008) *The 2007–2013 European Cohesion Policy – A New Strategic Approach by the Commission?* Bonn: Zentrum für Europäische Integrationsforschung.

SEA (Single European Act) (1986) *The Single European Act*, 17 February, available at: http://ec.europa.eu/economy_finance/emu_history/documents/treaties/singleuropeanact.pdf (accessed 21 May 2013).

Sikorski, Radosław (2011) 'Poland and the future of the European Union', Speech by Mr Radek Sikorski, foreign minister of Poland, Berlin, 28 November 2011, transcript available at website of the Ministry of Foreign Affairs of the Republic of Poland, http://mfa.gov.pl/resource/33ce6061-ec12-4da1-a145-01e2995c6302:JCR (accessed 18 March 2014).

Sosvilla-Rivero, Simón, Bajo-Rubio, Oscar and Díaz-Rolda, Carmen (2006) 'Assessing the Effectiveness of the EU's Regional Policies on Real Convergence: An Analysis Based on the HERMIN Model', *European Planning Studies*, 14 (3): 383–96.

Sutcliffe, John B. (2000) 'The 1999 Reform of the Structural Fund Regulations: Multi-level Governance or Renationalization?', *Journal of European Public Policy*, 7 (2): 290–309.

Tarschys, Daniel (2003) *Reinventing Cohesion: The Future of European Structural Policy*, Swedish Institute for European Policy Studies (SIEPS), Report No. 17, Stockholm, September.

—— (2011) 'How Small are the Regional Gaps? How Small is the Impact of Cohesion Policy? A Commentary on the Fifth Report on Cohesion Policy', *European Policy Analysis*, 1 (January): 1–8.

Tavistock Institute (2011) February, available at: http://tavinstitute.org/news/evaluation-of-an-esf-communities-of-practice/ (accessed on 3 March 2014).

TEU (1992) *Treaty on European Union*, 27 February, available at: http://eur-lex.europa.eu/legal-content/EN/TXT/PDF/?uri=CELEX: 11992M/TXT&from=EN (accessed 25 June 2014).

Tondl, Gabriel (1995) *Can EU's Cohesion Policy Achieve Convergence?* IEF Working Paper No. 9.

Trón, Zsuzsanna (2009) 'Evaluation Methods of European Regional Policy and Reasons for Different Outcomes', *The Romanian Economic Journal*, 12 (32): 149–85.

Ujupan, Alina-Stefania (2009) *Reform Perspectives for Cohesion Policy in the Budget Review Process*, European Union Studies Association 11th biennial international conference, 22–25 April, Los Angeles, USA.

Vida, Krisztina (2004) *New Modes of Governance in EU Cohesion Policy – Emergence, Evolution, Evaluation*, New Modes of Governance, Integrated Project, available at: http://eu-newgov.org/database/ DELIV/D01D16a_Background-Emergence_Cohesion_Policy.pdf (accessed 24 October 2012).

Vogel, Toby (2012) 'Fight over EU's budget for 2014–20 intensifies', *European Voice*, 26 July.

—— (2013a) 'A budget deal for all?', *European Voice*, 4 July.

—— (2013b) 'Funding, flexibility and frontloading', *European Voice*, 4 July.

Volynsky, Masha (2012) 'EU criticizes Czech Republic for inefficiently drawing funds', *Radio Prague*, Cesky Rozhlas 7.

Werner Report (1970) 'Report to the Council and the Commission on the realization by stages of economic and monetary union in the Community', Luxembourg, 8 October, available at: http://ec.europa.eu/ economy_finance/emu_history/documentation/chapter5/19701008en7 2realisationbystage.pdf (accessed 5 October 2012).

Wozniak Boyle, Jennifer R. (2006) *Conditional Leadership: The European Commission and European Regional Policy*, Lanham, MD: Rowman & Littlefield.

Index